The Ulster Tales

To those Britons engaged in the Service of the Crown who lost their lives in Northern Ireland during the Troubles of the last three decades of the twentieth century

The Rifles Regimental Trust (Care For Casualties Appeal, C4C) will benefit directly from each book sold. C4C raises money to support battle casualties sustained in Afghanistan and Iraq by Riflemen, as well as their families, and the families of those Killed in Action.

The Ulster Tales

John Wilsey

Pen & Sword
MILITARY

First published in Great Britain in 2011 by
Pen & Sword Military
an imprint of
Pen & Sword Books Ltd
47 Church Street
Barnsley
South Yorkshire
S70 2AS

ISBN 978-1-84884-524-4

A CIP catalogue record for this book is available from the British Library.

Typeset in 11pt Ehrhardt by
Mac Style, Beverley, E. Yorkshire

Printed and bound in the UK by the MPG Books Group

Pen & Sword Books Ltd incorporates the imprints of Pen & Sword Aviation,
Pen & Sword Maritime, Pen & Sword Military, Wharncliffe Local History,
Pen & Sword Select, Pen & Sword Military Classics, Leo Cooper, Seaforth
Publishing and Frontline Publishing.

For a complete list of Pen & Sword titles please contact
PEN & SWORD BOOKS LIMITED
47 Church Street, Barnsley, South Yorkshire, S70 2AS, England
E-mail: enquiries@pen-and-sword.co.uk
Website: www.pen-and-sword.co.uk

Contents

Acknowledgements

It was thanks to Tony Whittome, then of Random House, that I wrote this book. After he had edited my biography of the late Lt Col 'H' Jones: *H Jones VC, The Life and Death of an Unusual Hero,* which Hutchinson published in 2002, Tony encouraged me to take up my pen again on a fresh subject relating to the Troubles in Northern Ireland.

We agreed that I should pay tribute to the work of all those Britons – from different backgrounds and professions – who left the mainland to cross the Irish Sea and work in Northern Ireland during those difficult years.

Primarily, my gratitude goes to the subjects of the ten chapters who gave me their trust and support. Two of them were the next of kin of men who had died in the service of the Crown. All of my contributors believed, as I do, that a tribute to the work we did during the Troubles was justified and, indeed, overdue.

To submit an account of one's own life and reputation for analysis by an outside author is risky enough; to permit that same process to be performed in respect of your late husband is particularly trusting.

I hope that none of my subjects, or their next of kin, regret doing so. I thank, chronologically, Simon Hoggart, Graham Crossland, Sir Philip Foreman, Peter Jones, Anne Blair, General Dickie Lawson. Sir John Blelloch, Lord King, Margie Deverell and Chris Albiston for their commitment and their forbearance of my efforts to record their stories.

I was helped by the memories of scores of people involved with Northern Ireland in various ways. For example, Professor Lord Paul Bew read my finished manuscript and encouraged my endeavours throughout the book's progression. Then there were those who assisted me in specific areas of research, such as identifying the financial costs of the Troubles. Here I valued the help of Peter Bell, formerly Associate Political Director in the Northern Ireland Office and now at Wolfson College, Oxford, and Dr Graham Gudgin of the Judge Business School (University of Cambridge), who, among many other appointments, was once Economics Adviser to Northern Ireland's Chief Minister. Together they guided me through that maze.

In the same vein, I am grateful to Air Commodore Mike Williams RAF (retd) who helped me understand better the intricacies and technicalities of the RAF Inquiries into the Chinook helicopter crash on the Mull of Kintyre.

Lords (Peter) Brooke and (Paddy) Mayhew shared with me their extensive knowledge of and wisdom in Irish matters and gave me generously of their time, which was as reassuring as it was helpful.

Likewise, Field Marshal Lord Bramall was solicitous about the progress of the book from its inception, and offered practical assistance as it progressed.

The provision of photographs and the negotiating of permission to use them are invariably painstaking tasks, so I am most grateful to Steuart Campbell for allowing me to use a plate taken from *Chinook Crash*, published by Pen & Sword Books, to Richard Doherty and to the *Belfast Telegraph* for allowing him access to their picture library; and to Nick van der Bijl BEM, author of *Op BANNER: The British Army in Northern Ireland* for allowing me use of his photographs. I am grateful also to those who have lent me copies of their private prints.

In the background and extremely supportive in practical ways was Dean Godson, Director of *Policy Exchange*; as was my sister Mary Venturini, a professional journalist. She encouraged me throughout, reading and contributing to most draft chapters as they emerged.

My thanks go to all those who helped as my task progressed, particularly my patient and supportive wife and family; my agent Michael Sissons and Fiona Petheram; and finally Henry Wilson and his dedicated team, which included my editor George Chamier, and the helpful staff at Pen & Sword.

Machrihanish

Mull of Kintyre

Portrush

Londonderry

NORTHERN IRELAND

Ballymena

Antrim

Aldergrove

Omagh

Lough
Neagh

BELFAST

Lisburn

Mullaghmore

Enniskillen

Armagh

Sligo

Monaghan

Newry
Warrenpoint

REPUBLIC OF IRELAND

Scale

| 0 | 10 | 20 | 30 | Kms |

| 0 | 10 | 20 | 30 | Miles |

DUBLIN

Foreword

The Rt Hon Sir John Chilcot GCB

Writing contemporary history is not for the faint-hearted. Making it, in Northern Ireland, through three decades and more of the Troubles, as these tales illustrate vividly, called for the sustained exertion of both moral and physical courage by very many men and women, British and Irish. These stories offer a few cross-bearings on what it felt like to those who crossed the Irish Sea to follow their various callings in those turbulent times. The years since the Troubles reignited towards the end of the nineteen sixties span most of a working lifetime for those who, like General John Wilsey, crossed and re-crossed that narrow strait, and all of us who lived and worked through those years were profoundly affected by that experience.

Much of the backdrop was dark, and the dreadful calendar of death, injury and pain tested the nerve and resolve of everyone involved. Particularly hard to bear were those tragic events, notably Bloody Sunday which the Saville Report has recently addressed, which could and should have been avoided. While they do not represent anything like the whole story, they are bitter reminders that conflict brings out ill as well as good.

That should not, however, obscure the extraordinary endurance, restraint and sacrifice both of the British Army and those serving in other institutions engaged in protecting the people of Northern Ireland; eventually resolving the conflict itself. It is the story of the sustained, determined, and ultimately successful pursuit of a humane and noble objective, making peace for a society long divided within itself. Only future historians will be able fully to assess the enduring quality of that achievement, and the contributions to it made from all sides, British and Irish. Even now, though, while the first rough drafts of the history are still taking shape, it is right to acknowledge, as these tales illustrate, that one vital contribution was that of the Crown Servants and their families who worked, and in so many cases suffered, to make today's and tomorrow's Northern Ireland the better place that it so evidently has become.

Preface

'Oh Lord, deliver us from an Englishman in a hurry'

Anon Irish Prayer

This book relates the stories and experiences of ten Britons who were involved in the Northern Ireland Troubles between 1969 and 2000. Some were public figures, others worked influentially behind the scenes. Several found their lives altered forever as a result.

That Great Britain's involvement in Northern Ireland's recent Troubles was creditable is my underlying assumption. It was generous, even-handed and altruistic, although those of strong Republican persuasion or Unionists of firm conviction may reject the premise. Republicans recall centuries of British oppression and alleged tyranny in Ireland, and there are Unionists who consider a lack of British resolve and a propensity to compromise to be at the root of the Troubles.

Yet, faced with prolonged intransigence and violence from Ulster's opposing factions, many consider British forbearance to have been remarkable and doubt whether any other nation would have exercised such patient restraint.

The events of Bloody Sunday on 30 January 1972 and, occasionally, other controversial incidents are said to undermine that assertion. In January 1998 Prime Minister Tony Blair commissioned Lord Saville of Newdigate's Bloody Sunday Inquiry to serve as an adjunct to the Peace Process then underway, and an 'Historical Enquiry Team' is currently reviewing other incidents where evidence is unclear or conflicting.

Twelve years later, Prime Minister David Cameron accepted Lord Saville's findings that serious mistakes and failings by officers and soldiers of the Parachute Regiment had caused the "unjustified and unjustifiable" death of fourteen unarmed and innocent civilians on Bloody Sunday. He also made the point that over a period of thirty-eight years "our Armed Forces displayed enormous courage and professionalism in upholding democracy and the rule of law in Northern Ireland during the longest continuous operation in British military history." Furthermore, successive British Governments pursued bi-partisan policies consistently supported by their electorate.

Words and definitions, particularly in the context of Ireland, are important, as ill-chosen ones can inflame passions. Dervla Murphy, the renowned Irish traveller and writer, takes seven pages of *A Place Apart* just to explain the significance of place names. She relates, for example, that some staunch Unionists talk proudly of Ulster, not Northern Ireland, while there are Republicans who refer to it as 'The Six Counties'. In doing so they express their desire to see the recreation of a single Irish entity, as existed prior to Partition in 1922.

Those from the British mainland, where definitions in this context do not carry such burdens, sometimes forget that 'The Queen's Realm of Great Britain and Northern Ireland' recognises two distinct entities. This book observes that same distinction; hence, the account which follows of the efforts of Britons in Northern Ireland refers to the endeavours of those from England, Scotland and Wales engaged on the other side of the Irish Sea.

It is not a history of the Troubles; neither is it an account of the policies of successive British Governments towards Northern Ireland; still less is it a definitive record of the operations of the Security Forces there. Rather, its purpose is to give an illustrative flavour of the lives and experiences of some British soldiers, policemen, officials and civilians, with whom I worked, over those difficult years in a beautiful but troubled place.

During my Army service, I spent longer there than anywhere else. Initially, I served in Belfast as a subaltern – the most junior category of officer. That was before the latest Troubles erupted in 1968. Thereafter, I came and went on short 'emergency' tours and on full-length postings of two years or more. Twenty-three years after first being sent there I was put in charge, as a lieutenant general, of the Army's overall effort during what in retrospect turned out to be the last consistently violent phase of these Troubles. In all, I spent over ten years in the Province on seven separate tours, serving in every rank except brigadier.

Some soldiers hated everything Irish, and there are those on the Mainland who felt the same. However, I found Ireland intriguing – its history, its politics, its people and their attitudes, both North and South. Indeed, I owed much to my service in Northern Ireland.

I remember, before crossing the Irish Sea as a young man, being warned to heed the old Gaelic prayer at the start of this Preface. It stuck with me and, although I have not been able to verify its authenticity, its sentiment is certainly true. I observed that brisk, busy Englishmen generally unsettle the Irish, no matter how well-intentioned they may be. By the same token, it is said that no prudent Englishman should write about Irish affairs. So it was with some trepidation that I began to do so once these latest Troubles subsided.

I wanted the book to answer the sort of question a generation untouched by the 'Troubles' – grandchildren perhaps? – might ask: 'What was it like to be in Northern Ireland at the end of the last century?'

I also decided to write because, after more than thirty years of armed conflict, I felt those Britons who crossed the Irish Sea to serve the Queen in Northern Ireland, in whatever capacity, whether in uniform or civilian clothes, deserved some recognition and understanding for what they faced and achieved – both individually and corporately – and for the sacrifices they made.

In the course of ten chronologically arranged Tales I endeavour to portray through my subjects' experiences what some of the issues were and what it was like to be there, or, in the case of The Widow's Tale, to be caught up in it consequentially. In an introduction to each Tale I explain my own involvement at the time and describe briefly how my subject fitted into the environment in which I was working.

I make no higher claim than that we did our best. We were – or at least we sought to be – altruistic, non-partisan, conscientious, patient, fair-minded and generous. Around 300,000 servicemen and women are entitled to wear the purple and green Northern Ireland campaign medal, and at least another 50,000 civilians from English, Scottish and Welsh homes crossed the Irish Sea to work in Northern Ireland during the Troubles. All were unsure – initially at least – of what to expect, and over 1,000 did not return alive.

Author's note
A glossary can be found on p. 178, explaining military, political and other specialised terms in an Irish context.

1

The Reporter's Tale

Author's Introduction

I first served in Northern Ireland, aged 23, in 1962, before the Troubles. The Province was at peace, although with hindsight it was clear that powerful tensions were submerged. Neither I nor my friends in The Devonshire and Dorset Regiment particularly noticed them. Based at comfortable Palace Barracks, Holywood, on the outskirts of Belfast, we were too busy enjoying ourselves. There were none of the restrictions that were later imposed. We could go down to Dublin for rugger Internationals at Lansdowne Road; the border was no barrier and we crossed it without constraint, something that was unthinkable later on. We marvelled at the sight of the Mourne Mountains and we could sail, fish, play golf or undertake any legal activity without restriction. Everyone appeared to welcome us with smiling Irish eyes, and we considered ourselves fortunate to be stationed where the community approved of soldiers and where, although it always seemed to be raining, or about to do so, at least the rain was soft and the countryside green and attractive.

My first inklings of underlying tension came when a distant, elderly relation, who had kindly invited me to lunch, lowered her voice and enquired how many Catholic officers we had in the Regiment. I did not know and said so, but she found my answer unsatisfactory and seemingly evasive. She could not accept that I had no interest in discussing the denomination of my fellow officers.

Similar jolts to our English ways of thinking were experienced by the parents of the regiment's school children. One mother recounted how the forearm of her Catholic daughter had been pinched by Protestant kids who declared their surprise that her skin went white "the same as ours does".

In 1968 the inherent tensions dividing the two communities broke out in Londonderry, where young Simon Hoggart, who was about my age, had just come down from Cambridge to start his first assignment as a reporter with the Guardian. His first big reports covered the aftermath of the Civil Rights March of 1968 and then the infamous Burntollet March of January 1969. He and his colleagues in the large press pack which, at times swollen with international, national and local media representatives, numbered more than a thousand, tried to explain the situation to their various audiences and put what was happening into some context. But, initially, stories from Northern Ireland were unpopular and fought domestic news to get space. Furthermore, reporters found it hard to convey simply the complexities of the issues at stake, and why a conflict was emerging. Was this a religious dispute or something less well defined? Were the attitudes and extreme utterances of people such as Dr Ian Paisley really the views of the law-abiding majority, and, if so, how strong was the following of such men? Much of the rhetoric emanating from across the water seemed so un-British that it jarred with readers at home. It was the task of correspondents like Simon Hoggart and television presenters like Peter Taylor to make sense of the complexities and convey the reality to their respective audiences.

I recall as a young officer the Army's uneasy relationship with the media early in the Troubles. Young and impressionable officers inherited as gospel, from a more staid yet experienced generation, that the media were untrustworthy and should be avoided at all costs. Indeed, it was instinctively frowned upon for an officer to feature in the media, and any hint of self-publicity was deplored.

Circumstances forced change. Initially, the Army's standard procedure, following a serious incident, had been for a senior officer or spokesman to give an interview or make a statement of the facts. But that person had not necessarily been at the scene and therefore could only offer a second-hand (and often inaccurate) account of what had happened.

After various embarrassments when the Army had been wrong-footed, then publicly criticised when its version of events was shown to be incorrect, the practice was abandoned and replaced by an arrangement whereby the best witness, irrespective of rank, gave an account of the incident. This propelled junior officers and soldiers to the fore. Generally they gave coherent accounts of the incidents, since there is nothing as authentic as someone who was present describing with conviction what he has seen. Credibility was restored and relations with the press improved, and to this day soldiers of all ranks are exposed to the media and give confident account of their actions.

Nationally, we should be grateful to Simon Hoggart and his colleagues for their reporting and for providing their readers and viewers, whose initial understanding of anything to do with Northern Ireland was rudimentary, with coherent accounts of the situation. The Government and those that acted in their name may not always have relished what was written or portrayed, but from the outset the public had access to every point of view and shade of opinion. This aided transparency and was to the overall benefit of the public, in whose name the Army and police acted.

The Tale that follows gives some feel for what it was like to be a reporter in the Province at the very start of the Troubles.

* * *

'The impossible has happened, and the Irish controversy, the oldest and deepest quarrel disturbing the peace and politics of the country, is to all intents and purposes settled ... Let us thank Heaven that that chapter of our history is closed and that a new one opens today.'

So ran the leader in the *Manchester Guardian* on 7 December 1921. The newspaper had been closely involved with contemporary Irish matters, and had been a strong advocate of Home Rule. The then editor, C.P. Scott, had been consulted by Lloyd George about preparing the public for the outcome of the tense, pre-Partition negotiations.

It was hardly surprising therefore that in the early months of 1966, alone among the quality newspapers, the *Guardian* alerted readers that Northern Ireland was becoming "edgy". The occasion was the 50th anniversary of the 1916 Easter Rising in Dublin, which would be celebrated by Catholics in the North with parades and speeches and flying of the Republican flag. To the neutral observer this commemorative celebration would seem to be no different in principle to the annual Orange marches in Belfast and Londonderry which traditionally celebrate the victory of Protestant William of Orange – 'King Billy' – over the Catholic King James II at the Battle of the Boyne in 1690. But that was not the perception of most Ulstermen.

In Ireland a protest can be quickly arranged, and the naming of a new bridge across the River Lagan in Belfast served this purpose. The bridge was to be named after the Queen and not, as originally proposed, after Lord Carson, the great Unionist leader of the early 1900s. The *Guardian* noted that the Rev Ian Paisley was incensed by what he interpreted as a snub and an insult to a patriot; and he suspected it was "just another sop to the Catholics."

The paper reported that Mr Paisley and his followers mounted street demonstrations in protest and that Prime Minster Harold Wilson had been urged in the House of Commons to call off the Queen's visit. Nevertheless, it went ahead amid some tension, and it occasioned a spectacular incident.

'Queen's car hit by block of concrete' was the *Guardian*'s headline on 5 July 1966. The story told of a twelve–inch slab hurled from a bridge, which dented the bonnet of her car. 'Thousands march with Mr Paisley,' trumpeted a headline, reporting how, within a few hours of the affront to the Monarch, Paisley had organised a march and demonstration, blaming the incident on Roman Catholics. The *Guardian* warned portentously: 'If Mr Paisley has his way there could well – and this is no exaggeration – be a religious war here quite soon.'

In fact, this was the first time in years that a Northern Ireland story had made the front page in any mainland newspaper. As a neglected province, neglected in the sense that those on the British mainland showed little interest in or understanding of its affairs, Northern Ireland rarely commanded media attention. But the situation was about to change.

Soon after this episode, Simon Hoggart, a twenty-two-year-old King's College, Cambridge undergraduate was taken on by the *Guardian*. Hoggart was one of a series of bright young reporters and leader-writers recruited straight from university. Hoggart, who was based in Manchester, had been educated at Hymers College, Hull and Wyggeston Grammar School in Leicester, and then went up to Cambridge, where he got a 2.1 degree in English. At Cambridge he worked on *Varsity*, the student weekly newspaper, reasoning that this would provide some fun and might be useful afterwards. It was.

Forty years later, Hoggart is one of the country's busiest and most versatile journalists, writers and broadcasters. Having had a spell with the *Observer*, he is again with the *Guardian*, where he is a columnist and parliamentary sketch writer. He contributes a twice-monthly wine column to the *Spectator*, and for twelve years was chairman of the BBC's News Quiz on Radio Four.

From 1979 to 1985 he was the political columnist for *Punch*. He then became the US correspondent of the *Observer*, a columnist and later the political editor of the same newspaper. Hoggart is also the author of numerous books, many with a political theme. Much of his success as a journalist is attributable, he claims, to his years in Northern Ireland covering the Troubles, initially as a trainee and then as the *Guardian*'s resident Northern Ireland correspondent from 1971 to 1973.

The late 1960s were marked by agitation on campuses throughout the western world. There had been disturbances at Berkeley University in California over the draft for Vietnam; a violent anti-Vietnam War rally in London's Grosvenor Square; race riots at Watts University, Oklahoma in support of Martin Luther King; unrest at the Sorbonne in Paris; and recurring student protests at most British universities.

A Civil Rights campaign in Northern Ireland followed this trend. Terming itself the Northern Ireland Civil Rights Association, or NICRA, it protested at discrimination against the minority community – mainly Catholic and Nationalist with Republican leanings – in terms of the franchise, housing and employment. Many of the minority's grievances, such as the demand for 'one man one vote', were justified. Householders only were entitled to vote in local elections, but the allocation of housing was in the very hands of those who might be unseated by a wider franchise. In the predominantly Protestant town of Dungannon, for example, where the Council was gerrymandered, not one new Catholic family had been offered a permanent council house in twenty years.

Equally unfairly, Catholics seemed much more likely than their Protestant or Unionist counterparts to work in industries of low status and high unemployment, such as construction. Indeed, in parts of Northern Ireland Catholic unemployment was running at sixteen per cent, twice the rate of their Protestant neighbours.

Historically, this was unsurprising. Two centuries earlier Edmund Burke had claimed that Ireland was 'profoundly unstable because of the denial of Catholic rights and the radical humiliation of that community.' In a pamphlet published in 1792 he argued that there were thousands in Ireland who had never conversed with a Roman Catholic in their whole lives. Indeed, Professor Lord Bew in his scholarly *Ireland – The Politics of Enmity 1789 – 2006* considers Burke to have possessed 'a profound insight into the vision of Catholic Ireland living cheek by jowl with an entire community that considered itself superior.'

By the late 1960s in the North, however, additional tensions were simmering. A substantial minority of Protestants were just as badly off as their Catholic neighbours, and they felt equally underprivileged. They formed a rival and vociferous group of malcontents, ready to take to the streets, especially if they felt Nationalist grievances would be addressed before their own. This added fuel to an already explosive and potentially unstable situation.

The timing of this disquiet was unfortunate because Northern Ireland's then Prime Minister, Captain Terence O'Neill, was the first genuine reformer to hold the position since the Province was created in 1922. It was O'Neill who invited his counterpart in the Republic of Ireland (the *Taoiseach*) to Stormont, the seat of Ulster's government, for the first meeting between leaders from North and South since Partition. It was O'Neill who was chiefly responsible for the unprecedented telegram of condolence sent to the Vatican on the death of Pope John XXIII in June 1963. Moreover, O'Neill made the first official visits by an Ulster Prime Minister to Roman Catholic schools and convents, initiatives, however, that were badly received by his Unionist Party. Nevertheless, O'Neill persuaded most of his Cabinet to accept some of the demands of the Civil Rights movement, although not the crucial principle of 'one man one vote'. But all this was to be too little and too late.

Mary Holland, the *Observer*'s campaigning journalist, summarised Northern Ireland's anguish and the unfolding tragedy:

> No one who spends any time in Ulster can feel anything but compassion for the pain and prejudices of the situation here. The Protestant majority has its fears, the Catholic minority its very real grievances. Reversing the process established for nearly half a century presents great difficulties. But for Great Britain to stand by and do nothing could be disastrous.

Initially, the Civil Rights protests took the form of peaceful banner-waving marches, mostly confined to areas where the cause would be understood and accepted. But after a series of clashes with the police that became increasingly violent the stage was set for a major showdown.

This occurred in Londonderry on 5 October 1968 where a Civil Rights march ignited what would become 'The Troubles'. That day the media gave widespread coverage to the unrestrained batoning by the Royal Ulster Constabulary (RUC) of the demonstrators, including Mr Gerry Fitt MP, without 'justification or excuse', according to Lord Cameron's subsequent Commission of Inquiry.

The next day, Simon Hoggart's front page article in the *Guardian* captured the mood:

> Ulstermen this morning have woken and found that Derry, the 'Maiden City', is on the same card index with Jackson, Mississippi, and Salisbury, Rhodesia. There will be pain, fury, frustration and bafflement.

In the prevailing mood of impending crisis, a flurry of political activity followed at Stormont, at Westminster and in Dublin. But attitudes in all three capitals soured rather than sweetened the atmosphere. The Minister of Home Affairs at Stormont, Mr William Craig, claimed simply that NICRA had been infiltrated by the IRA, for which there was scant evidence. Moreover, Ulster Unionists at Stormont were unable to defend coherently to the political elite in London the peculiarities of their system of government. They overlooked – even ignored – the fact that it was from London that the Province was largely funded. As for Dublin, Stormont viewed their strictures as irrelevant, if not deliberately malevolent, and, not for the first time, Dublin resented this implied snub.

Prime Minister Harold Wilson told Northern Ireland Ministers on 4 November 1968 that, if further reforms were not forthcoming, HMG would feel compelled to propose a radical course involving the significant withdrawal of financial support for Northern Ireland.

Forced to make some concessions, the Stormont government announced a reform package on 6 December, but only after O'Neill had secretly given a commitment to his Unionist Party Council not to introduce any further reforms, especially of the local government franchise, without their prior consent.

However, three days later O'Neill appealed to the general public over the heads of his Cabinet and party critics in a celebrated TV broadcast. "What kind of Ulster do you want?" he asked. "A happy and respected province in good standing with the rest of the United Kingdom? Or a place continually torn apart by riots and demonstrations and regarded by the rest of Britain as a political outcast?"

He implied support for the crucial measure of 'one man one vote' in local government. Two days later, having sensed positive support from within both communities, he sacked his hard-line Cabinet opponent, William Craig.

Support for O'Neill did increase over the following days, and all might have been well, and these 'Troubles' might never have ignited, had he implemented his promised changes speedily. But the advent at this very moment of a new, student-based, radical faction of the Civil Rights movement – the People's Democracy (PD) – put paid to any further measured progress.

PD organised a symbolic seventy-mile New Year's Day march from Belfast to Londonderry, modelled on Martin Luther King's historic Selma to Montgomery march in Alabama. This was provocative because the route wound – as it does naturally – through many Protestant areas, where trouble was almost inevitable.

The failure to take steps to avoid, or at least minimise, conflict at these potential flashpoints was one of Stormont's most far-reaching errors. Perhaps they were lulled into a false sense of confidence that the march would be a damp squib, because initially there was little support for it – only a few dozen turned up at the start at Belfast's City Hall. Arguably, a sensitively enforced ban might have been successful.

On its fourth day, however, when the seventy remaining marchers – the young PD firebrand Bernadette Devlin among them – accompanied by some eighty police, neared their destination, they were ambushed at the village of Burntollet by about 200 Protestants – some allegedly off-duty B Specials – wielding sticks and stones. A dozen or more marchers were injured, and some were driven into the nearby river, an event which was dramatically screened on TV.

Afterwards the Royal Ulster Constabulary was heavily criticised for its failure to protect the marchers; but more lasting damage was caused by the compelling media reports and images flashed around the world which further polarised local attitudes along sectarian lines. As a consequence, Premier Terence O'Neill lost his appeal to the many Catholics who had earlier believed he could deliver on his promises. He never recovered their support and, following other setbacks and electoral reverses, such as the election to Westminster, as MP for Mid-Ulster, of Bernadette McAliskey (née Devlin) in March 1969, O'Neill resigned as Prime Minister on 28 April 1969.

Major James Chichester-Clark, a kinsman of O'Neill, succeeded him; but he lacked the guile and political skill to handle an increasingly fractious and turbulent Province. Furthermore, the annual summer marching season – the so-called 'madness of July and August', when traditionally the worst bigotry and sectarian excesses are displayed – precluded modernising initiatives.

On 12 August 1969 the emotional, commemorative annual parade of the Protestant Apprentice Boys in Derry was stoned by Catholic youths, which in turn led to violence between Bogside Catholics and the police. The RUC were egged on by a large Protestant crowd. With the Bogside in a state of virtual siege, and the RUC over-stretched after striving to contain the violence for 48 hours, the *Taoiseach*, Jack Lynch, added to Chichester-Clark's difficulties by appealing for a UN Force to be dispatched to Northern Ireland. Meanwhile, he announced that Irish Army Field Hospitals were being mobilised along the border as "we can no longer stand by and see innocent people injured and perhaps worse."

The effects within Northern Ireland of this broadcast were destabilising. Many Protestants, recalling the Republic's hostile stance during the Second World War, genuinely feared an Irish Army invasion. Moreover, RUC stations in Nationalist areas of Belfast, as well as in the already troubled Londonderry, had begun to come under attack. So, on 14 August James Chichester-Clark formally asked London for Army reinforcements to be flown in and for those soldiers already garrisoned in the Province to be deployed in aid of the civil power. By midday soldiers were on the streets, where they were to remain for the next thirty-eight years.

Hoggart, now in his second year in Ulster, was developing a good feel for both the place and the issues. Contemporary photographs show him as a young man of medium height with long black hair and wearing large round spectacles. Completing the picture is an open face with a relaxed – almost unworldly – expression.

The *Guardian* at that time had a relatively low daily circulation of around 180,000. Standing to the left of the Unionist position, it was the quality newspaper of choice both for those of a Nationalist persuasion and for those wanting an insight into that viewpoint.

First posted as leg-man to the legendary Geoffrey Moorhouse, the travel writer occasionally sent to cover great events, Hoggart recalls: "Initially I was sent over to Ireland on a rota basis for a few days a week, catching the awful early morning flight out of Manchester at 6.40 am, on which most of the passengers were still hung over."

Hoggart reported to the paper's Northern Office in Manchester, from where Ireland had traditionally been covered. His editor was John Cole, later the BBC's political editor. Cole was an Ulster Protestant, but a Labour supporter who often found Unionist attitudes disagreeable and their rhetoric distasteful. Nevertheless, he never altered Hoggart's filed articles; at most, he might urge him to cross-check a fact or opinion on the basis that both sides could be "somewhat selective"!

Hoggart recalls:

The paper took the job seriously, placing as much importance upon the elegance of the writing as on its strict accuracy. I was expected to file a report every day, almost all of which were used. It involved a 24 hour/ 7 days a week commitment, with one week off in three. It was unbelievably good training.

You would report on everything; you made lots of contacts and learnt never to take anything at face value so, where possible, I double-checked on everything. Waking to the sound of a bomb, you would follow that up; then you could be driving to Stormont with the other hacks for a briefing over drinks and lunch. Everyone was available and eager to get their point of view across. We would take Army officers for lunch at the Europa Hotel, where they would be delighted to get out of their squalid bases and have a nice meal.

This was the first time the British Army had been closely scrutinised by the British Press; previously they had always been 'the good guys', even when they were fighting colonial operations in Cyprus, Aden or Kenya. No one had gone up to them and said 'this is wrong, it shouldn't be happening.' For example, we would query the statement that 'a man, who had been shooting at an army patrol, had been shot dead.' Often the report was true and quite often it was wrong; or more likely one could not tell either way. But the army had not been questioned like that before and they were outraged.

I got into terrible trouble writing an article saying that the Parachute Regiment were so unpopular that other infantry regiments had asked not to have them ever sent in as back-up because they would undo months of hard painstaking community relations by coming in and thumping people – or worse; Robert Fisk and I interviewed a woman in hospital who had been blinded by a rubber bullet.

I wrote this and it caused a terrible fuss. Six days after the article appeared was Bloody Sunday and that made life easier for me because I felt vindicated, as I testified to the Saville Inquiry.

I had been given the story by an officer who was very astute and realised that hearts and minds mattered more than it had in any British Army operation in living memory ... Others were plain stupid and imagined it was the job of the media to give uncritical support to the army. If they claimed something was true then as far as they were concerned, it was true.

When such an impression was prevalent, journalists would insert into their articles a piece, similar to Hoggart's of 14 August 1971, following a post-Internment briefing at the Army Headquarters at Lisburn:

The Brigadier's statement was received with a good deal of surprise at a press conference yesterday.

Rightly or wrongly, the credibility gap between what the army says it was doing, what it is believed to be doing and what it is actually doing is now greater than at any time in the recent operation.

On the other hand, Hoggart recalls occasions when trust with individuals was established to the benefit of all parties. One such incident followed a complaint to Gerry Fitt, a local MP, that one of his constituents was under pressure from the Army to become an informer against the IRA. It was a case of possible entrapment. Such allegations would normally elicit a non-committal official response along the lines: of "we don't discuss intelligence matters in view of their potential sensitivity."

Hoggart got to hear the story and tackled the Army's local press officer who confirmed the allegation and promised that the complainant would receive no further attention from the Army. Thereafter, Hoggart felt, when seeking confirmation or denial of a current story, that trust had been established with that individual, and he would get the truth. This benefited both parties: the reporter did not waste time pursuing untrue or incorrect stories; and the press officer did not have to respond to the rumours that inevitably circulated at busy times.

Of the various bodies' relationships with the press, Hoggart recalls that those with the RUC were virtually non-existent, as the police were generally tired, demoralised and on the back foot. Dealings with the many paramilitaries were haphazard. The IRA was split into the Provisional IRA (PIRA) and the left-wing Marxist-inclined Official IRA (OIRA). The Loyalists were even more diffuse: the Ulster Volunteer Force (UVF) was pre-eminent; but the Ulster Freedom Fighters (UFF), Ulster Defence Association (UDA), the Red Hand Commandos and others were sporadically active. Generally, the Loyalists' dealings with the media were poorly organised and unsubtle.

The purpose of all media activity, whether by the Government, its agencies, or by paramilitary forces, was to influence a specific target audience. Those involved in conveying and reporting that message were regularly confronted with the issue of moral equivalence. Did the media have a moral duty to treat the agents and report the activities of an elected democracy more or less favourably than those who sought the violent overthrow of that democracy? In other words, should both be treated the same?

Hoggart explains:

At my level the issue of morality was not a factor. I saw my job – and I imagine my colleagues from the Mainland would generally agree – was to try to establish the truth in a fast moving and complex situation, wherever that led. I hope I treated everyone the same.

Often this caused trouble. When the Government or Army did not like our reporting or our behaviour they complained to our editors or they excluded us from briefings, or they did both.

Aggrieved paramilitaries, on the other hand, posed the threat of violence – including death – to reporters. But our job – and our duty to readers – remained to report on events as accurately as we could. And arguably, in democracies, the public is best served by this approach.

Two operations occurred early in Hoggart's tour which altered local attitudes sharply and adversely affected relations between the Catholic community and the Army.

The first was the 'Falls Road Curfew' in early July 1970 when the Army was ordered to mount a cordon-and-search operation in the heart of one of Belfast's Nationalist ghettos. The second was Internment in August 1971 when, despite Army misgivings, soldiers were ordered to mount a dawn swoop to arrest 300 people, mainly Nationalists suspected of being active IRA members or supporters. These events (recalled in the next Tale) altered the level and intensity of violence and ended the Army's generally harmonious relationship with the minority community, who until then had viewed them as protectors. Moreover, they breathed new life and purpose into the IRA as an effective terrorist organisation.

During this time Simon Hoggart was promoted to be the *Guardian*'s Northern Ireland correspondent based permanently, along with most of the Press Corps, in Belfast's regularly bombed Europa Hotel. His annual salary started at £1,050, plus expenses, and he reflects wistfully that a bottle of Chateau Latour cost only £5.00.

For a bachelor, as I then was, it was fantastic because in the hotel you had every meal cooked. I would be woken at, say, 9 am with a full breakfast and every single British and Irish paper. I had TV, record player, everything I could possibly need.

I got on well with most of my colleagues and we collaborated on stories and shared quotes and statements. But 'exclusive scoops', such as revealing the army's intention to crater the border crossings, were hard earned and carefully protected.

I became totally absorbed by the variety in the job. I had never done any politics before and found the interplay of personal rivalries and obsessions fascinating. It was almost like Westminster, only with the added violence. William Whitelaw was the first Secretary of State to run Northern Ireland from Stormont (after Direct Rule was imposed in March 1972) and he was good at briefing the press; I think he quite liked journalists because they were convivial, and he was a great toper himself.

But local politicians were generally of poor quality and most were regarded with complete contempt on the Mainland. You could see why: some of them were very limited intellectually. Intelligent people weren't attracted to Northern Ireland politics very much.

John Hume, the Social Democrat Labour Party (SDLP) leader, was an exception. I gave him a lift from Dublin to Londonderry one day, not because I needed to go there, I just thought it might be useful to talk to him for a couple of hours in the car. We drove into an Ulster Defence

Regiment (UDR) roadblock. I thought: 'this might be difficult!' not because we might be stopped and searched but because they might warn their 'friends' in less official organisations up the road that a nationalist MP, and an awkward reporter, were heading their way. I did my 'I'm from England; I think you'll find my driving licence in order' routine; meanwhile John was faking a coughing fit so they didn't actually see his face in his handkerchief.

Despite that incident, I never felt remotely threatened because of whom I was. Occasionally, I'd stray near gunfire or otherwise into danger, and then stray right out again as quickly as I could. In fact, we reporters had a simple way of minimising risk. We had an informal arrangement for protecting each other under the umbrella of a paper's allegiance. For example, as the *Guardian* was considered on the Republican, Catholic, non-Unionist side, it was very useful for colleagues from other papers to pretend, when necessary, they were from the *Guardian;* likewise the *Telegraph* was perceived as Unionist, which more or less it was. I remember an IRA bomb had gone off in a Protestant residential area – a very bad business and contrary to all the IRA's cynical protestations that they abhorred sectarian violence – and about six of us went there all saying we were from the *Daily Telegraph.*

"You've sent an awful lot of people down here", the minders said. So, James Brady, who really was with the *Telegraph*, replied: "The news editor was so shocked and appalled by what had been done to you people today that he sent every available reporter. They seemed to feel this was no more than their due."

Hoggart's work regularly took him to Dublin.

I actually thought Belfast was a nicer place; Dublin was so smug and pleased with itself. I knew a lot of people down there; we had a link with the *Irish Times* and they were very good to me. But the Troubles hadn't really affected them. They were happy to sit back in nice safe Dublin and say 'It's all the fault of the Brits.' Well, up to a point, but only up to a point! 'What about you lot?' I thought. 'You could have helped a great deal as well.'

I remember the first time I went to Dublin, leaving mayhem behind me in Belfast. The bellboy in my hotel asked "You're from the North? Leeds United is doing well this season!" That's all they wanted to talk about. The Troubles were as distant to Dubliners as they were to anyone in

London at the time. When I watched the British Embassy being torched after Bloody Sunday, people were amazingly kind to me.

It was from Dublin that Hoggart wrote one of his most perceptive pieces under the headline 'Ireland's most perplexing peacemaker', in which he predicted accurately what admittedly took another thirty-five years to come true:

> The name of one unexpected peacemaker for troubled Ireland is emerging in the minds of several people close to the Dublin Government. Three years ago the Rev Ian Paisley was a demon king to every Roman Catholic in Ireland. Now those who make it their business to study Ulster politics from the South are beginning to see him in a very different, subtle and moderate role ...
>
> Mr Paisley's record over the past few months has been a fascinating and in many ways a very impressive one ... He has been a model constituency man, and his constituents, both Catholic and Protestant, can say that on local issues they have had the most effective and sympathetic representation.
>
> Mr Paisley has spelt out in some detail the ways in which there could be greater cooperation between North and South ... and the theory in Dublin is that Mr Paisley is ... biding his time ... to emerge as the man ... prepared to seek actively a means of making the two communities in the North live together ...

Hoggart was not the first to find Irishmen imprisoned by their history. During interviews he found it virtually impossible to discuss an issue or initiative without the past being dragged up. "Moreover," he recalls, "it seemed that Irish history went back just as far as it took to prove that the community the speaker was from had been done down by the other side. And if Britain could be convincingly blamed along the way so much the better!" Hoggart remembers Roy Bradford, a prominent Unionist, "always grumbling ungratefully about HMG, whoever was in power."

Hoggart further recalls:

> Another thing about the people in Northern Ireland is that they are fantastically solipsistic. Theirs was the only story that mattered, as far as they were concerned. I remember there was some huge news story elsewhere – I think it was the terrorist attack at the 1972 Munich

Olympics – something which every paper covered with banner headlines – except the *Belfast Newsletter*, which led with 'IRA blows up letterbox.' I was sitting in a pub watching that night's TV news and the regulars there were furious when the story moved off Northern Ireland.

I came to believe that a lot of people in Northern Ireland loved the Troubles. I know this is a terrible thing to say but hating your neighbour is a luxury that you can only afford when there is someone else holding the ring.

Reggie Maudling, who was Home Secretary some of the time I was there, talked of 'an acceptable level of violence', and was much mocked for it – 'disgraceful, no such thing', etc – but, in fact, that applied in Ulster for a very long time: an acceptable level of violence that people were prepared to tolerate. Calculations show that if you excluded the participants: that is the army, police and all the paramilitaries; the likelihood of genuine civilians being hurt was statistically very low. In fact, they were ten times more likely to be killed in a road traffic accident in Northern Ireland than to be killed by a bomb or bullet. That's a pretty stunning statistic. Nobody wakes up and says 'I could be knocked down by a car today!', you just assume you won't be. Northern Ireland was like that; you didn't wake up and say, 'Oh, I could be cut down in a hail of sectarian bullets today!' That made the risks acceptable and so people could carry on safely voting for extremists.

I used to despair when I heard British politicians saying that the people of Northern Ireland yearn for peace. No, they didn't; they yearned for victory! That sounds outrageous and horrible, but it went on for 37 years.

Notwithstanding such occasional negative impressions, Hoggart concluded:

After a while I realised I liked the place very much and I got totally absorbed in it. I know it's a cliché, but the people in Northern Ireland are the nicest in Europe, or perhaps the world, except when they are trying to kill you!

2

The Soldier's Tale

Author's Introduction

By the summer of 1971 the atmosphere and the operational situation had changed. Two events had altered forever the perception of the minority community towards the Army. That community was largely, but not exclusively, Catholic, Republican-minded and inclined to nationalism – it is widely referred to for simplicity (but not always accurately) as the Catholic community.

Initially, the British Army had been welcomed by Catholics as their protectors against what they perceived to be a sectarian police force and hostile Loyalist neighbours. But the Falls Road Curfew of July 1970 and Internment in August 1971 were interpreted by the minority as the Army turning against them under the direction of a sectarian government in Stormont. As a consequence, the IRA, consisting then of two factions, the Provisional IRA (PIRA) and the Marxist-inclined Official IRA (OIRA), were galvanised into protecting their community by confronting the British Army directly with force.

The result was the most violent and destructive period of the Troubles. In 1971 the number of deaths from terrorist incidents reached 174, a sevenfold increase on the previous year. By 1972 the figure had risen to 467 deaths, before falling back annually thereafter.

To stem this tide of violence, soldiers were sucked into Northern Ireland from Germany, and even from as far away as Malta, where I was serving at the time. In the summer of 1970, as a young captain, I had been enjoying with my regiment a precious overseas posting in the sun, without much thought for what was happening at home. Suddenly we were warned for immediate deployment to Belfast, where in the wake of intense inter-communal violence the Ministry of Defence had run out of home-based troops.

Historically, this was perverse. Traditionally, when unrest had erupted in places for which the Government had responsibility, overseas garrisons were reinforced from home. But the Army had become so small and overstretched (even then) that 'robbing Peter to pay Paul' was no longer feasible. Reinforcements had to be summoned from overseas to support the home base.

Within hours we had exchanged the sun and beaches of Malta for the drabness and drizzle of West Belfast. Such was the ad hoc nature of our deployment and reception that we slept where we could find cover – some in buses, some in school classrooms and some on the straw in pens at an agricultural hall. Patrolling the streets, conspicuous in our sand-coloured helmets, we formed five of the twenty-four infantry companies needed to conduct the controversial cordon and search of the Lower Falls in the summer of 1970. That search is described below by a non-commissioned officer (NCO) who was present, as I was.

It was upon our shoulders that the daily burden of operations and leadership fell – the conflict was primarily conducted at junior officer and junior NCO level, which meant that most of the engagements involved decisive action by a handful of well led men, rather than being settled by force of numbers under the direction of senior commanders.

Still a captain, I was just in the category of junior officer when we embarked on my second emergency tour. We deployed in mid-1971 from our (then) base in Gillingham, Kent, to Gough Barracks in the centre of the city of Armagh. From here we were tasked to patrol a length of the border with the Republic of Ireland; to protect the police stations there; to provide reinforcements at Armagh Jail if needed – as they often were; and to quell the rioting which emanated nightly from Armagh's Nationalist housing estates. The initial welcome and pleasantries, accompanied by offers of tea, which the Army had earlier enjoyed, were replaced by the certainty of bricks and missiles flying through the air in our direction.

Relationships got worse when Operation Demetrius was launched. Demetrius was the codename for internment, which the Army had opposed as ill-advised. But our generals had been overruled by the Provincial Government at Stormont, then still in being. The mounting of internment and its consequences are graphically described below.

Corporal Graham Crossland MM, of the Green Howards, is a proven leader and a man of strong Christian faith, who commanded a section of eight men on three separate tours in Belfast during the years of greatest intensity and highest danger.

Before joining the Army, Crossland had been a tough, deep-seam Yorkshire miner. He now holds the rare and prestigious Military Medal for his courage and leadership. He took part in both the Falls curfew and Internment, as well as numerous routine engagements which never got publicly reported. This is his Tale.

* * *

Sailors enjoy serving in a happy ship. Likewise, soldiers relish membership of a good family regiment. The Green Howards was one such: one of three infantry regiments from Yorkshire recruited almost exclusively from that county that attracted into its ranks generations of the same families. In the Second World War the Regiment raised twelve battalions, and the Green Howards were renowned for the brave, proud and independent qualities which characterise Yorkshiremen.

Many organisations promote cohesion because the need to belong is itself a powerful human instinct, which reinforces a corporate identity. Indeed, the more challenging the enterprise the greater the need for cohesion and the sense of belonging. Hence, the Army deliberately fosters a strong regimental ethos and actively promotes loyalty. Over the centuries, the Green Howards had nurtured a deep affinity with Yorkshire, and it has been warmly reciprocated.

Unfortunately, these intangible bonds were ignored by the Army Board of 2004, who capitulated to political pressure and either failed to articulate successfully the benefits of such bonds or did not attempt to justify them. So a decision was taken to weaken or sever the links which most infantry regiments enjoyed with their local counties to the benefit of both. Historic regiments such as the Green Howards, the Devon and Dorsets and others equally distinguished were lost, and in four cases whole infantry regiments were arbitrarily extinguished. Moreover, this occurred when the nation's need to meet its increasing defence commitments had never been greater.

In August 1965 – well before these cuts were made, and when local identities and ties were still prized – a twenty-two-year-old miner from Barnsley named Graham Crossland joined his county regiment. After training at Strensall in Yorkshire, at which this fit young man excelled, he was nominated Best Recruit and posted to the Green Howards, who were shortly to go to the Far East, initially to Hong Kong.

It is not easy for a recruit to make an impression on his new Regiment. When an overseas posting is in prospect it is particularly difficult, because the young man will have almost nothing to contribute; no shared reminiscences of a previous tour or worthwhile views on the next.

Unusually, however, Crossland left his mark on three counts: firstly, he enjoyed the prestige afforded to any ex-deep-seam coalminer in a Yorkshire regiment. Secondly, he was already a boxer of some renown who would be a useful light heavyweight fighter for the Green Howards; and thirdly, he possessed a strong Christian faith which he observed unselfconsciously by kneeling nightly in prayer by his barrack-room bed with plenty of hard-bitten old sweats looking on.

Only a respected and popular man of strong conviction and self-assurance could carry this off. Remarkably, Graham Crossland, softly spoken, mild in manner and modest of habit, did so without challenge. Equally commendable was the ethos within the Green Howards which allowed young Crossland to be himself, and to flourish.

In the late 1960s British Army units were still deployed extensively around the world on what was often termed 'colonial policing', a legacy of Empire. Their principal role was to support the local authorities should British or Commonwealth interests be threatened.

Hence, in early 1966 some eight hundred men and families of the Green Howards, including Private Graham Crossland, arrived in the Crown Colony of Hong Kong to acclimatise, prior to their eventual deployment to Borneo, whose territorial integrity was being threatened by neighbouring Indonesia.

In Hong Kong's heat and humidity Graham and his comrades prepared for this task and were instructed like generations before them in what the Army termed 'Keeping the Peace' and 'Military Aid to Civil Power', in other words the procedures, techniques and skills required for low-intensity operations against insurgents, which had consistently stood British garrisons overseas in good stead, at least since the end of the Great War.

Private Crossland was drilled, both in theory and practice, in the methods of riot control, crowd dispersal, curfews, anti-ambush drills, and cordon and searches. The same basic principles were drummed in: every action must be legal and proportionate; only the minimum necessary force must be used to achieve one's aim; strict impartiality must always be observed; and tight control must be exercised at all levels. It was emphasised that the British Army would never bluff by firing warning shots over the heads of a crowd. Therefore, so it was taught, belligerents would clearly understand that soldiers would only be deployed as a last resort – lawfully and in deadly earnest. So, if forced to open fire on a mob, the consequences would be lethal.

Three years after leaving Hong Kong, and following a home posting in Colchester, the Green Howards joined the British Army of the Rhine (BAOR) in West Germany. BAOR was the Army's shop window where its brightest officers earned their spurs, its latest equipment was deployed and where the conflicting ideologies of East and West met along the Inner German Border which then divided the two halves of Germany. Crossland was stationed in the small garrison town of Minden where the regiment was kept at a high state of operational readiness – as were all units throughout the Rhine Army – to deploy to prepared battle positions in the event that the Warsaw Pact Forces made a hostile move. Occasionally, as during the

'Prague Spring' uprising in Czechoslovakia of 1968, such hostilities appeared frighteningly imminent.

At other times, life off-duty in Minden was generally unexciting. The armoured vehicles with which units were equipped needed constant maintenance; soldiers were restricted in what they could do and where they could go. Many found their duties dull and monotonous and their social life away from home lonely and boring. Consequently, time in BAOR for many hung heavily.

But not for Graham Crossland, who saw service in Germany as a new adventure. Now a lance corporal, he throve and was soon appointed to command a section in the rank of full corporal. He was now on the second rung of the promotion ladder which would one day earn him a commission.

Events in the United Kingdom now unexpectedly intruded. In the summer of 1969 public order in Northern Ireland rapidly deteriorated and, as described in the previous Tale, the Army was deployed in aid of the civil power for the first time since the General Strike of 1926.

Initially, BAOR was considered immune from such a commitment because of Britain's sacrosanct obligation to NATO to keep 55,000 soldiers stationed permanently in West Germany. However, in the wake of a deteriorating situation in Northern Ireland, the pressure on units already there was so intense that the Ministry of Defence was reluctantly forced to call upon the Rhine Army to provide reinforcements.

As a consequence, between the summer of 1970 and late 1972 the Green Howards deployed to Belfast three times on emergency tours each lasting around four and a half months, leaving their families behind. Corporal Crossland was there on each occasion, commanding the first section of 11 Platoon in C Company (call-sign 33 Alpha), consisting of eight riflemen.

Like most soldiers, Crossland was initially excited at the prospect of going to Northern Ireland. At the outset, pre-tour preparation was rudimentary. Regiments went 'as they were', each preparing for what lay ahead as best it could. It was several years before sophisticated training packages were devised which prepared units and individuals for their task.

Some units deployed to Belfast by ferry from Liverpool or Stranraer; others, like the Green Howards, flew into Nutts Corner, an old RAF wartime flying boat station on Lough Neagh. On arrival they took over requisitioned schools, factories, or public buildings like the Ulster Hall, where soldiers could be protected, administered and briefed.

The Green Howards' task was to restore law and order in the riot-torn areas of Belfast. They were to work alongside the demoralised local police force, the RUC, which was still reeling in those early days from a series of blows to its standing and pride.

The Regiment were confronted almost at once by widespread street disorder. Corporal Crossland and his section were ordered to prevent the erection of barricades between the two opposing communities of West Belfast. Crossland recalls:

The place was in chaos and the situation very tense. Our 'patch' looked like a war zone with burnt-out buses and cars in the streets, houses gutted by fire, severed gas mains roaring, falling masonry everywhere and the streets littered with the debris of days of fighting. Every conceivable form of missile from bottles to iron bars was lying around.

It was quite a shock; if we had been back in Hong Kong it would not have been so strange – but this was 1970 in our own country, for heaven's sake!

We were greeted as protectors by the Nationalist community and offered tea and biscuits – all nice and friendly. Yet, attitudes towards us were inconsistent. I recall in the heart of a Catholic area a boy coming up saying: 'Me ma says would youse all like a cup of tea?' Later he returned and asked another soldier: 'Me ma wants to know if youse English bastards want sugar?'

We ourselves had no allegiance one way or the other. We were there solely to separate the two rioting factions and support the police.

Yet we must have looked [in] a sorry state for we weren't dressed or properly equipped for what we were doing. We still had the old olive green uniform. Body armour was not issued initially (and when it did come it was ex-US Army kit issued for Vietnam with their names still on it). We had Self Loading Rifles (SLRs) with bayonets but soon had to remove the bayonets because they were seen as too offensive.

Initially we carried only one radio per platoon; we wore uncomfortable steel helmets and carried one blanket each to sleep on. We slept where and when we could; in fact, after 48 hours we were so exhausted that we 'crashed out' almost at once whenever we stopped.

I remember our first proper meal was fish and chips which our Colour Sergeant produced somehow – perhaps he bought it locally with Company funds. It was a nice idea but, by the time ours arrived, it was just a greasy, congealed mess because he couldn't get through the various riots. He kept being diverted and couldn't find us.

Similar incidents occurred in Londonderry or wherever the adjoining communities were at each other's throats. Although the two factions were at odds, they had much in common. Both comprised poor, ill-educated, badly housed and under-employed families. At the heart of their mutual antagonism was a history of distrust. The Catholics believed that they suffered institutionalised discrimination whilst the Protestants perceived that their unwanted neighbours were intent on undermining the Union of Great Britain and Northern Ireland by force and replacing it with a United Ireland.

The initial welcome from the Nationalist community that the Army had enjoyed ended before long. Corporal Crossland's section took part in two major operations which, whatever else they may have achieved, destroyed the Army's standing within that community for at least the next two decades. Furthermore, these operations resuscitated the Irish Republican Army (IRA) and its offshoots that, until then, had been largely dormant following their earlier unsuccessful campaign in the 1950s which, ironically, had ended with the introduction of internment in the South.

The first of these major operations was in July 1970 when the Army was ordered – ill-advisedly, many thought – to conduct an extensive cordon and search of the slums of the Catholic Lower Falls Road, where intelligence had it that weapons were hidden. In order to complete the search thoroughly, a four-day curfew was imposed, from Thursday to Sunday, which prevented any free movement into or out of the area.

Crossland and his men found the task of searching highly intrusive – almost degrading – as they poked into dark corners and beneath often rickety beds, exposing intimate belongings under the hostile gaze of the occupants. During the search of hundreds of shabby dwellings 107 weapons, 25lbs of explosives and 21,000 rounds of ammunition were found.

Corporal Crossland remembers his section coming under fire from the roof-tops. His Company Sergeant Major ordered the street lights to be shot out. These lights assisted IRA snipers by illuminating soldiers. But the resulting rifle fire only added to the confusion as to who was shooting at whom.

The whole operation stirred up a hornets' nest, and hundreds of complaints were received. Corporal Crossland recalls the accusations that Scottish soldiers in particular had vandalised homes whilst searching them and had desecrated Catholic symbols such as crucifixes – accusations which were formally investigated but never proven. One certain result, however, was that the honeymoon with the local Catholic community in West Belfast had abruptly ended.

A year later, during which time the IRA had been revitalised, violence had escalated and the political situation deteriorated further, internment was ordered. The Army had warned Stormont, the de facto government of Northern Ireland still in place, against the imposition of internment because, among other things, it would alienate a whole community and provide a further boost to the IRA. Moreover, senior officers suspected – correctly it transpired – that the intelligence from which the list of those to be interned would be drawn was based on suspected Republican families from earlier IRA campaigns, and would by now be largely out of date. Moreover, arrest and detention without trial – for that is what internment meant – would play badly internationally.

Unfortunately, the Army's advice was not heeded either at Stormont or at a higher level by Home Secretary Reggie Maudling in London, who was ultimately answerable to Parliament for security throughout the whole United Kingdom.

At dawn on 9 August 1971 Corporal Crossland was ordered, along with thousands of other soldiers across the Province, to knock at various listed addresses and arrest the wanted occupants. They were often asleep alongside their young children, who were understandably terrified by the intrusion. Those arrested were bundled into lorries and taken off to be interrogated and, if appropriate, interned.

This was a disagreeable task for Graham and his men, who reflected uneasily – as most thoughtful soldiers did – that during the war alien occupying regimes had engaged in similar dawn swoops. Although the circumstances were not comparable, most soldiers nevertheless remember internment as a distasteful task. Moreover, it was not particularly successful from an operational point of view. Many of the wanted men had already fled south; and among those discovered at home there was often confusion over identity. An elderly grandfather, for instance, might carry the same Christian and surname as a youth being sought. Crossland recalls being ordered over the radio to bring in any suspect over whom doubt existed so that the RUC could sort it out later. As he remarked at the time, "We're certainly making a lot of enemies today."

Predictably, internment was loudly and widely condemned in North America, much of Europe and especially in the Republic of Ireland, where the British Embassy in Dublin was set on fire. The repercussions were soon felt by soldiers on patrol as the rejuvenated so-called 'Belfast brigade' of the IRA became increasingly active.

In the aftermath of internment, notwithstanding an improvement in the quality of intelligence, the darkest days of the Troubles occurred. Rioting would rage for days on end, gun battles could last for hours and it was quite common for more than 10,000 soldiers to be deployed on the ground at any one time. In 1972 there were 1,853 bomb attacks and 10,564 shootings, and 1,264 weapons were found along with more than 27 tonnes of explosives. That year 130 soldiers were killed as a direct result of terrorism. Indeed, the Army lost more soldiers killed in Northern Ireland (241) in the years 1971–5 than at the height of the action in Afghanistan thirty-five years later.

Graham Crossland remembers the dangers he faced in West Belfast following internment. He and his section felt most at risk when patrolling in a PIG – a large, lumbering, armoured vehicle which carried eight men. In a typical attack, a gunman would fire an explosive grenade as the vehicle slowed down to negotiate a corner, its occupants cooped up in the back and unable to see out or dismount quickly. Furthermore, soldiers knew that if the projectile hit the right spot it would penetrate the PIG's armour-plating, killing or wounding them.

In one such attack the grenade failed to penetrate the protective plates, yet its detonation created a massive shock wave which perforated the eardrums of two soldiers. They were all enveloped in a blue haze of cordite and smoke which temporarily blinded them.

Through this haze, Crossland, who was the first to recover his wits, remembers seeing a man running towards them. He assumed this to be the gunman, or an accomplice, coming to finish them off by tossing in a hand grenade or spraying automatic fire into the back of the stricken vehicle. But, as so often with 33 Alpha, luck – or, as Crossland would have it, the Almighty – was on their side. The man was a Protestant from an adjoining estate who had seen the attack and had bravely run over to assist.

This incident was a typical nightly occurrence to be logged at Company Headquarters as just another failed ambush. But Crossland recalls the tough reaction of his superiors when he got his soldiers safely back to base. Instead of being stood down for the night and getting the sympathy and attention they thought they deserved, their Company Sergeant Major barked: "You didn't complete your patrol, Corporal Crossland. Get out there again and finish your task!"

On active service soldiers want to be with lucky commanders. Corporal Crossland's section was considered to be fortunate because their leader, as well as being able, calm and popular, had developed a sixth sense for impending danger. Perhaps, his section deduced, Crossland's strong religious faith was behind it. Whatever the reason, they were pleased to be in Call-sign 33 Alpha, because on numerous occasions their commander had a 'hunch' or experienced something that alerted him to danger.

Once, when patrolling the Ballymurphy on foot, Crossland instinctively sensed a threat and deviated from his planned route. Quietly moving his patrol down a parallel alleyway instead, he approached from an unexpected direction and came upon a bomber at the end of a command wire waiting to detonate his explosive device. The bomber was now facing in the wrong direction, and the ensuing red-handed arrest further enhanced Crossland's growing reputation.

In an area of Belfast where the Green Howards had earlier had five soldiers killed, 33 Alpha was patrolling in a PIG. They were engaged by a gunman who had been given the signal to attack by an accomplice watching from a vantage point further along the street. Bullets entered through the vehicle's open back doors and ricocheted around inside, but amazingly no one was hit. It was a nasty near-miss, which badly shook the section.

Following the incident, a routine contact report was broadcast on the Green Howards' radio net. Hearing it, an alert sentry, who had noticed a man waving his arms about, realised that this had probably been the pre-arranged signal for the gunman to fire. Accordingly, the sentry guided 33 Alpha by radio on to the man.

Corporal Crossland duly arrested this apparent accomplice, although he was unarmed and had no incriminating evidence upon him. Still shaken and furious at so nearly having taken casualties, Crossland knocked the man down with his rifle butt.

In no time a complaint was lodged with the local Army HQ; and when 33 Alpha returned to their base in Flax Street Mill the Royal Military Police began an investigation by taking witness statements. Corporal Crossland was arrested and jailed in the bowels of the building. Giving evidence to the RMP, he confessed: "I done wrong. I shouldn't have hit him, I know; but I just lost it."

The complainant refused to give evidence in court on the basis that it would mean recognising British jurisdiction, which Republicans were loath to do. The case therefore had to be dismissed. But Crossland's suspension and the investigation were unpleasant experiences from which he and all concerned learnt salutary lessons about self-control and what happens if you act outside the law.

This illustration of the strict nature of Army discipline on patrol may appear to fit uneasily with the findings of Lord Saville's Report into the events of Bloody Sunday, when individual self-discipline and training broke down. Yet Crossland's experience is the true reflection of the Army's attitude to confrontation and the expectations and demands that good infantry regiments have of their soldiers. Regiments whose officers remain tightly in command and do not abandon control of their more excitable and headstrong soldiers ensure that their discipline holds, even under pressure. As the Chief of the General Staff wrote following publication of the Saville Inquiry: "The overwhelming majority of those deployed conducted themselves with utter professionalism, restraint and humanity." Likewise, Prime Minister Cameron commented: "Our Armed Forces displayed enormous courage and professionalism in upholding the rule of law."

That is not to say that soldiers found the sheer hatred which they regularly experienced on the streets other than disconcerting and even sometimes frightening. Soldiers recall the banging of dustbin lids and the whistle-blowing that heralded the approach of any patrol. Pye-dogs were specially trained – or so it seemed – to follow and bark ferociously at those wearing uniform. Military vehicles were invariably pelted with stones, rocks and garbage. On foot patrol, Corporal Crossland recalls being spat at by coarse-looking women, and his patrol was subjected to the foulest-mouthed abuse, even from toddlers. After any incident in which a soldier had been killed or wounded by the IRA, harridans, often dishevelled in their nightdresses and curlers, would spill on to the streets gleefully yelling a tally such as, "IRA 5: Green Howards 0", and chanting personal taunts about the dead soldier. Occasionally soldiers reacted, but mostly they ignored the provocation. However, these hateful scenes and the jarring Belfast accents were given nightly publicity on TV. Viewers at home were affronted by what they saw, and this contributed significantly to the wave of anti-Irish sentiment and despair that circulated on the mainland.

Even Mother Teresa, who visited the Ardoyne around this time at the behest of a Catholic housing organisation, appeared disconcerted at the vehemence generated by the presence of soldiers and the hostility to them. The company commander of Crossland's neighbouring sub-unit recalls this saintly person expressing her horror at such displays of violence and hatred; yet she felt unable to remonstrate or express her feelings lest her remarks be used for political purposes.

Crossland was the instigator of one retaliatory incident which came to national prominence. Graffiti were regularly daubed by locals on the walls of their slum estates. One new scrawl in the Green Howards' area read, 'Join your local IRA unit.' Crossland drew from the QM's stores a brush and a pot of white paint. On patrol that night, whilst passing the slogan,

33 Alpha quickly amended it to read, 'Join your local unit – the Green Howards!'

There was uproar locally when the fresh graffiti was revealed in daylight. Complaints poured in, priests and other representatives demanded to see the commanding officer, and the media relished the story. It served to illustrate the gulf between opposing attitudes. On the one hand, it could be portrayed as an insensitive provocation by ill-disciplined British squaddies; and on the other, it could be written up as a bit of cheeky but harmless fun at the IRA's expense.

The Army, always sensitive to something which might reflect poorly upon it, declared the matter to be under investigation, thereby gaining a breathing space. Meanwhile, the Green Howards had already begun their own inquiry, and Crossland had admitted to the deed.

To nip the complaint in the bud, Corporal Crossland was ordered to remove all trace of his offending slogan. But did that mean he was required to restore the original one? Returning to that same spot incurred the risk of being booby-trapped or ambushed. Surely the area should first be cleared and 'staked out'? But that would require a large presence of soldiers, which in turn would almost certainly provoke another disturbance. Resolving these practical considerations became the preoccupation of commanders at various levels, and even engaged the Ministry of Defence back in London. What began as 33 Alpha's harmless bit of fun had repercussions which Graham never anticipated.

Eventually, the issue was resolved. The local community lost patience and replaced 33 Alpha's slogan themselves with an even more vitriolic one.

Those on the Mainland were sometimes surprised to discover that privately many officers and men were sympathetic to the lot of the minority community. Crossland was among them. It was indicative of a malaise – or so the Army felt – that no senior politician or official from Stormont visited the slums on the Falls Road during the controversial four-day curfew. The Stormont government's urging of the Army 'to sort out the ghettos' on their behalf jarred with soldiers who are quick to spot something phoney or unfair.

Many soldiers who had experienced deprivation and hardship in their own early lives were appalled by the poor living standards and discrimination found in the ghettos of West Belfast. From the outset of the Troubles, soldiers tended to view the Catholic community as an oppressed minority with genuine grievances. Few soldiers got to see the substantial improvements made in the area in later years which went some way to removing the original grievances.

Privately, soldiers like Graham Crossland even reflected how easily they themselves, had they been fit, young Catholics living in West Belfast, could have succumbed to the call of the IRA. However, these same sentiments rarely extended to members of the neighbouring Protestant community, who, although equally socially deprived, were generally perceived as bigots and bullies. Their strutting demeanour during the 'Marching Season' in particular was held by soldiers to be partly responsible for the prevailing discord. When soldiers' morale touched bottom, they tended, unreasonably perhaps, to pin responsibility for being in 'this Godforsaken spot' upon Unionist intransigence.

For soldiers on operations it is important to feel that they have national approval and popular support for their endeavours. Crossland, like his comrades, was gratified – and often uplifted – throughout the Troubles by the understanding and encouragement they received from home. At Christmas the Forces Post Office was overwhelmed by thousands of extra cards and food parcels sent by the public to anonymous soldiers 'on duty away from home'. At no stage did Crossland's men feel they had lost the support of those on whose behalf they were engaged.

Admittedly, the *Mirror* group of newspapers ran a half-hearted 'Troops Out' campaign in the mid-seventies, and occasionally a bereaved mother or widow would make an impassioned plea for the withdrawal of troops from Northern Ireland. But by and large the Army enjoyed a strong degree of public support – albeit mostly unstated – for their patience and resilience in difficult circumstances. This was an important factor in maintaining soldiers' morale.

Politically too, the campaign was underpinned by the bi-partisan stance maintained by both major parties. Furthermore, the Army enjoyed the encouragement and appreciation of successive Northern Ireland Secretaries and Defence Secretaries. Shining examples were held to be Roy Mason (Labour's Northern Ireland Secretary in the mid-seventies) and George Younger (the Conservative Defence Secretary 1986-89). At home, opinion formers of all hues were perceived by the Army to be generally sympathetic to their needs and understanding of the pressures upon them. Such support may never be taken for granted; yet Crossland and his men, whilst politically unaligned, understood the importance of maintaining public support.

Meanwhile, on the streets there were many trying days and moments. Corporal Crossland recalls the sheer physical exhaustion, and numbing boredom of routine patrolling. His section mounted up to eight patrols, each of two hours' duration, in a 24-hour period. They repetitively circled their 'patch'– no more perhaps than six blocks and half a dozen streets – comprising the interfaces between the two warring communities. At times Graham had to drive himself and his section – physically and mentally urging them on – as another patrol was scheduled just hours after completing the last one, with only time in between for a snooze.

Most patrols passed off uneventfully. Soldiers built up an intelligence picture along their route, as much to maintain their interest as to satisfy the need for more information. For example, 33 Alpha was given tasks to perform like counting the milk bottles outside each house and comparing the result with the previous count. From this, a broad tally of the occupants of every house could be ascertained. Any subsequent increase or decrease in deliveries might indicate a significant change at that address.

Other indicators would be noted too, and a comprehensive local picture was built up over time, especially when supplemented by intelligence from other sources. Graham's section might be amused to see an apparently innocent packet of Omo washing powder visible in a downstairs window signalling 'Old Man Out'. But they had been briefed that such a seemingly insignificant observation might indicate more than just an invitation to a neighbour to pop round. If the absent man of the house was a suspected terrorist, this might indicate something significant to those checking alibis or trying to anticipate terrorist activity.

Such work was basic and unexciting, but when explained properly it appealed to the natural inquisitiveness of soldiers and helped maintain their interest and their sense of being valued.

The main grumble of Corporal Crossland's section was their appalling living conditions. They were billeted in factories, public buildings like the Ulster Hall (where the famous boxer Terry Downes used to fight) and empty schools and university buildings. During the Falls Road curfew, Crossland even recalls snatching a couple of hours' sleep on the top of a burnt-out double-decker bus. Wherever soldiers were temporarily billeted, conditions were cramped, hygiene was basic and catering rudimentary. Yet, perversely, Crossland's men – as is the way of soldiers – throve on extremes of discomfort and hardship, especially when they were demonstrably worse than those in cushier billets elsewhere.

For instance, the Army fortress at Crossmaglen, in South Armagh, was renowned for its austerity and vulnerability. A massive concrete blockhouse had been built there as a base – which had to be routinely reinforced – against frequent mortar attack. With no windows, and doors made of steel, it was hot, smelly and cramped. Off-duty soldiers often had to 'hot-bunk'. Yet a stint at Crossmaglen was considered to be the most prestigious duty in Ulster, and few would have swapped it for the safer and more commodious facilities at nearby Bessbrook Mill.

Crossland's three unaccompanied roulement tours lasted four and a half months each. Later, in order to provide better continuity, the Army extended these to six months. Operational effectiveness increased and the continuity of support to the RUC improved if units changed round less frequently. However, the corollary was that an upper limit of six months' absence from home was all that could be reasonably tolerated by families without adversely affecting morale.

Besides, as the campaign dragged on, Crossland and others became somewhat sceptical about what 'providing support for the RUC' really meant in practice. Whereas soldiers admired the brave and resolute local police, who were at much greater risk off-duty than themselves, they grumbled about some of the RUC's so-called 'Spanish practices' and their misuse of soldiers.

Military patrols were meant to be accompanied by an RUC officer to provide a 'legal' presence on the ground. But at weekends and during popular television programmes such as Match of the Day, quizzes and soaps, policemen, well-paid and on generous overtime, wanted to remain inside and watch TV. So supposedly 'off-duty' soldiers had to be sent out on patrol to replace them, but without legal cover if they got into difficulties.

Conversely, the RUC had their justifiable grumbles too. Senior policemen felt that some army colleagues could not be relied upon to keep to themselves what they had been told in strictest confidence. It was said that loose talk by army officers had blown the identity of various sources, thereby imperilling the intelligence effort. This criticism, in so far as it was occasionally justified, was a product of the Army's taut chain of command, which required important information to be passed upwards for a higher headquarters to distil. In contrast, police officers acting as individuals traditionally cultivated their own informants and kept their identities to themselves.

Other than the Victoria Cross, the Military Medal (MM) was, at the time, the most prized operational medal for gallantry in the face of an enemy. Unlike the VC, the MM was reserved exclusively for soldiers (until John Major's modernisation of the Honours system), and holders of the MM are especially admired and respected throughout the Army. Graham Crossland was awarded his MM for a series of brave actions during the late summer of 1971, a period of intense violence in West Belfast. Corporal Crossland's citation depicted a typical engagement which took place in September 1971.

During a night attack on the Green Howards' base, Corporal Crossland, already occupying a well protected, sandbagged position, observed through his night-sight two armed men closing in on some soldiers in an adjacent but exposed position. Crossland assessed that the only way he could protect his colleagues was by engaging the enemy. To do this he had to move out of his protected position and risk exposing himself to their fire. Without a thought, he left his hide and crawled into the open. He was now in a position properly to protect his comrades, within the terms of the Yellow Card, if the enemy opened fire on them, which they did. In the words of his official citation Corporal Crossland:

> at great risk to himself, was able to engage the enemy accurately thereby neutralising their attack on the neighbouring position.

The citation alluded to the fact that Corporal Crossland had killed one of the gunmen and wounded the other. His citation was endorsed by his brigade commander, the renowned Brigadier Frank Kitson, then the Army's foremost counter-terrorism expert, who wrote:

> This NCO's courage and initiative over a long period in an area of continual violence has done much to deter the terrorists.

After completing his three tours, Graham did not return to Northern Ireland again. This was not because he had fulfilled his quota of duty there – some men completed eight or more separate tours in Northern Ireland – but because his career path now took him in other directions: service with the United Nations in Cyprus, then back to the Green Howards in Berlin.

Prior to his returning to Germany, his first wife, Iona May, left him for an officer who was teaching her German. In any small community, particularly a regiment, where such scandals attract comment and humiliation in equal measure, this was a devastating blow for a sensitive man possessed of strong Christian principles and belief in the sanctity of his wedding vows.

However, this setback to Crossland's morale was alleviated somewhat by his promotion into the Warrant Officers' and Sergeants' Mess – a threshold and major accomplishment for any soldier. As Sergeant Crossland, MM, he continued to contribute widely to his Regiment's success. At the age of thirty-eight he was still undefeated in the Green Howards' boxing ring.

By the mid-1980s the end of Graham's regular service of twenty-two years beckoned. This is a difficult and uncertain time for any soldier because, still only in his forties, he has to decide where to settle as a civilian, what job to pursue and whether to buy or rent a home. Former soldiers often find that comparable jobs and environments with the same degree of comradeship and fulfilment are elusive.

Regiments, however, try to assist this transition into civilian life; so Graham was offered the job of a Senior Permanent Staff Instructor with one of Yorkshire's Territorial Army units in Guisborough. Although not a unit of the regular Army, many of its Permanent Staff were regulars like Graham. The appointment carried with it promotion to Warrant Officer Class 2. For Graham it was an ideal posting. He was back in Yorkshire, and he would benefit from local access to housing and to civilian jobs when he was finally discharged.

Graham wisely obtained two civilian qualifications against that day: a Heavy Goods Vehicle (HGV) driving licence followed by a licence to drive a Public Service Vehicle (PSV). On leaving the Army he secured a job as a bus driver with Darlington City Corporation.

However, the job did not require the experience and character of a highly decorated former soldier. Before long Graham found that the work was repetitive, and he felt that the Corporation's standards and management left much to be desired. By chance, one evening he met a former colleague from the Territorial Army who had heard of a vacancy with the Cleveland Army Cadet Force (ACF) as an Instructor.

Graham applied for this post in the rank of Second Lieutenant and was duly commissioned. Back in uniform, Graham felt reinvigorated. Happily, he met Pauline Johnson, a Yorkshire girl from Northallerton with two sons from a previous marriage. On 28 June 1986 they were married and have a daughter of their own.

Further professional good fortune was to follow. The appointment as Cadet Administrative Assistant in the rank of Captain became vacant and Graham was promoted into that post.

Captain Crossland, MM looks back on his time in Northern Ireland as one of the most fulfilling periods of his life. When he and his Regiment arrived in Belfast shortly after the onset of the Troubles, Ulster was imploding. Violence was widespread and fear stalked the polarised communities of West and East Belfast, of Londonderry and the larger towns. The only disciplined force preventing widespread anarchy was the British Army, itself attacked and abused. At the outset it provided some stability and order so that eventually moderate influences could take root. Yet, for almost three decades these influences could not become established.

Graham Crossland makes no exaggerated claims of his own contribution. He was but one of more than a quarter of a million Service personnel who served there during the Troubles. Thousands of Soldier's Tales similar to Graham's could be told – some served there longer, and many were engaged in more hazardous exploits. Others were just as brave and committed as Crossland. Indeed, at his Buckingham Palace Investiture in 1972 Crossland recalls that ninety-seven recipients of Northern Ireland service or gallantry awards were being honoured by the Queen.

Several regiments experienced a greater number of casualties than did the Green Howards; some units adopted higher profiles and claimed more spectacular success. But for sheer dogged determination and for consistency of effort, coupled with patient good humour, Graham's performance and that of his Regiment was emblematic of the Army's even-handed and disciplined commitment. Arguably, no other Army could have held the ring so staunchly and so effectively for over thirty years.

3

The Chief Executive's Tale

Author's Introduction
Harland and Wolff's 'Samson' and 'Goliath' are the massive twin cranes which dominate Belfast's skyline. Below their yellow gantries, 300 feet above Queen's Island, a 2000-acre industrial site sits. It was from here that Harland and Wolff fitted out and launched the Titanic *prior to her ill-fated transatlantic maiden voyage. Here too the renowned Short Brothers, now owned by the Canadian company Bombardier, was located. Shorts were the manufacturers of numerous aircraft, such as the giant Belfast freighter and Sunderland Flying Boat, and were world-class contributors to the international aerospace industry.*

The Chairman and Managing Director of Short Brothers was an Englishman, Sir Philip Foreman CBE. I did not know Sir Philip at the time but I was aware of the significance of Belfast's largest employer and knew that what Harland and Wolff was to shipbuilding, Short Brothers was to the aerospace industry.

I was also well aware of the importance of Northern Ireland's industrial base and of the Province's need for a buoyant economy and full employment, if the Troubles were ever to be resolved. Our pre-deployment background briefings had explained the Government's strategy, which rested on four supporting pillars – political progress, social fairness, a strong economy and effective security – which, when achieved and suitably robust, would enable a return to 'normality', a condition that no one ever managed to define convincingly.

One attempt at industrial investment had already failed spectacularly. The American DeLorean Car Company had been encouraged to invest in West Belfast with the offer of a purpose-built factory. But the predominantly Nationalist local workforce's lack of skills, exacerbated by poor quality control, led to unreliability and eventually to bankruptcy after John DeLorean himself was arrested on drug charges. As a consequence, the factory closed and, according to Westminster's Public Accounts Committee Report (dated 18 July 1984), the British taxpayer lost £77 million.

In contrast, Shorts' large skilled workforce was mostly from the other community – the Protestant one – and drawn from the hard-line Unionist heartlands like Ballymacarrett in East Belfast. Knowing the nature of such communities, I was able to appreciate the adverse effect that the crippling Ulster

Workers' Strike of 1974 must have had on both Shorts and Harland and Wolff. Furthermore, I could visualise the management's difficulties in adhering to the Government's 'equal opportunity' and 'fair-employment' legislation, which were important tools in the fight against discrimination.

At the time, I considered the Army's challenges were hard enough but I did not realise, until I invited Sir Philip Foreman to contribute, just how tough it was to be responsible for managing Northern Ireland's largest and pre-eminent industry. The worsening political and security climate of the early seventies drove lesser men than Sir Philip, from all walks of life, to up sticks and leave the country altogether. But Sir Philip, whose Tale follows, was made of tougher stuff, and he persevered despite the difficulties.

* * *

By the mid-seventies the tensions and violence that Simon Hoggart was reporting (Tale 1) and that Corporal Crossland experienced daily on patrol in Belfast (Tale 2) had affected attitudes throughout the Province, and on the Mainland too.

Locally, those working in Belfast's important industrial communities were critical of the deteriorating security situation, and disliked the attitudes and the policies emanating from Westminster – which had exercised Direct Rule since March 1972 – and they made their dismay felt.

Many of their concerns were shared – but not always for the same reasons – by HMG who had taken over Short Brothers in 1943 under emergency wartime provisions, as an industry of strategic national importance. Shorts was directly accountable through a local Executive Committee, beneath a main Board in London, for its internal affairs and its financial viability. But HMG held ultimate responsibility, and alarm bells were ringing in Westminster at the alleged inequality of job opportunities and at the sheer power, in terms of influence and possible industrial action, concentrated in Northern Ireland's key industry.

The financial health and economic stability of the Province was reliant on the inward investment and revenue generated by companies such as Shorts. Furthermore, throughout the Troubles HMG sought to demonstrate internationally that 'normality' prevailed in Northern Ireland. Any significant industrial or civil unrest of a sectarian flavour undermined this claim.

Since 1967 Shorts' Chief Executive had been Philip Foreman, an Englishman recruited originally from the Royal Naval Scientific Service. In

1983 Philip was appointed to the combined posts of Chairman and Managing Director. So, for twenty years, throughout the worst of the Troubles – he retired in 1988 – Foreman was responsible for the day-to-day running of this world-class company which was Northern Ireland's most prestigious manufacturer and the Province's largest employer.

Philip discovered at the outset that Short Brothers were proud of their history. Their story had begun in 1909 when three brothers, Horace, Eustace and Oswald Short, with eight years' engineering expertise under their belts, were building the *Wright Flyer* for those famous pioneers of US aviation, the Wright Brothers.

That same year, a War Office committee, established to consider the possible future use of military aviation, decided that there was no place for aeroplanes on the battlefield; for one thing, it was said, they would frighten the horses!

Undeterred, the Short brothers turned to the Senior Service and, thankfully from an Allied point of view, successful experiments took place with sea planes flying from warships and torpedo-carrying Royal Navy aircraft in time for combat in the 1914–18 War.

As aviation developed, the business prospered and by 1936 Short Brothers had expanded production from their factory in Rochester, Kent to a second manufacturing base in Belfast at Queen's Island, on the south-eastern shore of the Lough. It was from here that Shorts became such an important national asset in the Second World War that HMG took the firm into national ownership in 1943, where it remained until 1989.

Philip Foreman's origins are English. He was born on 16 March 1923 in the small Suffolk village of Exning, where his father Frank worked as a tractor driver on a nearby farm. Philip's early life centred on the farm. His father undertook the installation, maintenance and repair of all the farm machinery, and this rubbed off on young Philip, who developed an interest in design and all things mechanical. Indeed, he treasured a Meccano set from which he constructed working models of farm machinery.

Philip's early education was at the local Church of England elementary school: first in Exning and later in the village of Fordham. Then, having passed his 11-plus, he obtained a scholarship to Soham Grammar School, where he took his School Certificate. He determined to leave school at sixteen to earn his living in Ely, where the family were now living. But he failed to secure either of the jobs he wanted, and so with parental blessing – his mother was the driving force, his father tending to endorse her line – he returned to school for a further two years and was encouraged by his woodwork teacher to apply for a British Empire Open Scholarship to Loughborough College. Although not the strongest academic candidate, the boy was single-minded and determined, particularly as his headmaster had predicted his "inevitable failure", suspecting aloud that Philip "would let the school down."

Foreman found the interview, conducted over several days in Loughborough, daunting. So he was overjoyed when notified of his success; however, provision for a scholarship only covered the cost of tuition and he had to seek financial assistance from the local education authority. Despite this, Philip felt the pinch financially throughout his residential study. Undeterred, he left Loughborough in 1943 with a first-class honours degree in mechanical engineering.

With the Second World War at a crucial stage, his ambition as he approached twenty was to become involved in the conflict before it ended. He applied to join the Royal Navy but to his dismay was rejected outright due to colour blindness. Instead, he was directed into the Royal Naval Scientific Service, which was then a specialised department of the Civil Service. This was a severe disappointment for a keen young man seeking to make his mark in uniform in wartime. But, despite his protests and appeals, Philip was drafted under wartime emergency regulations to the Admiralty Research Laboratory at Teddington as a Temporary Experimental Assistant Grade 3 on a salary of £200 per annum.

Allocated to a department charged with the design and development of future hydraulic servo-systems for the Royal Navy and Army, Philip found the work surprisingly stimulating. It involved projects such as the stabilisation of the mirror deck-landing system for aircraft carriers, the trials of which afforded him his first ever flight, from Lee-on-Solent to land on HMS *Illustrious* in the English Channel – a never-to-be-forgotten experience for an impressionable young man. Later, Philip conducted research fundamental to the successful guidance of many remotely controlled weapon systems. This work was at the leading edge of technological development and was immensely satisfying.

Philip prospered both at Teddington and later at Portland, where a new Admiralty Gunnery Establishment had been built to carry out this specialist and secret work. In due course, Philip was given his first major responsibility: to design the four-barrelled launcher from which the *Seacat* missile could be fired on board ship.

This project brought him into close contact with Short Brothers, the designer and chosen manufacturer of the missile. Now aged 35, married, and a Senior Scientific Civil Servant of fifteen years' experience, Philip was offered the newly created appointment of Head of the Ship Equipment Department in the Precision Engineering Division of Shorts in Northern Ireland.

The appointment, which gave him responsibility for designing all the non-flying equipment associated with the company's guided weapons, meant that Philip had to relocate from London to Belfast in the late fifties. This was a decade before the start of what came to be known as 'The Troubles', and Northern Ireland appeared to be serenely at peace.

Away from Belfast and the major towns, the beautiful countryside was strikingly green and bathed in a soft light. When it rained, it was as if a soft garden spray was lightly falling. Everyone seemed open and friendly – never too busy to stop and chat, or to enjoy a good joke. To the casual observer there was no sense of a divided community, or any indication of the intensity of the feelings and hatreds which were to erupt and afflict the Province in the decades ahead.

Notwithstanding this appeal and Philip's own rosy prospects, he recalls arriving in Belfast on a Sunday afternoon in the autumn of 1958, walking with his wife Elizabeth, whom he had married six years before, through the deserted city centre, and feeling downcast. The October skies were grey, a cold wind was blowing and the shop doorways were strewn with newspapers and the general detritus left by overnight revellers. He momentarily harboured doubts about the wisdom of his decision to leave comfortable England and settle in what seemed that afternoon like a run-down and distant outpost of the kingdom.

Furthermore, as they settled in and adjusted to their new surroundings, the Foremans sensed that their reception was mixed. Although most of the senior staff were friendly and cooperative, Philip and Elizabeth knew they were not fully accepted. At his first Christmas party, Philip remembers the caustic remarks of one staunch Ulsterman who was a senior member of the team Philip now headed. Ostensibly welcoming the Foremans, the man reminded his listeners that their new boss was a "bloody-Englishman" – clearly a hyphenated word, as far as he was concerned.

Had the Ulsterman but known it, Philip's uncle had served with the notorious Black and Tans in Dublin in 1920. This would have been considered an accolade in parts of the North and would have greatly enhanced the reputation of the new Head of Department, making Philip much more acceptable in bigoted eyes. But his impartiality and apolitical attitude were ingrained, and he never alluded to the fact.

By 1967, after only nine years with the Company, Foreman, aged only forty-four, was appointed Managing Director and Chief Executive Officer. Now the destiny and direction of one of the most important parts of Northern Ireland's industrial base, employing 8,000 people, was his responsibility. Foreman's rise had been meteoric. But he now faced some severe management and commercial challenges.

Industrially, Northern Ireland was depressed in the late fifties. Unemployment was in double figures and the first signs of future difficulties facing the nation's heavy manufacturing industries were apparent. The once high wartime level of orders had declined, and Shorts had to adjust to the commercial demands of peace. Orders were becoming increasingly hard to secure and the cost of raw materials, especially steel, was often in excess of the overall value of finished foreign imports.

Shorts, along with the rest of the British aircraft industry, was not immune from these difficulties. The 1965 Plowden Report, commissioned to analyse and find solutions to these difficulties, had recommended that the airframe industry should be consolidated into two main groups – the British Aircraft Corporation and Hawker-Siddeley Aircraft. Shorts, along with Handley-Page, would be part of neither. This was a depressing moment at which to take over the reins of a major company.

Foreman and his board had to restructure the company. One option was to retrench, cut back and concentrate on Shorts' growing and successful missile business. However, the board decided not to pursue this route, which would have ended the company's proud history as an aircraft manufacturer. Rather, Foreman advocated a balanced approach, making the missile business one facet of a tripartite structure. The other two components would be a small civil transport aeroplane – based on the Skyvan – and lightweight aero-structures, such as wings, flight controls and engine cowls.

The building blocks were already in place, and the proposals could be swiftly adopted. However, one painful decision was necessary first: to close the general engineering division that had become commercially uncompetitive. This was locally unpopular, and Philip caught a taste of the Ulsterman's wrath, as he was to do more severely later.

Around this time, HMG decided, without consulting Shorts, to decentralise and transfer the shareholding of their plc from the DTI to the Northern Ireland Department of Commerce. The latter had no experience or expertise in the aerospace industry and therefore had to seek advice from Whitehall on all major technical and commercial issues. To Philip's irritation, this lengthened and sometimes duplicated the decision-making process, resulting in cumbersome and highly frustrating delays.

Moreover, the imposition of Direct Rule in 1972 had resulted in an influx of Westminster politicians and Whitehall civil servants to run the Province, few with any feel for industrial engineering.

As Chief Executive, Foreman had two worries which he tackled head on: levels of employment and the size of wage packets.

Rumours that jobs might be at risk prompted the shop stewards to seek immediate political support from Stormont. Foreman recalls:

This ritual was usually met with smooth words but no commitment from the politicians, but at least the union leaders could report back that they had exerted their influence to good effect, even though in practice nothing had changed. As far as wage demands were concerned the politicians rightly refused to become involved.

Foreman's other worries concerned the low levels of productivity and the excessive overheads in calculating 'dues'. He learnt that the individual reward for each worker (i.e. 'the dues') was based on the estimated time taken to complete a given task. The system relied on a host of 'estimators' to set the times and arrange fair, realistic targets. But the arrangement was open to manipulation by many of the estimators who, Foreman judged, were in the pockets of the workers.

Foreman's solution was to abandon individual piece-work and replace it with a system of rewards based on the performance of discrete groups of workers. But this made Foreman unpopular with some who could no longer determine their own wage levels. Conversely, it earned him the respect of many more who had long recognised the abuse and were delighted to see it challenged and rectified.

At the same time, Foreman decreed that Shorts would move from payment by weekly pay packet to payment by cheque. This would be cheaper, for it reduced the need for clerical staff to make up and distribute pay packets, and obviated the requirement for an armoured van, with police escort, to deliver cash. An unintended spin-off from the change was that the men could not so easily hide from their wives any bonus payments.

By now the Troubles were underway and sectarian tension was running high. Traditionally, Shorts' workforce had been drawn from nearby East Belfast, where a small Catholic workforce, living in the Short Strand on the east bank of the River Lagan, coexisted with the much larger Protestant community of Ballymacarett. By the early seventies their peaceful coexistence had evaporated after a series of violent incidents in which the homes of Catholics in the Short Strand were set ablaze and had to be abandoned. Violent retaliation heightened the tension, and its effects bedevilled relationships at Shorts for many years.

It was the issue of discrimination in the workforce that Foreman found most difficult to handle, because of its long history and sectarian connotations. As a government-owned industry, Shorts had to operate an open, non-discriminatory policy. But its implementation was dependent on the cooperation of the staff who managed the workforce.

Foreman thought he understood the staff procedures and morale within the company until one day he discovered that employment application forms were routinely being intercepted by a senior shop steward who was an influential Loyalist on the Ulster Workers' Council.

"This was dynamite," Foreman explained, "and was extremely difficult to rectify. Decent employees were being intimidated and induced to behave in a way they would not normally have contemplated."

The whole issue of discrimination had wide ramifications impacting on commercial contracts and politics. Quangos and executive bodies, like the Fair Employment Agency and the Equal Opportunities Commission, became involved in seeking to keep the company free of bias. Other pressure groups with more sinister and radical agendas, such as the Irish National Caucus in Washington DC and the local Ulster Workers' Council, also made their presence felt. Philip found this to be both commercially and morally unwelcome.

For example, throughout the Troubles influence was exerted by the Irish National Caucus, an umbrella group for the majority of Irish-American organisations. Some 42 million North American citizens claim Irish extraction, and their influence, when well focussed, is powerful. Many are still resentful of Britain's role in Ireland's history and are burdened by tales of past tragedies like the potato famine.

Father Sean McManus was the Caucus's national coordinator, and Philip recalls that the priest "spared no opportunity to stir the pot on the issue of alleged discrimination against Catholics."

"Shorts had no such discriminatory policy", Philip insisted, "and I found McManus's bitter prejudice unwelcome. His malign influence was felt during the competition to supply a small number of aircraft to the USAF for their Strike Force in Europe."

Foreman recalls McManus trying to have Shorts' bid excluded. However, after months of deliberation, the US Air Force rejected all competitors other than Short's Sherpa and the Spanish Casa 212. A delighted Foreman felt that technically either could do the job but that his Sherpa was marginally superior.

But to win we had to deploy all our strength to head off Father McManus's influence. He had already tried to influence adversely our own airline customers as well as our commercial ones, such as Boeing, and their airlines. Fortunately, some months previously, we had engaged a professional US lobbyist, John O'Malley, a Catholic ex-US Marine Corps pilot, to press our case. He was highly respected on the Hill in Washington and was also acceptable to the Irish Embassy.

O'Malley was instrumental in securing their invaluable political support and Shorts won the contract.

A series of security scares were about to involve Foreman, and this eclipsed his concern about the activities of the Irish National Caucus. He recalls:

Without doubt, by far our worst situation was triggered by the Sunningdale Agreement in late 1973 which created the Power Sharing Executive and provoked the defiant Ulster Workers' Strike. Inspired by the Vanguard Party and by Ian Paisley's Democratic Unionist Party (DUP), the trade unions took to the streets and brought life in the Province to a halt. There was no power and no fuel; food was in short supply; no transport services operated; and as a result industry came to a complete standstill.

I was even physically barred from entering my own office by barricades at the entrance to the factory manned by my own employees.

From our family perspective what was worse was that our son had been born that summer. Domestically we were anxious and greatly inconvenienced – as were many others of course – by the practical effect of the strike in terms of the essentials needed to care properly for a baby: no power or heat; absence of warm milk, no petrol for post-maternity visits, or for travel of any sort.

Direct threats against individuals were serious too. Like many others in the public eye, I received regular visits from the police, as well as from Special Branch, to warn that my name was on some list or other, and to advise me what I should and should not do. Security briefings stressed the importance of not setting up predictable patterns of activity or behaviour, and always to vary one's route. But almost everyone at risk was confronted by unavoidable practicalities when leaving or returning home – the choice of alternatives was extremely limited. However, physical surveillance devices were installed and other security measures were put in place, and soon our home resembled a fortress.

For one particular period I was not even allowed to cross the City en route to Aldergrove Airport without a police escort. Yet, despite all such precautions, a CBI colleague, Geoff Agate of DuPont, was shot dead as he arrived home by car one evening. This shook us all, as did the kidnapping of Don Tidey, a senior supermarket executive, in Dublin.

Tidey was later released, presumably on the payment of the ransom demand.

Earlier, Thomas Niedermayer, who was Head of Grundig as well as Honorary West German Consul in Belfast, had been kidnapped.

He was never seen again, although it was revealed years later that his body had been buried in what was known in IRA circles as the 'Mulberry Patch', between Monaghan and Donegal in Eire.

Such disconcerting incidents affected the morale of the families of the Province's senior businessmen and industrialists; and they themselves contemplated their potential vulnerability. In all there were six kidnappings during that period, of which the most widely reported was not that of a prominent citizen but of a famous race horse: Shergar, owned by the Aga Khan and stolen on 8 February 1984 from his stud farm in Co Kildare.

Foreman recalls the commercial repercussions of such tension:

Our customers became restive. Those in work-sharing agreements, such as Boeing, wanted to distance themselves from the Troubles. Boeing, for example, threatened to send an aircraft from Seattle with a team of mechanics to rip the jigs from the Shorts factory floor and re-site them in Seattle. Fast talking was required to persuade them that not only would this be unwise, but unsafe too. Eventually, we agreed that once the factory reopened we would establish a contingency stock of completed components and store them – at our own expense – in a safe haven off-site.

To add to our difficulties, just as the Company was staving off allegations of discrimination against Catholics, the predominantly Protestant workforce was festooning the factory with provocative flags, bunting and other items demonstrating their 'loyalty'. When, in accordance with Company policy the flags and symbols were removed, the demonstrators accused the Company of stealing their property and demanded them back! Seven hundred workers walked out in protest at our action.

The *Guardian* picked this up and reported Philip's robust response:

In a tough statement sent to his 7,200 workers, Foreman asserted the Company had an obligation to provide an atmosphere free from intimidation. [If the walk-outs continued] he could not guarantee to keep the factory open.

Then, the usual mischief-making occurred. The *Irish Times* reported that Philip's blunt letter evoked an angry response from the Rev Ian Paisley, who condemned it as "high handed and arrogant". The DUP leader proclaimed:

There is a concerted effort to drag the national flag of our country into the gutter. This is a clear result of the Anglo–Irish Agreement and is a symbol of the joint authority under which Ulster is governed at the present time.

Episodes of defiance and other unpleasant incidents occurred at the factory. The Harland and Wolff Band, which traditionally had performed for the 12th of July celebrations, was coerced into playing the most provocative sectarian songs on the public road below Philip's office, so that he was unable to work.

More sinisterly, a senior Shop Steward, a rabid Loyalist, sidled up to Philip one morning and advised, "Mind you take good care of your young son." The boy, then aged six, was at Rockport, the local preparatory school. The implication was that he had been specifically traced there and targeted.

On another occasion, shortly before Shorts' HS 125 Executive Jet took off with Philip aboard for a meeting in London, a foreign object was found to have been placed in one of the intakes. Had the engine been started the result could have been catastrophic. In a separate incident, sabotage was discovered on the aircraft assembly line, where some electrical wiring had been severed during the night shift.

Earlier in the Troubles, the Army's General Officer Commanding, Lieutenant-General Sir Frank King, had alerted Philip that Loyalist weapons were being manufactured in Shorts' machine shop. Philip was unable to find any direct evidence but concluded, "there must have been some truth in it, maybe some precision parts were being machined there for assembly elsewhere."

Finally, as all other methods had failed to persuade Philip to soften his line on flags and sectarian symbols, he received a letter delivered by hand from the 'Loyalist Action Force' prior to publication in the *Belfast Telegraph*:

> The LAF demands that flags and bunting removed by the management at Shorts be replaced immediately and the lock-out of loyalist workers ended.
>
> Failure to comply with these demands will leave us no alternative but to take punitive action against those guilty of trampling over the rights of Ulster Workers.
>
> We warn the Shorts Management, in particular Sir Philip Foreman, that the patriotism of loyal Ulstermen will be neither bought nor intimidated and that the safety of anyone attempting to do so cannot be guaranteed.
>
> We also warn the would-be Lodges of the CSEU [Confederation of Shipbuilding and Engineering Unions] that their despicable sell-out of their members rights will not be tolerated.
>
> Signed Capt TA Calderwood LAF HQ

Underneath in biro had been scrawled:

This document must be destroyed after copying.

According to Foreman, the organisers wanted a Province-wide display of flags. Additionally, they had arranged strikes within factories in the DUP heartlands, where they would have most impact. Shorts, as the largest employer in the Province, owned by HMG and with a worldwide customer base, was naturally a prime target. Foreman further explained:

> Being English, I was neutral but the Catholics saw me as unsympathetic and the Loyalists as suspect! My strong belief was that flags and bunting had no place in the workplace and, indeed, they presented a factory hazard which we could not condone. Despite considerable pressure from the DUP, we stood firm and eventually the threats subsided.

In my opinion the Confederation of Shipbuilding and Engineering Unions (CSEU) had behaved most responsibly throughout what was, essentially, a political strike. In effect, they guided the workforce successfully away from a damaging and escalating confrontation.

Once the Ulster Workers' Strike, which succeeded in fatally undermining the Sunningdale Agreement, ended, the bad blood and tensions at Shorts, and the violence generally in Belfast, subsided.

It should have been a time of calm consolidation; but Philip's preoccupation became catching up with lost time and orders. When the strike was over Shorts expanded, taking on more staff. Their turnover quadrupled between 1974 (£24.6 million) and 1980 (£90.7 million). Ten SD330 aircraft, a 30-seater passenger/freighter for the overseas commuter market, were in scheduled service with five airlines in USA, Canada and Europe.

That year's Chairman's Annual Statement reported that these aircraft had carried between them 335,000 passengers, and Shorts had firm orders or formal letters of intent for sales of a further eighteen. By 1980 the firm orders and options for the aircraft had increased to 77, involving 25 operators in 11 countries. Meanwhile, the Missiles Systems Division secured a repeat order from the MoD for over £20 million of *Blowpipe* systems for the Territorial Army. Lastly, the Aero-structures Division secured the largest single order ever placed with the company – the multimillion pound contract for the supply of 400 aircraft sets of inner wing-flap assemblies for the Boeing 757.

On the face of it, therefore, despite under-capitalisation and the burden of Government debt, Shorts appeared to be flourishing, and reflected one of the few positive images emanating from Northern Ireland.

Domestically, too, it was a good time for Foreman. His first marriage had been dissolved in 1970, and he had been living on his own in Helen's Bay, an attractive residential area on the shores of Belfast Lough. During this time he met and married Margaret Cooke, who was the personal secretary to Shorts' commercial director.

But storm clouds were gathering. Despite Shorts' favourable order book and its new-found industrial calm, the reality, largely unrecognised outside the company, was that by the second half of the 1970s Shorts was in trouble commercially.

Five adverse situations afflicted virtually the whole of British industry at the time. Interest rates were unusually high; inflation was rising; the

Government's statutory pay restraint policy from 1977 onwards sharply reduced bonuses and incentives to the workforce, which adversely affected morale and production; exchange rates – especially against the dollar – were unfavourable, reducing Shorts' annual profitability by some £1.5 million, according to the 1979 Report and Accounts. And finally, international aviation was experiencing a worldwide recession.

Each of these factors had a negative impact on Shorts' profitability, and they accounted for the balance sheet's showing a £9 million deficit after tax in the last three years of the decade. The Chairman's 1979 Statement concluded:

> The past year has been difficult and the financial results reflect a set of circumstances, both internal and external, which we would not want to see repeated.

Mainly in response to the difficult economic, security and political situation, HMG unveiled another Northern Ireland initiative in 1977. Its purpose was to promote and develop a more coherent economic strategy for the Province to support HMG's political and security aims. These were founded on four pillars – a coherent political structure, a fair social system, a strong security pillar and a healthy economy. All four pillars needed to be strong and in good repair if terrorism was to be defeated and if Northern Ireland was to resume its place as a peaceful and prosperous province of the United Kingdom.

One economic initiative was to create an Economic Council to advise on the potential commercial strengths of the Province, with a view to identifying and supporting new business opportunities. The Council comprised representatives both of the employers, nominated by the CBI, and of the trades unions, appointed by the CSEU. Shorts, as the largest employer in the Province, would inevitably become involved. Hence Philip was invited to join.

The Council considered matters requiring urgent treatment, such as investment opportunities, along with long-term economic or structural defects in Northern Ireland's industrial base. But Philip, who did not care for bureaucracy in any guise, doubted whether the Council could achieve anything worthwhile. However, he accepted that membership could promote informal dialogue between employers and trades unions on issues of potential disagreement, without violating the formal positions of their parent bodies.

By 1983 Philip had become something of an industrial doyen. He now had a platform from which he could point out the uncomfortable truth (for

HMG) that for a quarter of a century a business owned by the British taxpayer had been starved of Government contracts for aircraft and aero structures. Worse, government policies had actually concentrated the work in the hands of rivals. These policies, coupled with the enormous interest payments levied on the Government's own debt at Shorts, were albatrosses around Shorts' neck. In his Chairman's Statement of 1987 Philip publicly spelt out this absurdity: 'The continued crippling level of interest charges results from the Company's unsatisfactory capital structure ... £12.5 million relates to the servicing of borrowings arising from losses in the previous year.'

By the late 1980s multiple privatisations were taking place on the mainland, and the process soon crossed the Irish Sea. Hence, the last phase of Philip's thirty-year involvement with Shorts was spent preparing the company for successful privatisation – or, more accurately, for its return to the private sector.

The intention to re-privatise Shorts was officially announced in the 1988 Chairman's Statement, covering Philip's last year in post. It pointed out that Shorts 'was bottom of the world league of capital investment per employee, and had an inappropriate capital structure.' Reassuringly, presumably for the benefit of potential acquirers, it went on: 'HM Government recognises that this is the case and has indicated that the Company will be recapitalised prior to privatisation.'

Two external bids had already been received. The first had come from the GEC-Fokker consortium and the second from the French-Canadian company Bombardier, based in Montreal. Bombardier wanted to keep Shorts intact and to ensure the continuation of aircraft design and production in Belfast. This settled the matter in their favour, and Bombardier became the preferred bidder. In June 1989 the ownership of Shorts was duly transferred to them from HMG.

A junior Northern Ireland Minister, the shrewd and energetic Richard Needham, who had local responsibilities for industrial matters, pointed out in his book *Battling for Peace* what he saw as the delightful irony of this privatisation:

Bombardier, whose origins were from the minority Catholic community in Canada, took over an essentially Protestant company in Northern Ireland. They brought in fresh ideas, fresh money – mostly taxpayers' – fresh hope and a new management style where before there had been stifling government bureaucracy and a measure of despair.

Bombardier was as delighted with their acquisition as were the workers with their new owners. This proved that East Belfast workers were perfectly content to work for Catholic masters, albeit French-Canadian ones.

On the eve of Philip's retirement, the then Secretary of State for Northern Ireland, Tom King, hosted a special dinner in his honour at Hillsborough Castle, his imposing official residence outside Belfast.

Mr King (now Lord King of Bridgwater) paid tribute to Philip's thirty-year career at Shorts and commented that he was one of those select few who had arrived hesitantly in Ulster as an imported Englishman and, despite the Troubles and some associated unpleasantness, had integrated fully.

That an Englishman sustained the leadership at Shorts, an iconic Ulster manufacturing giant, for so long despite all the impediments thrown up by the Troubles, by the Government and by the industry itself, is worthy of tribute. The fine personal qualities of Shorts' chairman became so admired by Ulstermen that on his retirement, having been awarded the CBE for services to industry and exports in 1972 and having been knighted twenty years later, he made his home among them.

4

The Source Handler's Tale

Author's Introduction
My fourth tour, in 1976, took me back to Belfast, this time as a Company
Commander responsible for the troublesome areas adjacent to the New Lodge
Road and Crumlin Road in the north of the city. This was a flash-point: one of
the places where the Catholic community felt threatened by their neighbours, and
vice versa. It was where IRA Volunteers lived, and from where they mounted
their attacks.

By now the Troubles had already lasted longer than the Second World War.
Pitched battles between the two opposing communities had reduced in frequency
and intensity, and the RUC routinely handled whatever residual disorder
remained. Reflecting greater confidence in the police, a new policy of 'Police
Primacy' had been announced whereby the RUC assumed the lead in the fight
against terrorism. In other words, the roles of the RUC and Army had been
reversed and the Army were subordinated to the RUC, except in the most difficult
areas like South Armagh.

The Army now set about revising some of its earlier priorities and methods.
Initially, in their urgency to restore law and order, soldiers had been too
indiscriminate and vigorous; too many citizens had been unnecessarily
inconvenienced and alienated, too many random arrests had been made, and some
wholly unjustifiable incidents had occurred, as the Saville Inquiry indicated. A
dilemma for the Security Forces in any democracy is to ensure that operations are
targeted at those who take up arms against the State, whilst those that do not
break the law but may sympathise with the cause of those perpetrating violence
are left alone. This requires subtlety, good discipline and, above all, accurate local
intelligence.

The absence initially of the latter (for the reasons explained in other Tales)
was what the Army had to rectify. Intelligence gathering became a priority;
consequently, it became imperative for those who directed and engaged in armed
conflict to thwart, by all possible means, the Army's endeavour to improve its
intelligence. They tried, and sometimes succeeded, by smearing the methods and
legality of intelligence gathering.

Recording what this concentration on intelligence meant in practice, I want to describe something of the work of Peter Jones of my Regiment, who had once been a young soldier in my platoon. He was one of those dedicated and brave soldiers with the rare aptitude and confidence to work undercover.

His is the Source Handler's Tale.

* * *

(In this chapter alone some identities have been disguised)

Peter Jones passes unnoticed in a crowd. Yet this dyslexic former Warrant Officer in the British infantry played so significant a role in Britain's fight against terrorism during the Troubles in Northern Ireland, that his work as a source handler – that is, a recruiter and controller of those prepared to assist the Security Forces – was formally recognised by the award, not just of the Queen's Gallantry Medal but later of the George Medal too. At the time, only one other serviceman – a bomb disposal officer – held this double distinction.

Notwithstanding his remarkable record, within a few years of leaving the Army Jones was divorced, bankrupt, living rough and forced to sell his medals to make ends meet. A proud and private man, he alerted no one to his plight. Friends and former colleagues, who noticed that he was drinking too much and did not seem himself, assumed this was part of a new undercover persona he had had to adopt, and did not enquire further.

Sadly, the reality, as will emerge later, was different.

Peter Jones, known as PJ, was a wartime baby, one of twin boys born in Poole, Dorset on 21 September 1944 shortly after the Allied Liberation of Paris. His shrewd, pretty mother was from the lovely Devon village of Lustleigh. His father, from nearby Moretonhampstead on Dartmoor, worked for an asphalt company in Parkstone.

The family's achievements were notable. Both of PJ's brothers went to university. The elder, David, now deceased, became a senior partner of accountants Price Waterhouse International and lived in comfortable retirement in the British Virgin Islands. PJ's twin brother is a physicist responsible for the research and development programme of Raychem, a US defence contractor.

Earlier generations of Joneses were interesting too. PJ's maternal grandfather fought at the relief of Ladysmith in the Anglo–Boer War of 1901, and his paternal great-great-grandfather, Richard Trevithick from

Helston in Cornwall, was the famous inventor who converted the first steam engine at a tin mine to run on rails. As PJ dryly recalls, one forebear was the Mayor of Penzance, another a pirate from Penzance.

An active and quick-witted boy with an enquiring mind, PJ was severely handicapped at school by dyslexia. No one recognised the condition then, or even that his learning was impaired. Thus his academic attainments were dismal. Yet a fit, inquisitive and gregarious boy like PJ was exactly the sort of young man the Army sought, although they might not have realised it until his formidable mother drew it to their attention.

One day the teenage Jones appeared before Poole magistrates for pilfering cigarettes from a beach kiosk. His powerful mother, likened by PJ to Margaret Thatcher in full flow, represented him and told the Bench that he would be joining the Army the next day. This was news to PJ. But the Justices were impressed and bound the boy over, enabling Mrs Jones to deliver her son the next morning for enlistment in his local County Regiment.

The Army brings out the best in certain types. It has had decades of experience in encouraging and developing practical and self-reliant young men and women who might, for lack of formal qualification, be considered otherwise unpromising. Army selection staff set greater store by emotional intelligence – EQ – than IQ. The former claims to identify useful practical qualities such as intuition, adaptability and the ability to relate to others, things not assessed by the more usual Intelligence Quotient.

Jones possessed EQ in full measure and easily passed selection. He was enlisted in Exeter on 10 June 1960 into the Devonshire and Dorset Regiment (subsumed into The Rifles in 2007) as a Junior Soldier. This regiment – not showy, but with a fine reputation – prided itself on its close affinity with its counties, its dependability and its family cohesion which, in all ranks, stretched back generations.

PJ's training began at the Nissen-hutted Heathfield Camp in Honiton, Devon where he made friends easily and relished a more practical and stimulating environment than he had experienced at school. On reaching seventeen and a half – the Army's definition of 'adulthood' – PJ joined the 1st Battalion of his regiment, then stationed on the outskirts of Plymouth. He was drafted into the Signal Platoon because ex-junior soldiers tended to secure the better jobs. Here Jones was required to receive and send Morse code at a minimum of twelve words a minute, but his still undiagnosed dyslexia handicapped his ability to record messages fast and accurately. The results were often incomprehensible, and so he was transferred to the Anti-Tank Platoon, where brawn counted for more than brains.

In the early 1960s the Army was adjusting to the end of National Service. Conscription had provided abundant manpower but this was often poorly directed, even misused. Furthermore, without a clearly defined role or challenge, garrison soldiering in Plymouth was dull, especially for a high-spirited young man. But Jones's fortunes were to change. In July 1963 his regiment was posted to Northern Ireland, where it was due to remain for the next couple of years.

Jones's unit moved into Palace Barracks, Holywood, in County Down, one of only four regular Army barracks then in the Province, and generally considered the best. Situated a few miles outside Belfast, it had sweeping views across Belfast Lough to the distant Antrim shore. Shorts' airfield at Sydenham and Harland and Wolff's shipyard were thriving, and vessels of every size and nationality plied the Lough.

Northern Ireland was then what soldiers called a 'plum posting'. New arrivals were struck immediately by the people's friendliness. It was a real pleasure to serve in a place where, unlike naval Plymouth, soldiers were popular. Smiling local girls queued at the barrack gate for the weekly NAAFI dances where the Swinging Sixties swung. There was kudos in marrying a soldier. It afforded opportunities and raised horizons otherwise denied to most local girls, many of whom felt claustrophobic in the Province. Girls single-mindedly pursued partners, and most young soldiers – PJ among them – could hardly believe their good fortune at finding such easy companionship and pleasure.

PJ should have lived in camp, but discreetly broke the rules and slept out locally. With other Devon and Dorset friends, he frequented the bars and night-spots of Belfast. It was through contacts made at Sammy Houston's Jazz Club in downtown Belfast that he met the twenty-one-year-old model, Margaret Power, daughter of a well known Belfast businessman and distiller of Powers whiskey. She would later become his wife.

There were few indicators in the early sixties that the community was deeply divided, or that so massive and ingrained were the resentments on both sides that, within six years, the peace would be shattered, never to be restored during the twentieth century.

Soldiers knew of the IRA, of course. That was why – unusually in the United Kingdom – the police were armed. Yet it was startling to alight from the Liverpool ferry and find a policeman armed with a heavy .303 rifle at the bottom of the gangplank. Equally, new arrivals were intrigued when playing local rugby sides to be told, with a conspiratorial wink, that their opponent's massively built front row were all good 'B Men' – in other words, 'B Specials'.

The security of military armouries in Ulster was taken particularly seriously, following various IRA break-ins, but otherwise the job was similar to soldiering in England. Yet life was a great deal more relaxed and congenial. Even the Republican pubs and clubs of Belfast, such as Dubarrys, were haunts where PJ and other off-duty soldiers in civilian clothes, as long as they were not quarrelsome, could safely down their pints and join in the rebel songs.

Jones's agreeable circumstances changed when the Devon and Dorsets were hurriedly deployed to a minor insurrection on the other side of the Atlantic. In the early sixties Britain's Armed Forces were still deployed around the globe policing the remnants of her former Empire. Trouble had bubbled up in British Guiana, the small Caribbean country on the north-east coast of South America, where the two indigenous communities – African and East Indian – had embarked on a campaign of riot, murder and intimidation. Nowadays this would be described as ethnic cleansing – and would probably involve the United Nations. But then, the colonial power – with the Governor representing the Queen's authority – had the responsibility of intervening and restoring order in classical colonial policing style.

In these circumstances, an eager young Lance Corporal Peter Jones arrived up-country at Mackenzie on the Esquibo River to find his Company confronted with the grisly aftermath of an inter-communal massacre, with hundreds of mutilated bodies floating down the river.

Here it was that PJ got his first taste of intelligence work. A native had been arrested, and in an amateurish field interrogation PJ invited him "to spill the beans."

"We have no beans to eat, man, let alone to spill!" exclaimed the poor suspect indignantly.

PJ's sojourn in British Guiana was short, but helped him mature. A more grown-up young man returned to Northern Ireland after nine months and rekindled former relationships in Belfast. In January 1966, aged twenty-two, he was married in the Belfast Registry Office to his previous girlfriend, Margaret Power. They honeymooned in Canada, with a week spent at Niagara Falls.

Later that year PJ and Margaret moved with his regiment to Munster in West Germany, which was then one of the British Army of the Rhine's largest garrisons. By now Jones had been promoted to corporal and was a section commander responsible for eight men in one of the rifle companies.

Service in Germany was monotonous for those who were slack or who had been stationed there too long. However, for the active and adventurous it could be most agreeable. Numerous sporting opportunities were available once the large annual autumn exercises were over. Skiing had the greatest appeal. Each year championships were held in the Alps, where regimental teams headed when the first snows fell. Competition at unit, divisional and army level was keen and standards were high. Even experienced racers found the Downhill Race – usually set on an Olympic or World Cup practice run – a formidable challenge. For novices like PJ, barely in control yet going flat out down seemingly vertical drops, the races were terrifying. Often unable to sleep before a big race and needing all his willpower and courage to get down the course, PJ nevertheless became the highest placed infantry novice. By the end of the season he had proved to himself and colleagues his determination and physical courage.

After four years in Germany, Corporal and Mrs Jones moved to Exeter, where PJ was to train young recruits joining his own and other West Country regiments. This was a normal career progression for a young NCO, offering wider experience and the chance of promotion into the Warrant Officers' and Sergeants' Mess. Two years later, PJ returned to his regiment – now back from Germany and stationed at Gillingham in Kent – as Sergeant Jones. That autumn he went to Kenya on exercise, where he was selected to be the Intelligence Sergeant.

The essence of military intelligence is inquisitiveness: burrowing around to make sense of the many random snippets of information gleaned from observation and other sources in order to build up, and hopefully complete, an overall intelligence picture. Another skill is making useful deductions from each new fact or development, by enquiring "So what?" After the novelty and glamour of being 'in intelligence' wears off, few soldiers show the patience and tenacity to stick at its painstaking processes. But Jones did. By the end of the Kenya exercise he had established a reputation as a skilled and alert intelligence sergeant. He was soon to be tested.

The most violent years in Northern Ireland were the early seventies. At their height, the Army deployed some 28,000 servicemen and women, some units returning within nine months of their previous tour. Soldiers' attitudes to service in the Province varied, depending on the number of tours served, whether they were married or single, and where they were deployed. Often they found the work more interesting than barrack routine in garrison towns. Moreover, many a soldier's career was advanced by a successful tour in the Province, as was the case with Jones.

In 1976 his battalion – already on their fourth emergency tour of Northern Ireland and unaccompanied by their families – was in North Belfast. Their Tactical Area of Responsibility (TAOR) covered the mainly Republican enclaves of the Ardoyne and New Lodge, along with the hard Protestant areas of Whiterock and the Crumlin Road, off which lay both the heavily guarded Law Courts and the austere Crumlin Road Jail.

Because of PJ's intelligence experience in Kenya and his impressive showing on previous tours in Northern Ireland, he was selected to be the Battalion's Intelligence Sergeant based at North Queen's Street Police Station. His commanding officer was the inspiring Lieutenant Colonel Colin Shortis, an officer with an unusually good feel for the subtleties of operations in Northern Ireland and the need to work in partnership with the Royal Ulster Constabulary. Furthermore, Shortis had a keener understanding than most of the importance of acquiring intelligence by the unit's own efforts, rather than expecting it to be delivered from on high.

To achieve this, he vigorously encouraged his Devon and Dorsets to engage with the community, irrespective of local attitudes or persuasions, by – among other things – chatting casually on patrol to passers-by. Many soldiers found this difficult, either because they were self-conscious talking to strangers, or because they considered it pointless in the face of hostile reactions. But Shortis's initiative broke important new ground and became widely adopted by the British Army as a good practice per se. Terrorists and their sympathisers seeking to impose total control locally were disconcerted by soldiers talking freely in their neighbourhood, for they could never be certain what was being discussed or passed on. Occasionally invaluable nuggets were.

PJ was naturally what the Army called a 'chatter-upper'. He liked the Irish – his wife was a local, after all – and he understood their colloquialisms and idiosyncrasies. He had a friendly, open and, for a British soldier on operations, unusually easy and relaxed manner. Furthermore, he had a remarkable memory for faces and places. He remembered all those he met, and recalled what they said. Everything he gleaned went first to his own headquarters then up the military chain of command and sideways to the RUC. He operated initially in uniform, but later, when confidence in him was established, was authorised to work in civilian clothes, grow a beard, grow his hair long – as was then the fashion – and mingle unobtrusively. Unselfconsciously at ease, PJ did not find it difficult to blend in, not least because he understood the social scene in Belfast, where he had spent many off-duty hours in the mid-sixties, and where he had courted Margaret.

His local knowledge and the information he gathered was such that he was tasked to identify anyone with existing or prospective links to the various paramilitary groupings who might be encouraged to assist the Security Forces. This was 'source recruiting', delicate work of a strategic nature. Not only was PJ putting himself in physical danger, he was opening up the whole national security effort to being manipulated.

Large areas of Belfast in those days – after internment in 1971, and well before the hunger strikes of ten years later – comprised two poor, polarised and disaffected communities in which many separate intelligence agencies trawled for information. At the time, the activities of both the Security Forces and the paramilitaries were poorly controlled.

Intelligence boundaries were ill-defined. Unauthorised efforts to obtain or thwart intelligence were haphazard on both sides, and the greatest risk to someone like PJ was coming to the attention of another undercover agency or a paramilitary gang. But PJ kept his wits about him and, patiently over time, succeeded in forging a drinking companionship with one of the many engaging characters in the clubs and bars of Belfast frequented by Republicans. PJ carefully nurtured this contact, sinking pints until the early hours, and over time their relationship matured into mutual friendship and trust. Neither PJ nor his companion was to know that one day the latter would occupy a position of trust and influence at the very heart of the Provisional IRA.

When the potential significance of PJ's access was eventually recognised, he was redeployed from his humble role as Battalion Intelligence Sergeant to a higher level, working directly under brigade control. This meant that when his Devon and Dorset colleagues completed their six-month tour and returned to Germany, PJ remained in Belfast. He was content to do so, for he relished the excitement and scope of his work and enjoyed his new status and responsibility.

If the relationship between a prospective source and a potential handler is to develop successfully, their chemistry must be right. This was where PJ's personality was significant, for there was – and still is today – something unusual about the man. He has a twinkle in his eye, a casual and unhurried manner, and a wry disrespect for authority; his whole personality attracts those who enjoy mystery and intrigue.

Certainly PJ's new Republican friend, himself unconventional, was attracted from the outset by this rebellious streak. He would have realised that PJ was not local but, in view of his friend's familiarity with all things Irish and the quality of his 'craic', there was no reason to suspect PJ was in the Security Forces, still less a soldier on duty. Moreover, PJ's relaxed and easy manner was unthreatening. He did not talk, act or walk like a soldier and he never once asked a direct question or pressed for information. Hence, the Irishman felt under no pressure or obligation. Yet, his curiosity was aroused and he became intrigued by this engaging, hard-drinking friend.

Drinking companions at ease in each other's company tend to exchange confidences during convivial evenings. It did not take long, therefore, for PJ to sense that his new friend, despite being a Catholic, a Republican and a committed Nationalist, was unsympathetic to the aims and methods of the Provisional Irish Republican Army (PIRA). This was not inconsistent. PJ knew the IRA was factional and riddled with dissent. Gradually it emerged that his companion had access to them, and occasionally was active on their behalf, albeit at a low level. Equally, at some stage, it must have dawned on the Irishman that his new friend was connected with the Security Forces.

Like a skilled and patient fisherman, PJ read the water well. He bided his time until, intuitively, he judged the moment right to cast his fly. He then hooked and landed his fish. This fish represented the Security Forces' biggest intelligence breakthrough at the time and, arguably, the Army's most significant single contribution to the whole campaign. PJ had secured a priceless asset that would run and run.

Within the intelligence community a formal process is routinely undertaken to upgrade a casual contact into a declared source. Its purpose is to register new informants, to verify their identity and authenticate them; to determine their potential value and to decide how and by whom the source was to be 'run'. This process was conducted at a level far above PJ. It was partly procedural – the proper legal checks and clearances had to be obtained – but also it was to ensure the best outcome by devising suitable cover stories and protection, for both source and handler.

Sometimes the intelligence community was faced by circumstances that required normal practice to be modified. For example, agent handlers from the RUC's Special Branch and from the Security Service, who constitutionally had responsibility for the job, could not effectively run informants everywhere, because they were unable to work alone safely in hard Republican areas. So some operations were passed to the Army, who could function anywhere, and who trained soldiers like PJ (and other service personnel) to undertake these dangerous tasks.

There were other inhibitions too. Some Republican sources refused to deal with any RUC officer because they distrusted members of what they perceived to be a hostile and sectarian force. Likewise, there were other informants who did not relish being 'run' by the Security Service because, they claimed, they had little affinity with university graduates, or others with unfamiliar backgrounds with whom they would have to work. Such perceptions and attitudes may seem absurd, but at ground level they were real enough, and their consequences created suspicions and jealousy and impeded the overall intelligence effort.

Having been formally checked out, PJ's source was given the codename *Kerbstone* to protect his real identity. This was standard procedure, which ensured that only a handful of people knew an informant's real name and personal details. Those holding high office were not among them; no government minister, civil servant or military commander would automatically be privy to an agent's true identity for good reason: source protection and credible denial. The well-tried 'need-to-know' principle was widely adopted, and was strictly observed at all levels. Moreover, speculation within the Army about a source's identity was considered – as it still is – highly unprofessional. As a consequence, the identity of almost all the Army's Republican agents remained secure throughout the campaign.

The motives of informants varied. Some were at ideological odds with the organisation or cause they once espoused, and wished to harm or destroy it. Others sought personal revenge against an individual or group, for past wrongs or present grievances. Yet others became informants for financial or material reward – though large sums were rarely offered – or through fear or favour. The principal motivation was often to take part in a clandestine enterprise; those living dull, humdrum lives in drab surroundings found the notion of pitting their wits secretly against others irresistible. Almost every source was driven by one of these motives. *Kerbstone* was no exception, although in his case financial enrichment did not feature prominently.

The credibility of the agent's handler – male or female – depends on the quality of the informant's 'product', and his or her survival. The handler's very reputation depends on the delivery of timely and accurate information. Equally, the source has needs too, such as the constant and credible reassurance that he has not been compromised or endangered. All informants agonise about their security being in safe hands. Some imagine that powerful forces are poised at instant readiness to pluck them from harm; and sometimes this may be true. Good handlers encourage such notions, positively radiating confidence, developing trust and getting to know their sources intimately. As PJ put it succinctly:

In this secret world, the relationship between agent and handler is a marriage – but, a one-sided one. The handler must know everything about his agent: his fears, his personal problems, his concerns about money, how often he has sex, and with whom; his relationship with his wife; and, who he hates within the IRA, and who he likes.

Most sources want to feel that what they are doing is right, or is at least justifiable in the circumstances; and that their contribution is properly valued. Moreover, they assume that their information is being acted upon. If they perceive that it is not, their morale and commitment is undermined.

PJ's and *Kerbstone's* partnership flourished. They met regularly in pre-arranged circumstances, their meetings initiated by either party. What passed between them remains secret. They were both aware of the dangers they faced: of *Kerbstone*'s being compromised in circumstances he could not explain and of PJ's running into a trap and being exposed. The result in either case would be torture and death. Both took prudent precautions under the supervision of an experienced controller or case officer. These extra pairs of ears and eyes, and the additional input to the planning and monitoring of each meeting, or 'meet' as it was termed, was reassuring, as was knowing that the resources of one of the Army's most professional and wiliest organisations were dedicated to their safety. Much thought and care, backed by the latest technology, supported every small detail of their meetings.

Their 'meets' might take place in pre-arranged locations, in vehicles perhaps. Each party might approach, as if by chance, on foot or by car from a different direction, and unseen back-up teams would check that neither man was being followed. These back-ups would then secure the meet within a cordon sanitaire. Well-rehearsed procedures existed for aborting meets if there was any question of a compromise. Finally, the informant would always be furnished with a credible explanation for his movements and activities. Nothing was left to chance.

Even so, informants remained anxious, and with good reason. They dreaded falling under IRA suspicion in the aftermath of a failed terrorist operation which could only be explained by some leak or betrayal from within. Traditionally, the IRA's factions were so prone to dissent and betrayal that suspicion was endemic, and investigations by its sinister 'Nutting Squad', charged with carrying out interrogations and executions, were in almost continuous session.

In practice, these personal animosities were the IRA's Achilles heel, and British intelligence was skilled at exploiting them. It was also adept at supplying credible alibis for sources who might be under investigation or likely to be cross-questioned. For example, a viable justification might be required for an unemployed informant who was known to be broke yet had been seen carrying cash. Even an employed source who was seen to flash unusually large sums of money about might come under IRA suspicion. In such circumstances his handler might provide a winning betting slip so that, when challenged, the agent could explain why suddenly he had money to burn. Furthermore, although informants never knew of the existence or the identity of a fellow source, it could be arranged that one informant would be able credibly to substantiate the alibi of another under suspicion.

An event in May 1977 profoundly shook the Army. Captain Robert Nairac, a twenty-nine-year-old Grenadier Guards officer who had been working undercover in South Armagh on rather too loose a rein, was abducted near the border at the Three Steps Inn at Drumintee, never to be seen again. Investigation revealed he had gone to the pub dressed as a local, and had chatted at the bar. Nairac was a delightful Irish Catholic of singular courage and charm who might have passed anywhere for a Republican, and indeed had done so successfully on many occasions.

It is not known who Nairac planned to meet at the Three Steps that night; possibly, like PJ, he was just hoping to make a casual contact. Whatever his aim, he was identified as an off-duty soldier by a Belfast Republican, who recognised him as a British youth worker who had taught boxing – which Robert indeed had – to lads in the Ardoyne. On impulse several men seized Nairac, bundled him into a car and handed him over to the IRA. After resisting prolonged, brutal interrogation, Nairac was murdered and his body disposed of south of the border. Afterwards, the IRA admitted that he had revealed nothing and had behaved with great courage and dignity.

Fateful swings of the pendulum determine the history of conflict in Northern Ireland and this intelligence setback for the British was counter-balanced by a lucky break in the opposite direction.

Around this time *Kerbstone* was elevated in the IRA from its fringe to a position where he was privy to its innermost secrets. The rise and fall of IRA volunteers was often abrupt, so this was not unprecedented. But first, the evidence had to be verified. When done, it was apparent that a significant new opportunity for the Security Forces had emerged.

Around the same time, PJ was awarded the Queen's Gallantry Medal (QGM), the first of his two awards for bravery. Instituted in 1974, the award of the QGM is a rare distinction and a mark of special bravery, of which every recipient can be justly proud.

PJ's citation records that he had run an agent successfully 'for longer than any other Army handler in the Northern Ireland campaign, and in ... particularly hazardous circumstances.'

Back in England for a break from operations and entirely unconnected with events on the ground, PJ's promotion prospects, future employability and impending retirement routinely came up for review by the Army Records Office, whose important duty it is to plan soldiers' careers and, as their service nears completion, their transition to civilian life. Ultimately, Records adjudicate between the Army's needs and the best interests of each soldier, and, as with a football referee, their decisions may not be gainsaid.

Army Records judged that PJ, now a staff sergeant, had the prospect of becoming a Warrant Officer before retirement. This would be a crucial advancement affecting both status and pension. With the end of PJ's service only a few years away, Records recommended that he be given the opportunity for promotion through wider responsibilities within his current area of expertise. Consequently, PJ became the Detachment Commander of the unit assigned to the secret collection of intelligence in the notoriously hostile area of South Armagh. In terms of professional challenge this was the equivalent of being given the chance to lead an assault on Everest.

Adjacent to the border with the Republic of Ireland, South Armagh was a uniquely hostile area for the Security Forces in which to operate covertly, as the Nairac case had illustrated. PJ's days as a 'loner' were now gone. Henceforth, he would be responsible for the actions of a small, select team working in the toughest part of the Province, where strangers and anything out of place were quickly reported to the IRA.

With PJ in South Armagh, a dilemma confronted those managing the intelligence war: who would take over responsibility for running his most valuable source? It was anticipated that *Kerbstone* himself, although not consulted, would not relish a new handler; he seemed only comfortable working with PJ. However, he related well to soldiers in general – visualizing himself as one. He would never accept an RUC handler, nor would he welcome being run by the Security Service. Hence, one of PJ's most significant duties became to persuade his informant, who could be stubborn, to accept change. He managed to do so, and *Kerbstone* accepted that he must be prepared to work with another soldier. Even so, it took six months to accomplish a smooth and effective transition.

PJ's marriage to Margaret had produced one daughter, Jenny. But it became a casualty of his unusual job and lifestyle. They had been living an ostensibly normal life in safe Donaghadee, a dormitory of Belfast, where on days off PJ played for the local rugby club. But his long, anti-social hours at work were not conducive to a stable marriage, his move to South Armagh widened further the gulf between them, and their relationship ended in divorce. As the year ended, PJ's focus was on taking command of what he assessed to be a somewhat demoralised Detachment in South Armagh, working from a damp, dark basement in Bessbrook Mill. The Mill was a former flax-processing plant near Newry, which had been requisitioned in the mid-1970s as the Army's main operating base in South Armagh. The Mill itself was massive and forbidding, conjuring up the 'dark satanic mills' of Blake's *Jerusalem*.

Commanding soldiers engaged in secret operations ('covert ops', as the Army terms them) is not straightforward. The unusual ways of the men and women involved – their initiative, independence and guile – made them uncomfortable bedfellows when living (as was the case in Bessbrook Mill) alongside more conventional soldiers, whose work was a great deal more monotonous. Furthermore, PJ's detachment was answerable to some distant power, hence the local CO had no authority over them. The potential for trouble existed.

Covert operators in civilian clothes, often unshaven and with long hair – coming and going in unmarked cars at all hours – were often dismissed as 'cowboys' by the Bessbrook regulars. In turn, the 'cowboys' tended to call anyone in authority 'Boss' rather than 'Sir' – something which particularly tried the patience of any traditionally-minded regimental sergeant major.

Whereas the need for good intelligence was widely understood, the practicalities of obtaining it and the decisions on whether to withhold or to disseminate it – fully or in part – were often criticised by conventional soldiers. Because of 'source protection' the 'Green Army' could seldom see any direct, practical benefit to themselves from the effort devoted to intelligence gathering; moreover, when these same soldiers were sustaining casualties tension ran high. This further aggravated the relationship between those operating covertly and those working conventionally.

Whatever the perceptions, the reality was that PJ's detachment worked extremely long hours under intense pressure and at considerable risk. Evidence shows that he and his team were successfully saving lives and thwarting the terrorists. His citation for the Queen's Gallantry Medal confirmed it:

Under Jones's leadership his team produced a number of highly valuable items of pre-emptive intelligence, including details of planned targeting of members of the Security Forces, bank robberies and locations of wanted terrorists.

An incident involving a well known terrorist, Dominic McGlinchy, illustrated the hazardous nature of PJ's work. McGlinchy, nicknamed 'Mad Dog', was a notoriously hardened terrorist who was for several years the successful leader of the Irish National Liberation Army (INLA), a rival Republican terrorist grouping to the IRA. It was INLA who in March 1979 were responsible for the murder of Margaret Thatcher's good friend and colleague, Airey Neave, then Opposition spokesman on Northern Ireland, by detonating a bomb under his car at the House of Commons.

A long-term task of PJ's detachment was to collect intelligence on McGlinchy, which was achieved in part through an INLA informant. Falling under suspicion, the informant was pulled in for questioning by McGlinchy, whose favoured method of inducing suspects to talk was to sit them on the two hobs of an electric stove, then turn the power on.

By this means McGlinchy extracted the time and location of the next 'meet' between the source and his handler, and determined personally to assassinate whoever turned up. Volunteering for the role of 'tethered goat', PJ took up position at the RV on the Newry Canal, covered by hidden 'back-up'. The plan was that Dominic McGlinchy's ambush would itself be ambushed. This was a very risky operation and therefore required authorisation from the highest operational level. Waiting there alone, PJ felt distinctly exposed.

As so often happens at tense moments, the unexpected occurred. PJ remembers a black Ford Fiesta approaching. Stopping, the occupants asked PJ the way to Newry. Was this, perhaps, part of McGlinchy's plan – a reconnaissance, or a distraction of some sort? Was it the trigger for the action to start? Perceptively, PJ quickly assessed that these were lost tourists – the driver a schoolteacher from Kent, accompanied by his young family – genuinely seeking directions. So to prevent his ambush being sprung, PJ barked the code to abort action into his radio, only to find that communications had failed. Fortunately, the back-up covertly protecting him had assessed the situation correctly and remained out of sight.

Dominic McGlinchy never showed up. Perhaps he had seen the car and the exchange and sensed a trap or something else amiss. Whereas that operation was called off, similar ones were mounted later, with PJ invariably acting as tethered goat. As for 'Mad Dog', he was subsequently murdered by an unknown IRA assailant in a revenge killing.

PJ's tour in South Armagh came to an end on completion of his twenty-two years of military service, and was marked by a rare award of the George Medal. In the words of his official citation:

> Warrant Officer Class 2 Jones has provided an outstanding example of leadership, courage and skill to the entire unit. Tasked with the improvement and expansion of the agent network within the terrorist gangs of South Armagh, he has worked tirelessly and with great success.
>
> He has led countless patrols with the aim of improving local contacts … in an area where roulement units spend 4½ months [against Jones's 3½ years] this has led to his identification by local terrorists. Despite this, he has on innumerable occasions returned to the area covertly and in civilian clothes to meet informers and agents.
>
> Warrant Officer Class 2 Jones personally directed an operation occasioned by information from his own agent, which resulted in the capture of two terrorists, the subsequent arrest of twelve more and the recovery of a large quantity of weapons and explosives.

On PJ's last day of service, he was invited to HQ Northern Ireland by a senior member of his regiment,[1] ostensibly to bid him farewell at the end of his service, but in fact to throw a celebratory party on the award of his George Medal, in which the Devon and Dorsets took natural pride.

As champagne corks popped, his host, who refrained from asking intrusive questions, assumed that PJ, as a civilian, would somehow be absorbed into the intelligence community to recommence the running of *Kerbstone* and others. In fact, PJ was to be interviewed that very afternoon for such an appointment. But, having celebrated too liberally, he made a poor impression. Nevertheless, on the strength of his reputation, he was invited back for another interview. But PJ, a proud man as well as an unconventional one, figured that if they did not want him tipsy, they couldn't have him at all. And so he returned home to Bournemouth without attending another interview.

Now a civilian, he was accountable only to himself. No one in Bournemouth knew of his past, and he mentioned to no one his plans – such as they were – for the future. Moreover, after years of living in danger and

---

1. The author

under the pressure of being responsible for others, he was enjoying his freedom.

However, he needed a job because he could not survive on an Army pension alone. So he capitalised on his two principal attributes: his ability to relate to people and his powers of persuasion. He approached Allied Dunbar, the local insurance giant, where on interview he was appointed as a self-employed representative selling life insurance.

PJ was a shrewd, hard-working salesman and, as insurance companies generally pay generous commission (sometimes up to 150% of first year premium) to their best people, PJ began to attract a substantial income. But he failed to declare his earnings to the Inland Revenue – not as deliberate evasion, but more through neglect.

For four years PJ prospered, but he lost touch with most of his former colleagues, not because he no longer valued them but because he was too absorbed by making money. Those friends who remained in touch presumed he was working for one of the various security agencies – under the credible cover of being an insurance 'rep' – and enquired no further. But eventually the Inland Revenue caught up with PJ and demanded a massive £85,000 in arrears of tax. A troubled PJ confided in no one; he began to drink heavily and to sleep rough. Then he lost his job.

In due course he reached a settlement with the Revenue by agreeing to repay a crippling £600 per month. But to clear his debt he had to resort to selling his medals. Devoid of cash, assets, employment and friendship, PJ had hit a low. PJ's George Medal was subsequently purchased by the Lord Ashcroft Trust (the Conservative peer being a well-known collector of VCs and conspicuous bravery medals; his book *Special Forces Heroes* features PJ and his George Medal).

One day a fellow down-and-out drunkenly extolled to PJ the merits of bankruptcy which, under recent legislation, had eased the recovery from debt. PJ duly went into voluntary liquidation, and, coincidently or otherwise, his luck changed.

He fell under two powerful influences. The first was an intelligent and pretty young undergraduate, Sarah Pennock, who became his girlfriend. The second was a successful former Devon and Dorset, Keith Crawford, who had retired from the Army and had enriched himself by means of some shrewd property redevelopment.

Sarah helped to stabilize PJ emotionally and to control his drinking. Crawford put PJ back on to his feet financially. By embracing these twin influences, PJ slowly regained his confidence and self-respect. He took a job as a Royal Mail postman and, in his spare time, started to write poetry. He wrote *Jenny*, an apology to his daughter – who he realised had been the real casualty of his broken marriage – for his long absences and his drinking:

> The eleventh hour
> eleventh day, a
> child of mine
> saw the world
> as cows do.
> She will never know
> the father who did
> not come home and
> cannot give the
> warmth of his skin.
>
> Jenny plays the games
> others will not,
> their fathers
> will never shout
> "ready or not".
> I had a good war
> afterwards
> fed my scarred ego
> with drink.
> Inwardly Jenny carries my
> red poppy, feeling
> the dilution into her blood.

With his dyslexia now understood, and the past behind him, he began to ponder the future. He enrolled at university as a mature student reading English literature and creative writing, the latter including prose, history and poetry. For a man of so little formal education, he found structured learning intriguing and satisfying. He was also stimulated by working and living alongside young undergraduates, and Sarah, at half his age, helped overcome any generational barriers.

In his new surroundings and in a climate conducive to learning, he began to record respectable academic results. He was suited to the process of continuous assessment, as opposed to the instant nature of the school exams he remembered of old. Moreover, as a diligent student who delivered his work on time, he enjoyed the support and encouragement of his tutors.

On graduation PJ gained a Second Class Honours degree. Subsequently he obtained a Masters degree in screenwriting at another university. He had come a long way since thieving from a beach kiosk in Poole half a century before. He has served his country with singular distinction and fulfilled his personal aspirations.

As for *Kerbstone*, he continued to provide invaluable information to the Security Forces after PJ had left the Province. He derived wry satisfaction from being told one day, by one of the few Army officers able to identify him and know of his remarkable contribution, that he was every bit as courageous as PJ, and as such merited equivalent recognition. But neither *Kerbstone* nor anyone aware of his circumstances imagined that such recognition could ever be bestowed.

5

The Widow's Tale

Author's Introduction

In 1972, serving in Armagh on my first operational tour, I recall hearing over the Army radio the report of our first fatality. Sergeant Ian Harris of my Regiment had been blown up by an IRA mine laid across the border with the Republic of Ireland at Cullyhanna in South Armagh.

In a small and close-knit county regiment such as ours all the officers and senior NCOs knew each other well, so this was a personal loss.

Harris was a particular friend of mine because we both came from the Channel Islands and I had recruited him as a young, enthusiastic teenager into the regiment. I therefore especially mourned his death, and was more than usually conscious of the effect it had on his wife and young son.

I wanted any book about British experiences in Northern Ireland to pay tribute to those killed there and their families. Hence the deaths of two friends feature in this Tale: Lieutenant Colonel David Blair OBE commanding 1st Battalion, The Queen's Own Highlanders, murdered by the Provisional IRA at Warrenpoint, and Mr John Deverell CBE, who was Northern Ireland's Director and Coordinator of Intelligence. As such, he was head of the Northern Ireland intelligence and security community – and is the subject of Tale 9.

Deverell died in the tragic Chinook crash on the Mull of Kintyre in Scotland. I knew many people on that helicopter, including my outstanding former adjutant, Chris Biles,[2] whom I still miss, and whose talent the Army misses even more.

In the early seventies the Army's attitude and approach to casualties had not altered much since the War. Whereas respect and sympathy were afforded to the bereaved, in practical terms widows were expected to show a brave face to the world and 'get on with it'.

Less time than is spent today was devoted to public support for the widows and the bereaved, and the nation was more matter-of-fact about the death of Service

---

2. Colonel (as he then was) Chris Biles was heading up the Operations and Intelligence staff in HQ Northern Ireland, and was an officer of such considerable talent that he would undoubtedly have reached the Army's highest ranks had he lived.

personnel. There was then no public expression of grief as witnessed during contemporary repatriations through Wootton Basset.

But the realities of sudden bereavement have not changed. Sergeant Harris's widow observed, much as contemporary widows testify, that the dutiful interest that Ian's sudden death had evoked contrasted with the isolation and awful loneliness that engulfed her after the top brass and dignitaries had left and she was on her own.

The Widow's Tale gives a flavour of what it must be like to learn of the sudden and violent death of your husband on active service. It features Anne Blair, David's widow, but similar tales could be echoed many times among the bereaved families of the Troubles. Her Tale reminds all of us who survived how much we owe to our families who bravely and patiently sustained us during that long conflict.

* * *

Traditionally, much is expected from the wives of those who serve their country in the Armed Forces. With little say in the major issues that affect their husbands, they are, nevertheless, bound up in the consequences of them. Recent changes may have improved matters – equal opportunities and social attitudes gradually take effect – but for most of the second half of the last century the lot of Army wives had barely altered since the end of the Second World War.

The wife of the commanding officer was the undisputed first lady of the regiment or unit; as such she would be widely recognized and deferred to. In a close-knit family regiment her unofficial influence would be immense, and its positive or negative effect on the corporate well-being and reputation of that unit would be significant. Good COs' wives were treasured; bad ones could be a menace.

The former enhanced their husband's reputation – indeed, many a commanding officer's cause was advanced by his wife – and the opposite was also true: occasionally commanders' wives impeded, and sometimes torpedoed, their husband's progress. Anne, the wife of Lieutenant Colonel David Blair, commanding 1st Battalion, Queen's Own Highlanders, a proud Highland regiment, was very definitely an asset.

In 1979 Anne Blair was thirty-six. A wartime baby, she was born in Scotland at her grandparents' home in Aboyne near Balmoral. Her mother was a Farquhar, so Anne's maternal antecedents were authentically Scottish. Her father, Dick Pinker, was a delightful, gregarious officer of the

Devonshire Regiment who loved parties. When Anne was born on 2 June 1943, Major Pinker, who had not been well, was serving on the staff of HQ Western Command in Shropshire, where he worked in secrecy on the planning for D-Day, then still a year off.

Regrettably for Dick, after the war he had to leave the Army, having being medically downgraded, and he joined a local wine merchant, Tanners of Shrewsbury. Subsequently he moved to Kent and commuted to London, where in due course he became Managing Director of Moet & Chandon, and later Bollinger. Later still he became a partner in a company called Metzendorf, but they folded, and Dick became the wine buyer for NAAFI, which provided him with an agreeable living until he retired.

Anne had an idyllic childhood in Kent. She had a French governess, and ponies to ride. Her adoring yet responsible parents ensured she was brought up properly, together with her brother Charles who was two years older. Although wanting for almost nothing, Anne was neither spoilt nor favoured. She boarded at a prep school near Salisbury, where she developed her equestrian enthusiasm and learnt archery. At thirteen she moved to an establishment – not academically demanding – where she received some of the best riding instruction available in the country, and became interested in art. As was then the convention among girls of her background and education, no thought was given to Anne's going up to university or obtaining a challenging professional qualification. Likewise, attending Art College or taking up riding as a career was hardly encouraged; so she enrolled at Queen's Secretarial College in London.

At the age of twenty Anne, by now an attractive and popular young lady working as a secretary in London, was invited to the Skye Balls, highlights of the 1964 Scottish social season. Here she met a good-looking, six-foot-tall, dark-haired, young Army officer named David Blair, of the Queen's Own Highlanders. David was not in the same party as Anne, but reeling parties intermingle, and David overheard another guest asking Anne for her telephone number. He was intrigued, and noted it down himself for future reference.

Captain Blair was about to begin what was arguably the most prestigious job in the Army for an officer of his age: ADC to the Chief of the Imperial General Staff (CIGS). The CIGS was then General Sir James Cassels (the 'Imperial' was dropped from the appointment title during his tenure). Formerly, General Cassels had been an officer of the Seaforth Highlanders, but his regiment had recently been amalgamated.

An ADC's job is to manage the social, administrative and domestic side of his principal's official life which, in the case of CIGS, was busy and complex. Essentially, David's task was to ease the burden on both the general and his family. Generals invariably chose an ADC from their own regiment. Duffers did not apply, and married officers were seldom accepted. David Blair, being single and highly regarded regimentally, fitted the bill perfectly.

Anne lived in London in Walpole Street off the King's Road, not far, she discovered, from where David was collected by the general's staff car every morning at the Duke of York's Headquarters in Chelsea. She was working at the time as a PA in the Press and PR department of Rootes Cars in their prestigious head office and showrooms in Piccadilly.

Anne recalls that her mother engaged in a little gentle matchmaking during her time in London, but whether or not this affected the outcome is unclear, as Anne had three suitors. What is certain, however, is that towards the end of David's appointment in London he proposed to Anne and they became engaged.

David also had a Service family background but it was not as straightforward as his fiancée's. His father was an RAF officer stationed in India before the war, when it was customary in the hot and sticky monsoon season for British officers and their families to move en bloc up to the cooler hill stations. It was in one of these – Dalhousie – that David was born on 18 July 1939.

By the time David was eight his father had been posted to Singapore, and from here David went to board at a prep school in England. For the next three years he never saw his parents.

Such a harsh arrangement would be unthinkable now, but then it was not that unusual. Indeed, in the austere circumstances prevailing after the war, it was almost unavoidable if a child whose parents were abroad was to be educated privately in UK. Young boys were packed off home to school at a tender age, where they learnt early to fend for themselves and where most developed a strong streak of independence and self-reliance. Occasionally a child was emotionally scarred by this experience, but most survived – even flourished – and David was no exception. In due course he passed Common Entrance to Radley, where he developed into a good practical all-rounder.

It was at Radley that David became a talented draughtsman and developed the ambition to become a naval architect. He hoped to join John Brown's Shipyard in Glasgow. But his father, now stationed in Cyprus, disapproved, presumably on the basis that this was not a proper career for a boy with a privileged education and a good start in life. David stoically accepted this, but somewhat dejectedly hung around in Cyprus working as a clerk in the local military HQ. At some stage he came under the influence of an officer from the Seaforth Highlanders, who lived next door and who introduced him to his regiment.

Good regiments – like successful football teams – are always on the lookout for talent and Blair, being a keen and presentable young man, was soon sponsored by the regiment for a National Service commission. His father approved.

The early 1960s were times of change, as National Service was phased out and the Army contracted. Downsizing invariably leads to the amalgamation of old and distinguished regiments with all the anguish that entails. In 1961 the Seaforth Highlanders amalgamated with the Cameron Highlanders to form the Queen's Own Highlanders, and Blair was invited to convert his National Service Commission to a regular one in the new regiment.

For the next four years he assumed the responsibilities, assimilated the skills and enjoyed the experiences of a typical young infantry officer. Within a couple of years almost all promising young officers stamp their mark on their new regiment. Blair is particularly remembered for an action in Brunei which demonstrated his strength of character and determination.

A rebellion there in 1963 was mounted against the Sultan by dissidents. The Queen's Own Highlanders, who happened to be training in Brunei, were deployed to support the Sultan. An armed group of insurgents in a boat were challenged by Blair's Support Platoon, and to conceal their hostile intent, dropped their weapons into the water. Proof of the armed nature of the rebellion was essential, so recovery of the weapons, now lying at the bottom of a deep, muddy, fast-flowing river, was crucial. Blair forced the reluctant rebels to dive into the torrent and recover their weapons. The 'Jocks' were impressed and spread word – suitably embellished – of their platoon commander's resolve. Blair's standing in the regiment rose.

By the time he took up his ADC's post in London Captain Blair was in his mid-twenties, so obtaining permission to marry – a customary formality in most regiments – was straightforward. He proposed to Anne, and nine months later on 10 December 1966 they were married at St Martin's Church, Brasted, from her home near Westerham in Kent. Their modest honeymoon, financed from the sale of David's VW Beetle, was spent in Portugal.

With their honeymoon over, David and Anne moved to Berlin where the Queen's Own Highlanders were now stationed. Predictably, the family-minded regiment welcomed them warmly. For his part, David was eager to present Anne for regimental approval, which was forthcoming unreservedly.

Early married life in Berlin, where the Regiment was now stationed, was agreeable. Their quarter in Charlottenburg was spacious; the facilities and amenities were excellent; and shopping was easy. The cost of living in a divided and occupied city governed by the (American, British, French and Russian) Quadripartite Agreement was cheap, and cultural forays to the East Berlin Opera House, or to enjoy the ballet, were memorable. Help was plentiful, and David's duties, although precise, were not onerous. This was an ideal place to start a family: Alexandra was born in 1969 and her brother Andrew two years later.

Some felt that Berlin was claustrophobic; but all agreed it was a well-ordered place in which to serve. Years after the war and after the dramatic 1948 Airlift, Berlin was still an active theatre of operations where border and other incidents involving the Russians and East Germans could suddenly erupt. Initially as the Regiment's Signal Officer, and then as Adjutant, David held high-profile posts which brought him into contact with senior officers.

On successful completion of his tour in Berlin, Blair advanced seemingly effortlessly up the military ladder. He was selected for staff training and volunteered for the year-long Australian Staff College in Victoria, which gave the couple an opportunity to explore. They had family connections with the Governor of Victoria and various Australian cousins, which ensured the Blairs an active social life. They attended the Melbourne Cup, and Anne made numerous equestrian friends, rode in beautiful country around Geelong, and enjoyed the exhilaration of riding in the bush on fine mounts.

The Blairs returned with a bump in 1973 to strike-torn England and later the three-day week. David, with his technical background, was appointed to an important but routine 'weapons staff' job at the Ministry of Defence in Whitehall, where he was primarily responsible for bringing the Army's MILAN anti-tank guided weapon into service. Anne, now the mother of two young children, looked after them, and her commuting husband, in an Army hiring near Crawley in Sussex.

Two years later, on David's next tour of duty with his regiment, he commanded a mechanized company (of about a hundred men mounted in elderly tracked Armoured Fighting Vehicles known as 432s) stationed in the old cathedral town of Osnabruck in Westphalia. This was one of the Army's largest garrisons, where the increasing demands to reinforce Northern Ireland were being adversely felt, just as they were in Great Britain.

The Army's response to what is customarily referred to as 'over-stretch', tended to be piecemeal, whilst hoping that the pressure worldwide on units and manpower would ease. It never did, and David Blair's B Company was despatched unaccompanied to Belize in Central America for six months where the Army had another residual commitment: to support that dependency against a threat from its southern neighbour, Guatemala. This made for an unusual tour in a poor, Third World country, but it was hardly a challenge professionally.

In 1977, at the end of his time as a company commander, David was selected for early promotion to Lieutenant Colonel and appointed to the Directing Staff at Camberley, the Army's prestigious Command and Staff College in Surrey, where the course was highly geared and the programme, including holidays, well devised. This was a delightful family posting among kindred spirits, with children of similar age and interests, and an active social life. The Blairs were particularly happy and popular at Camberley.

After Camberley came command. To command the regular battalion of one's own regiment is considered to be the pinnacle of any officer's career, and David was enormously proud to have been appointed to lead 1st Battalion, Queen's Own Highlanders. He and Anne moved with the children to a quarter in Redford Barracks, Edinburgh to begin a two-and-a-half-year tour during which, as the CO and his wife, they were the very embodiment of the ethos and traditions of the Queen's Own Highlanders. They would remain in the military limelight throughout his tour in command.

Like many incoming commanders, Blair assessed his new unit to be somewhat jaded and in need of a challenge. The battalion had been languishing in Edinburgh for several years, engaged mainly on what the Army terms Public Duties: such commitments as the Castle Guard at Edinburgh and the Royal Guard at Balmoral.

Just the sort of wider challenge the new CO desired came with the MoD's announcement of the battalion's deployment to South Armagh in mid-1979. David was delighted, while Anne, with her stoical Service background, took the news in her stride. She viewed it, as did most wives, as just one of those things, and certainly not something to be unduly concerned about – in public at least.

Unusually for an infantryman so steeped in his profession, David had no previous operational experience of Northern Ireland, even though by 1979 the conflict had been going for over ten years. So he consulted widely those who had and submitted himself and his battalion to the rigorous and sophisticated training package that was by then mandatory for all units and individuals deploying to Northern Ireland on operations.

During this pre-deployment training, David and his men were taught, and tested in rigorous and realistic conditions, the Army's latest counter-insurgency skills and techniques. He and his subordinate commanders tasted the sometimes devastating nature of operational setbacks, and were urged not to overreact to them.

Importantly, they discussed how new terrorist tactics could be countered by reappraisal, coupled with technical developments. However, the main focus was on how to wrest the initiative from terrorists who always had the advantage either of being able to choose the time and place of an attack, or of postponing it until more favourable circumstances pertained.

Their teaching stressed that they would be forced on to the back foot unless they were subtle and proactive. There was a dilemma here in terms of public confidence. On the one hand, the community had to feel secure, so reassurance was an important military task. This was best achieved by lots of soldiers being evident on patrol. But on the other hand, proper reassurance could only be delivered by stealth: physically confronting and defeating the terrorist in well-planned operations had to be based on good intelligence, and mostly took place out of sight of the public.

The events of August Bank Holiday 1979 provided spectacular evidence of how public confidence could be eroded. Two major incidents occurred in separate jurisdictions – Eire and Ulster – demonstrating the presentational skill and technical competence of the IRA, and gravely damaging the public's perception that the Government was on top of events.

Using the same technique that operates the controls of model aircraft or electrically opens garage doors remotely, the Provisional IRA detonated three massive bombs. The first went off just before lunchtime on Monday 27th August 1979, when an air-rending explosion, which could be heard for miles around, shook the sleepy little fishing village of Mullaghmore, County Sligo in the Republic of Ireland. Within minutes news was broadcast worldwide that Lord Mountbatten, on summer holiday in the Republic of Ireland, had been blown to pieces with others when their small fishing boat had been destroyed by a 50lb bomb.

Those killed with Mountbatten were his fifteen-year-old grandson Nicholas Knatchbull, the boy's paternal grandmother, the Dowager Lady Brabourne, and a sixteen-year-old local boy, Paul Maxwell, who was acting as boatman.

The next incident occurred some six hours later over 100 miles to the east at Warrenpoint, near Newry, in the North. The hamlet of Warrenpoint in County Down nestles in beautiful country separated from the Irish Republic by a strip of water some 200 metres wide. From a safe vantage point in the Irish Republic on the southern side of the water it was alleged that two members of the IRA, Brendan Burns and Joe Brennan, watched a Land Rover and two 4-ton lorries in convoy lumbering up the road from the east towards Newry. These vehicles carried soldiers to a routine changeover of duties under command of the Queen's Own Highlanders, who were in operational command of all soldiers in South Armagh.

A 700lb bomb had earlier been hidden behind the bales in a hay trailer innocuously parked overnight in a lay-by off the main road. The perpetrators knew that at some stage a military or police patrol would pass that way. As the convoy drew level with the trailer, a radio-controlled device was activated remotely, and the bomb, packed in milk churns and surrounded by petrol cans concealed in the straw, exploded and a ball of fire enveloped the trailer.

The full force of the explosion hit the rear Army lorry which carried nine soldiers of the Second Battalion, the Parachute Regiment. Of these only two survived. The human carnage was horrendous, with body parts strewn in trees, hedges and on the grass verge. A fireman at the scene remembered: "It seemed unbelievable that something so terrible could have happened in such a beautiful spot."

A yet more devastating and even bloodier sequel was to follow. From their vantage point, the waiting IRA men watched the carnage and chaos resulting from their first atrocity – the human debris flying through the air, the screams of the wounded and dying, and the panic as survivors struggled to get into cover and react as they had been trained. Burns and Brennan would have watched the standard Army procedures used to respond to any major incident being put into action. They bided their time.

They observed a large RAF Wessex helicopter bringing in reinforcements and medical teams to evacuate the wounded, and shortly afterwards they noted a smaller Gazelle helicopter land on a flat grassy patch near the scene. Unbeknown to the terrorists, this Army helicopter was bringing Lieutenant Colonel Blair and his radio operator, Lance Corporal Victor MacLeod, to ascertain what had happened and, if necessary, to take command of the follow-up operation.

It is unlikely the terrorists realised the significance of the helicopter's passenger, because commanding officers tended not to become embroiled in the immediate post-incident follow-up.

So they continued to watch as soldiers clustered around a derelict stone gate lodge that the IRA had assessed to be the most likely potential Incident Control Point (ICP). Here they had earlier concealed an even larger second bomb – of 1000lbs – which they would initiate by a simple variant. They had attached a twenty-minute clockwork timing device – as found in parking meters – which would trigger the explosion when the timer ran down. This was intended to give the bombers a twenty-minute head start to effect their escape.

The force of this massive second bomb completely demolished the gate lodge and killed a further twelve soldiers, including the Commanding Officer of 1st Battalion, Queen's Own Highlanders and his radio operator. Blair's death was instantaneous – just a fraction of a second during which his body was vaporised; all that remained were two epaulettes. In this way Lieutenant Colonel Blair became the most senior Army officer whose death in Northern Ireland could be attributed directly to terrorist action.

Debris from the explosion also severely damaged the Wessex helicopter that was in the process of taking off with the casualties from the first explosion. However, it just managed to remain airborne, despite damage to all four main rotor blades, and it clattered back to its base at Bessbrook Mill, ten minutes' flying time away.

It had been an appalling day for the British Establishment and the forces of law and order in both the North and South of Ireland. Faced with two major incidents commanding world headlines, the aftermath of three massive explosions, the death of a total of 23 people – soldiers and civilians alike – there was a public outcry and demand for tougher action.

Prime Minister Margaret Thatcher flew to the Province. She listened acutely to what had happened and why, and subsequently addressed robustly the complaints of local police and military commanders at the lack of cross-border cooperation in South Armagh which had bedevilled intelligence and security from the outset. The fact that the explosions had undeniably been triggered from across the border reinforced the Prime Minister's affront.

Furthermore, Mrs Thatcher tasted the frustration and emotion generated in the wake of such a major setback. At one stage, Brigadier David Thorne, David's brigade commander, dramatically drew Blair's epaulettes from his pocket and threw them down exclaiming, "That's all that is left of a fine commander and a brave man, Prime Minister."

Earlier, Anne Blair, with her children and parents, had been staying with friends at Glengarry on the west coast of Scotland. But on 24 August, following the news of a fatal helicopter accident – unrelated to any terrorist incident – in which two of Blair's soldiers had been killed, Anne had agreed with her husband over the telephone to return to Edinburgh and comfort the widow of one of them, a Mrs Lang, who was now left on her own with a young daughter.

This was one of those distressing duties that befell the wife of a commanding officer. After having tea with Mrs Lang and comforting her as best she could, Anne returned to her quarter in Edinburgh where the children and her parents rejoined her. Naturally compassionate and sympathetic, Anne reflected what "a terrible job" it was visiting widows, and how hard it was to keep one's emotions in check.

Army families who have relations and loved ones on active service tend to stay tuned to the news round the clock. So it was on 27 August that Anne first heard the shocking reports of the explosion that morning at Mullaghmore, and of the death of Lord Mountbatten and others; and later that there had been one, then another, massive explosion at Warrenpoint, a name that meant nothing to her. Anne was clearly anxious, so her father got out a map to find Mullaghmore, County Sligo and Warrenpoint in relation to South Armagh.

Although the geography heightened Anne's anxiety, she had no premonition of what was about to follow; indeed, David had seemed close at hand, as she had already enjoyed several long, relaxed chats on the telephone with him since she had returned to Edinburgh. Among other things, they had discussed Anne's visit to Mrs Lang and the feasibility of her attending the funeral.

At around 5 pm she resolved to share her anxiety with David and rang his office in Bessbrook Mill. Someone picked up his telephone, and when Anne asked to speak to her husband she was told, after a momentary pause which did not seem significant at the time, "The Colonel is unavailable, Ma'am." She had got a similar response on previous occasions, and thought little of it. She realised he must be busy and knew he was often away from his desk and on the ground. They would talk later.

Meanwhile, their ten-year-old daughter, Alexandra, and her eight-year-old brother Andrew were enjoying being back at home in Edinburgh. Alexandra recalls the latter part of that evening well. Now grown up and writing for the *The Times*, Alexandra recounted there the ghastly episode on the 25th anniversary of Warrenpoint:

In the evening a man came to the door. He was the Unit Families Officer, who the family knew as a friend and so thought nothing of his visit, even at this late hour.

Alexandra with Andrew her brother continued watching *The Great Escape,* the bank holiday film on television in the adjoining room.

"David's dead."

The words were barely audible, but I heard my mother sobbing in the next room. Numb with shock and disbelief, I carried on watching the film with my brother. Then my grandfather came to us. He, too, was in tears and he confirmed what we had already heard through the wall.

My father had been my hero. Dark-haired, six foot, with green eyes, he was fit strong and handsome, and always with a ready smile ... Before going to Ireland he had tutored me every night at the dining-room table for my 11-plus on the six ways of doing a fraction, and with his lessons I passed.

My father treated me as an adult, encouraged me to explore and learn. The last words I remember him telling me before he left our home in Edinburgh, where we lived with the rest of the regiment, were: "Look after Mummy and Andrew."

Next of kin, as those bereaved in the Services are defined, recount similar experiences after the dreadful news has been broken to them. Service widows are invariably young and often with small children. Usually their bereavement is unexpected, although some will claim to have had some kind of premonition. Irrespective of the circumstances, the full panoply of pastoral and professional support from their regimental or Service organisation quickly arrives on the scene.

When a death occurs on active service, there will inevitably be media interest. Suddenly thrust into the spotlight, the privacy of the next of kin is shattered and they feel exposed and vulnerable. If this is not sensitively handled, resentment can occur, since the bereaved person begins to feel caught up in, or even subordinate to, some wider military or political interest. Sometimes, too, the nature of their loved one's death can generate distressing public controversy played out in the media.

A death on active service traditionally invites ceremony and solemnity, to bestow a sense of dignity to the event and allow respects to be paid. Military funerals can have a momentum of their own, which sometimes leaves bereaved widows and families feeling that some powerful external force has taken them over and hijacked their private grief.

On the other hand, most principal mourners, struggling with a mixture of grief and pride, are thankful to be relieved of the decision making involving orders of service, attendance, protocol, timing and cost. However splendid and dignified the arrangements made on their behalf, most recall their emotional turmoil and the upheaval in their lives. They feel numb as they stand momentarily in the spotlight before the world moves on. Then they are alone, left with their fears and tears.

Anne was no different. She and her children were shattered and grief-stricken. The events of 27 August 1979 made world news, and for a short time they were at its centre. The death of Lord Mountbatten alone ensured that international condemnation and outrage were widely expressed. Equally, heartfelt condolences and genuine expressions of sympathy were widely offered to the Blairs.

Perversely, the families of those killed in Northern Ireland, especially at Warrenpoint, were aware that elements of the worldwide Irish Nationalist community would rejoice at their loved ones' deaths. This was hard to bear, is not easily forgotten and is difficult to forgive, even for a sophisticated journalist like Alexandra Blair. She wrote in her article that this was 'sweet revenge for the IRA, for Bloody Sunday, seven years earlier, when 14 civilians were shot dead by soldiers of the Parachute Regiment in Londonderry.'

In their grief, Anne and the family were in a state of deep shock; the days ran together and their memories of events are blurred. Visitors arrived and went, decisions were made and well-wishers wrote. Of huge comfort were the hundreds of letters and gifts sent by strangers. Prince Philip, as the regiment's Colonel-in-Chief, who was himself mourning the death of his uncle, Lord Mountbatten, wrote warm and understanding letters in his own hand twice to Anne.[3]

Alexandra recalls, "A travel agent paid for every bereaved family to go on holiday to Tenerife, while London members of the Royal British Legion paid for Christmas presents for my brother and me."

She further recollects that, "Of particular comfort were the good wishes and prayers sent by Roman Catholic priests."

Yet all this kindness could not assuage her distress. Alexandra recalls her powerful emotions back at a boarding school, where "I hid my father's photograph among jumpers and would not talk about him."

---

3. Many years later Prince Philip himself presented the newly created Elizabeth Cross, awarded to the next of kin of those killed on active service, to Anne at a private ceremony on 15 July 2010 at the Palace of Holyroodhouse.

David's funeral, with full military honours, took place on 5 September at the Army's beautiful seventeenth century Kirk of the Canongate on Edinburgh's Royal Mile. Military funerals are full of ceremony and tradition. David's coffin, draped in the Union Flag, entered the Kirk high on the shoulders of six non-commissioned officers from his regiment, and, as customary, his Service hat and medals lay on top. The route down which the military cortège drove was lined by thousands: silent well-wishers as well as those many tourists who just happened to be there that day, and who took the opportunity to pay their respects.

It was a daunting occasion for Anne. She recalls it passing as a blur, with any outward sign of her distress and emotion eased by a kindly doctor. Friends remember her in the front pew standing upright, proud and dignified with the children by her side. She was supported lovingly by her parents.

The church was packed with a 500-strong congregation – a sea of uniforms with black armbands, hats and sad faces. The poignancy of the event and the sorrow touched everyone present, yet stiff upper lips prevailed. The atmosphere mixed pride, grief and defiance.

The short, moving service concluded with Widor's *Toccata in F*, to which Anne and David had come down the aisle at their wedding thirteen years earlier. The funeral was attended by Lieutenant General Sir Chandos Blair (no relation of David) representing Prince Philip, who was himself attending Lord Mountbatten's funeral in Romsey Abbey that same day. A Scottish Office minister represented the Government, and there were wreaths from the Prime Minister, the Secretary of State for Northern Ireland, Sir Humphrey Atkins (later Lord Colnbrook) and the Secretary of State for Defence. Lieutenant General Sir Timothy Creasey, the GOC Northern Ireland, was represented, and numerous senior Army officers attended.

The senior company commander, Major Nick Ridley, who had had to take command of the Battalion in the field on that fateful day – an unusual event in peacetime – paid a short tribute, saying that David "had been greatly respected and admired throughout the regiment." Among other reflections Ridley mentioned how the CO had often attached himself to sections going out on patrol in South Armagh, and how afterwards David had always hand-written a note of thanks to the patrol commander. Ridley observed that such niceties were unusual in the hurly-burly of contemporary operations, and hence were doubly appreciated and remembered.

Security at the funeral was conspicuous and tight and, as this pre-dated the time when such precautions became commonplace on the mainland, it heightened tension and accentuated the public affront.

The funeral was followed by a private interment in the military cemetery at Glencorse on the southern outskirts of Edinburgh. As Anne – a slim and lonely figure – stood over the open grave, David's coffin was lowered into it. It was many years before someone had the courage to explain to her that the coffin had been empty, her husband's identifiable remains, other than his badges of rank, never having been found. Six soldiers in full Highland dress fired three volleys over the grave which startled Anne and those unused to the tradition. The *Last Post* was sounded and all those in uniform saluted. Finally, a piper played a Lament, the hauntingly beautiful *Flowers of the Forest*, which gradually faded into the distance and out of earshot, leaving Anne alone among the mourners, contemplating her loss. A dreadful sadness enveloped the cemetery.

For Anne reality was about to intrude. Tomorrow, on her own, and in the months ahead, she would be faced with the mundane domestic daily round: selling their flat and moving home, fixing the leaking roof, buying a car and paying the bills – things that David routinely had done. In such little ways Anne was reminded of him, perhaps a hundred times a day.

Although with the passage of time the pain of her loss eased, she still reflects daily on David's death:

It was as if a large boulder had been dropped into a still pool. The ripples reached places where the water has rarely been disturbed, and everything – large or small – was put in motion. David had been a most wonderful husband and father. He took all the important decisions and I relied on him far too much.

So the moment he was gone the huge weight of responsibility for the welfare of the children, where we should live and where they should go to school weighed heavily. Our backs were against the wall and we all had to grow up fast, or go under. For me sleeping became a big problem.

We had our crises, but somehow we got through them and are now probably the stronger for the experience. Perhaps one of the toughest moments was when Andrew, our eight-year-old son, returned to his prep school. Having been a happy, laughing little boy, the death of his father silenced him. He shut down, and neither laughed, nor cried, and barely spoke for two years afterwards. Sensitive to his personal turmoil, his prep school, Caldicott, near Burnham Beeches in Buckinghamshire handled him with the utmost sensitivity and gently coaxed him back to normality.

As his mother, I could only nurture him so far. I felt David's loss most keenly when, later, Andrew made demands on me, or asked questions that were simply beyond my experience. By now at Radley, his public school were brilliant too. And under the wise and benign supervision of the Warden, Dennis Silk, Andrew evolved from a sad little character who academically had achieved little, to going up to Cambridge and getting two Blues for boxing. David would have been so proud of his son who had been through so much.

Equally I know that Alexandra also felt the loss of her father profoundly, particularly when it came to choosing her A Levels when she broke down in tears desperate for his sound advice. Despite having been unwell in her last year at school, she was accepted for Bristol University from where she joined the BBC in Berlin. But after the relative safety of Germany, she later worried me to distraction by becoming a Foreign Correspondent for the *Scotsman* covering anything from wars and earthquakes to the plight of refugees in the Western Sahara. Thankfully, for me, after a further stint in Brussels she moved to a desk job on *The Times* in London.

One of Anne's important practical decisions was where to live. She had to vacate their Army quarter as, following David's death, the family were no longer entitled to Service accommodation. She decided to remain in Scotland and not to move south where she would have been nearer her children and parents. Thanks to a generous friend's surety, she bought a delightful, comfortable house in Newington, Edinburgh from where she enjoys a busy life and keeps in touch with family and friends. She has not remarried. She suffered a not unexpected loss when both her beloved parents, on whom she relied heavily, died recently. However, her supportive children – both married and living in London – keep in regular touch.

Sadly, financial worries beset most families whose breadwinner is killed in action. The Blairs were no exception. The Northern Ireland Criminal Compensation Fund eventually paid a miserly £80,000 to Anne for the loss of her husband, of which £20,000 was for the benefit of each child. This settlement was manifestly inadequate compensation in every sense. David's prospective annual earnings alone would have been much higher than £80,000 had he survived and completed a full career. He was assessed as future Army Board material – with the potential for an annual six-figure salary.

The children's school fees could not be met from the capital, let alone the interest, of the Criminal Compensation settlement, and had it not been for the charity of the Army Benevolent Fund, the generosity of Radley College, and the financial assistance of a relative, the children would have had to have been taken away from their schools.

Simon Hoggart (kneeling) attending an Army Familiarization Day at Ballykinlar. He is one of the few journalists still working who covered the Troubles from their outset. *(S. Hoggart)*

An anti–internment rally. Hoggart covered numerous such protest marches. *(Belfast Telegraph)*

Corporal Graham Crossland MM, Green Howards, after his Investiture at Buckingham Palace. He had been a deep-seam Yorkshire miner before enlisting in the Green Howards, with whom he served three emergency tours in Belfast. (*Press Association*)

The IRA graffiti on a West Belfast wall which Crossland and Callsign 33 Alpha amended. (*G. Crossland*)

Soldiers on duty in Belfast during the height of the violence in the early 1970s. (*Belfast Telegraph*)

Soldiers chatting to shoppers as the Army tried to adopt a more 'approachable' presence. (*Belfast Telegraph*)

Sir Philip Foreman CBE, Chief Executive and then Chairman of Shorts throughout the worst of the Troubles. (*P. Foreman*)

Protesters outside Shorts factory during the Ulster Workers' strike of 1974. During Power Sharing, some Shorts workers had been dismissed for 'intimidation'. (*Belfast Telegraph*)

Peter Jones GM, QGM, BA on graduation day, years after his remarkable contribution to British intelligence in Northern Ireland. (*P. Jones*)

Anne Blair and her young children Alexandra and Andrew, prior to her husband's death. (*A. Blair*)

The late Colonel David Blair OBE, commanding The Queen's Own Highlanders, murdered at Warrenpoint on 27 August 1979, the same day as the murder of Lord Mountbatten in the Republic. (*A. Blair*)

The site of the first explosion at Warrenpoint. (*N. van der Bijl*)

The shattered remains (left) of the 4-ton truck on the Warrenpoint to Newry road. (*N. van der Bijl*)

The GOC, Lieutenant General Sir Richard Lawson KCB, DSO, OBE, KCSS, greets the RUC's Chief Constable, Jack Hermon. The two men formed a close friendship and an effective partnership under the 'Way Ahead' policy. (*Crown copyright*)

Lieutenant General Lawson at Belfast's Cenotaph on Remembrance Day. He had previously distinguished himself in the Congo and in Aden. (*Belfast Telegraph*)

Supporting the RUC along the Peace Line. Under the 'Way Ahead' policy the RUC took over the lead from the Army in countering terrorism. (*N. van der Bijl*)

Sir John Blelloch KCB. On his first posting to Stormont he was involved in attempts to resolve the 1981 hunger strike. In 1989 he was appointed Permanent Under Secretary in the Northern Ireland Office. (*J. Blelloch*)

A 'blockade' of Stormont, a routine event during the Troubles. (*Belfast Telegraph*)

The firing party at Bobby Sands's funeral, 7 May 1981. The RUC estimated that 30,000 people attended. (*Belfast Telegraph*)

Tom King MP, CH, Secretary of State for Northern Ireland 1985–9. (*Belfast Telegraph*)

The *Taoiseach*, Dr Garret FitzGerald, and Prime Minister Margaret Thatcher sign the Anglo–Irish Agreement in Belfast on 15 November 1985. Tom King and the Foreign Secretary, Geoffrey Howe, look on. (*Belfast Telegraph*)

The late John Deverell sailing on Strangford Lough. (*M. Deverell*)

The memorial cairn on the Mull of Kintyre commemorating the names of the 29 Service personnel and intelligence specialists killed there. (*N. van der Bijl*)

Loyalists making their presence felt. (*Belfast Telegraph*)

A Republican funeral. (*Belfast Telegraph*)

ACC Chris Albiston inspecting an RUC Reserve passing out parade. After serving in the Metropolitan Police and the RUC, and with the UN in Kosovo, he was an internal candidate for Chief Constable of the new Police Service of Northern Ireland. (*C. Albiston*)

The shattered RUC Station at Loughgall after eight IRA attacking it were themselves ambushed and killed by the SAS on 8 May 1987. (*N. van der Bijl*)

Two further developments accentuated the family's financial unease. First, and disgracefully, David had by chance elected to increase his insurance premium to provide the highest level of cover on his Army Dependents Trust life policy just a week before his death. But after he was killed the insurance company evoked some technical clause by which the beneficiary could be denied the enhanced benefit. This was widely seen as outrageous (and injurious within the Services to the reputation of the insurers), yet Anne was advised not to waste legal fees fighting what would probably turn out to be an unsuccessful action.

Secondly, and to Anne inexplicably, the provision understood to be in the will of David's father, Air Commodore Blair, to provide for his grandchildren, never materialized. Hence, Alexandra and Andrew were virtually excluded from the will in circumstances which would never have met with David's approval.

Finally, the denial of natural justice arose as, invariably, it did with the families of those bereaved in the Troubles. Relatives and loved ones understandably sought justice, or at least the satisfaction that all had been done to bring the murderers of their loved ones to account. But, like many others, the Blair family – neither vindictive nor bitter by nature – were to be cheated in this respect. No prosecution has ever been brought in connection with the Warrenpoint atrocity.

In the immediate aftermath of the explosions, Brendan Burns (20) and Joe Brennan (21) were stopped by the Garda outside Omeath in the Republic. They were riding a Suzuki 100 motorcycle without registration plates; a hollow compartment, the shape of a radio transmitter, had been cut into the seat but it was empty. Traces on their clothes and hands tested positively for the explosive and the ammonium nitrate which had been used in both bombs. But because of the noise of the soldiers' rifle fire the Garda believed that the incident at Warrenpoint had involved shooting not bombing; and as Burns and Brennan had been picked up so soon after the attack without weapons, it was assessed that they could not have been involved. Hence the Garda let them go.

In 1988 Brendan Burns blew himself up when a radio–controlled bomb he was loading into a van exploded prematurely; and records indicate that Joe Brennan was convicted and jailed in Northern Ireland after being caught in the aftermath of a mortar attack in 1994. However, he was released four years later under the Good Friday Agreement.

Of greater and long-lasting significance were the decisions taken and the direction given following the Prime Minister's post-incident visit to Warrenpoint. These marked a turning point in the campaign.

First, Mrs Thatcher directed that increased effort was to be invested in technology that would enable the Army to master the new threat posed by radio–controlled bombs. This subsequently saved many lives. Secondly, she ensured that a much closer and more effective relationship was established with the authorities in the Republic and the Garda in particular. Thirdly, she appointed a Security Coordinator, Sir Maurice Oldfield, previously the Head of MI6, to improve intelligence and security coordination. This turned out to be controversial and generated little enthusiasm from the then Chief Constable, who considered it was his responsibility to exercise this function, which he was already doing. Nevertheless, the existence of Sir Maurice's team with its power of direction ensured that the Police, Army and Intelligence Services chose to work together more effectively.

The significant legacy of the deaths at Warrenpoint and Mullaghmore was that urgent measures were taken to improve the penetration of the IRA over the months and years ahead. After these two major incidents, it became increasingly difficult for them to function without compromise. Hence, an apparently successful day for the IRA sowed many of the seeds of their eventual neutralisation.

6

The General's Tale

Author's Introduction
Commanding one's own battalion is the apogee of any officer's career, and to command on operations in South Armagh, as I was fortunate to do for six months in 1979, was a rare privilege and a frontline challenge.

Whilst I was there, my overall military boss in the Province, Lieutenant General Sir Richard Lawson, the GOC, flew in on routine visits. Invariably he had refreshing ideas to impart, many of which seemed unconventional, even heretical, at the time. But with a lightness of touch and a twinkle, he conveyed his policies in such a manner that his visits were relished and his policies generally adopted.

He urged us, for instance, not to act as an army of occupation and reminded us that it was not the Army but the police and civil authorities who would have to remain in Northern Ireland long after we had left. Hence we should do all we could to support and encourage the RUC.

As ever, there was a history to this. In 1976 the Government had introduced a new 'Way Ahead' security policy, known as 'Police Primacy'. The RUC would assume the lead in the fight against terrorism and the Army would be subordinate to them. This would reverse the existing arrangement under which the Army was in charge.

The new policy had political and presentational attractions from the government's viewpoint: no homeland 'war' had to be declared; RUC confidence would arguably be restored and the police, back on the front foot, would be seen to be upholding the law, just as in the rest of the United Kingdom; thus 'normality' would gradually return.

Lawson's predecessor as GOC, Lieutenant General Sir Timothy Creasey, considered the change was premature and that the RUC was not yet ready to take the lead. Terrorism was too far advanced and sophisticated, and the terrorists themselves too 'hard' and well armed to be confronted successfully by police-led methods and attitudes. Tackling them, in Creasey's view, was a job which still demanded the experience, fire power and resilience of the Army, who, he considered, should remain to the fore. Furthermore, the change could have a demoralising effect on the Army as it potentially exposed soldiers to greater risk because police control could not be as direct or tight. In short, Creasey felt, it clipped military wings without adding benefit.

General Creasey was an experienced and tough fighter whose views carried weight. He had recently commanded the Sultan of Oman's Armed Forces and had successfully defeated in the Dhofar a communist insurgency from neighbouring Yemen.

But Sir Brian Cubbon, the Permanent Secretary in the Northern Ireland Office, considered Creasey to be a prisoner of his past and was critical of Army doctrine, writing that that it "took some years to move the leadership on from Staff College teaching derived from Malaya and Cyprus."

In practice, during this period, the essential tripartite cohesion and harmony between the Northern Ireland Office, the Royal Ulster Constabulary and the Army had broken down, and the nadir of the campaign had been reached.

Lawson set about repairing it. His appointment had come at a pivotal time. He believed in Police Primacy and understood how he would implement it. Not only was the change inevitable, he felt, but it was the surest way to release soldiers from the day-to-day conflict.

At the time there were few in the senior ranks of the Army with the vision, determination and subtlety to put a new policy into effect. General Lawson's legacy, coupled with his unusual background and interesting career prior to going to Northern Ireland, made him an obvious choice for my ' General's Tale'.

* * *

'I would not recommend polio. As a disease it does have its disadvantages. But as a release from hell it had its value to me.'

This was Officer Cadet Richard Lawson's calculation of the balance of advantage between sustaining a life-threatening disease – the polio which he caught in 1944 – and his enforced release from the rigours of Sandhurst.

The mischievous and diminutive Lawson went on:[4]

The nurses fussed over me, and I loved it. I could never understand why my mother cried so much at my bedside; assisted by drugs I was having a ball!

---

4. Extracts from *Strictly Personal*, first published as *All the Queen's Men* by CIO in 1972.

It was only after weeks of being strapped down in a hospital bed and a trial run in an iron lung that I began to realise that I might be congratulating myself on my good fortune a little too prematurely. When I first tried to move I appreciated that I had another battle on my hands. It took me most of eight months to get back to my beloved drill instructors and to enjoy once again the mad rush from classroom to classroom and from extra drill to extra drill that, for me, was Sandhurst.

By a miracle I was allowed to graduate with my contemporaries and in July 1948, after three and a half years of trying, I was commissioned as a Second Lieutenant in the Royal Tank Regiment.

After two weeks' commissioning leave, I sailed to join the 4th Royal Tank Regiment in the Suez Canal Zone,

It was early in the morning when the ship's tannoy announced that we would be docking at Port Said in two hours. As the troopship moved slowly through the narrow canal to its berth, the palm trees along the waterfront, the minarets towering above the low silhouette of the town and the picturesque dhows rolling at anchor created an initial impression of calm serenity. This illusion was quickly shattered by the raucous noise of the dockside, and it was to be the violent struggling mass of street vendors that I was to remember when, a few months later, the riots broke out and the terrorists began to take their toll of our garrisons in the Canal Zone.

Thereafter, Lawson never stopped being a 'frontline soldier' until thirty-one years later he became the General Officer Commanding and Director of Operations in Northern Ireland in the aftermath of a crucial change in security policy which he implemented with subtlety and flair.

In the intervening years Lawson got into and out of scrapes which in contemporary terms might well have qualified him for an ASBO, or, as actually did occur in the Congo, a medal for bravery second only to the Victoria Cross.

Lawson first experienced terrorism in Egypt's Canal Zone in 1948. Like many an intelligent soldier, he saw at once the essential dilemma it posed, which was as apposite then as it was in Northern Ireland three decades later. He described it in these terms:

This form of hidden terrorism skulks in the dark and you cannot find it. Often you are not even allowed to try Ever since I first became a soldier I have never been allowed the luxury of an enemy. We were not at war with Egypt any more than we were at war with Israel. Nobody could give us a licence to kill. Of course if you saw an Egyptian fire at you, you could fire back. But you could not fire first. Nor could you fire first the next day. They did not play the game by the rules; they used grenades, booby-traps or delayed charges. The risks were ours – not theirs.

Notwithstanding, Lawson was attracted to the Middle East and showed a flair for service there. Eight years later – now a Captain and widely known as 'Dickie' – he was back, this time in the Lebanon as a language student at the renowned Middle East Centre for Arabic Studies (MECAS). Of his experiences there he wrote:

The Middle East Centre for Arabic Studies, MECAS, used to sit precariously on a ledge in the mountains overlooking Beirut ... People were always suspicious about MECAS; they used to call it 'The Spy School'. (It was blown up and destroyed by Lebanese in 1960)

In a way I suppose it was natural that they should think of us as spies. Why else would Englishmen isolate themselves in that tiny village in the mountains, so far from the luxury and excitement of Beirut? For what other reason would we bother to learn their Arabic language, their ancient culture and their customs?

They may have been right but I do not think so. If it was a spy school, I must have failed the course, because I have never been asked to act as a secret agent. No one has issued me with a cloak or a dagger, and my regiment will not even allow me to wear dark glasses in the brightest sun! No, it was not a spy school. It was just another case of rumours which come out of the Beirut souk and spread through the villages at an alarming speed being wrong – they nearly always are.

The Centre was run by the Foreign Office with a retired ambassador as its Director. The instructors were all Arabs and the students came from the Foreign Service, the Armed Forces and several Middle Eastern based business firms ... Most of the year's course was spent studying in the classrooms at the Centre. Then twice during the year we were sent off to different areas of the Middle East to practise local dialects.

I went to Jordan ... and persuaded General Glubb Pasha to let me stay for a month with the 4th Battalion of the Jordan Army, which used to be known as the Arab Legion in the days of the British Mandate. They were guarding the border with Israel at Jerusalem ... and then I spent two weeks in the house of a tailoress on the outskirts of Jerusalem.

Arabic, based on a series of mathematical computations of three consonant root forms, is a particularly accurate language and the vowel endings of many words change when one talks to a woman. Those two weeks of practice with the tailoress were essential, but I never overcame my background fear of a shotgun wedding. The nervous strain of ensuring that there was a chaperon present at all times was far greater than that imposed by the front line tension of the Jordan Army.

Back at MECAS ... after the final examination, I was graded a second class interpreter in Arabic and posted as Aide-de-Camp to the Governor General of the Sudan, Sir Knox Helm.

On 18 December 1955 Sudan declared independence, and so the Governor no longer held the appointment. However, his ADC remained in Khartoum for a chaotic few days to act as a conduit to the new regime. Eventually Lawson left the country through Port Sudan on a ship on which an attractive, young Swedish girl named Ingrid Montelin was embarked with her parents on a Middle East tour.

Dickie and Ingrid's ensuing courtship culminated in their wedding in Stockholm five weeks later. Outside observers considered the Lawsons to have a very close and interdependent relationship throughout their marriage. Ingrid died in Devon in 2006 with Dickie at her side.

Meanwhile, Lawson had been selected to take up a new appointment in May 1956 as Military Attaché to the British Embassy in Baghdad – as a major. It was here that he was to experience the reality of Middle East intrigue and coups.

The main task of a Military Attaché is to obtain a comprehensive knowledge of the Armed Forces of one's host, mostly obtained by visits.

Describing his initial round of visits in Iraq, Lawson wrote:

On one trip, I stayed with an Iraqi Brigade some hundred miles to the North of Baghdad. The Commander, Brigadier Abdul Karim Qasim was a most extraordinary man. I spent two days with him but he never admitted that he could speak English. I could not understand this as I knew he had spent several months at our School of Infantry at Warminster. He had also commanded the Iraqi troops in Palestine during the Arab/Israeli war in 1948, yet he persistently refused to discuss the subject.

In fact, whatever subject you tried to draw him out on failed. He was a morose character for an Arab. A Sunni Moslem, he spoke very little to his officers, and spent most of his time in his office, where it was said he used to compose poetry ... He was the only Arab I ever met who was not only a bachelor but who was never even rumoured to have attempted the usual string of conquests which are the great source of pride and the main topic of conversation for most Arabs.

This background and the impression I formed only began to make sense after 14 July 1958. On that day Qasim was ordered[5] ... to move by night through Baghdad to carry out manoeuvres in the desert ... His leading troops entered the city at three in the morning but did not pass through. Instead, they took over the airport, occupied the radio station and telephone exchange, mounted machine gun posts at every street intersection and surrounded the Royal Palace and the barracks of the Royal Guard. By eight o'clock the Royal Family had been massacred and Brigadier Qasim was in control of Baghdad. Two days later he was the accepted dictator of Iraq.

Subsequently, in 1959, although Lawson's account was written earlier, Qasim himself survived an assassination attempt. But in due course he was overthrown by the Ba'athist coup of 8 February 1963, which allegedly had the backing of the British Government and the CIA and in which the young Saddam Hussein was implicated. Qasim was given a short trial and was quickly shot. His overthrow paved the way several years later for Saddam Hussein's dictatorship.

As an observer at the start of the series of incidents which eventually grew into events of world significance, Lawson had witnessed the Middle East raw in tooth and claw.

After a year as a student at the Army's prestigious Staff College at Camberley, Lawson's next formative experience occurred in another violent continent – Africa.

In July 1961 he was seconded voluntarily to the Royal Nigerian Army and by the end of that year was serving on the headquarters of the Third Nigerian Brigade as part of the United Nations Force in Congo. His Brigade had been given the task of re-establishing peace in Congo's Kasai Province. Tribal strife had bedevilled the Province after Independence, and recently some 400 people had been massacred in a village about a hundred kilometres from Luluabourg, the capital.

---

5. It has not been definitively established who was behind the coup, or from whom Qasim received his orders.

Lawson described the situation on his arrival:

> There were five different groups of armed soldiery operating in the Province and relations between them and the UN Forces were strained. Wherever the Congolese troops or police were stationed the local population lived in a state of terror. The soldiers were completely undisciplined and pillaged at will, while the police were generally self-appointed and extremely corrupt. If a soldier was hungry, he would kill to get food; if a policeman wanted money, he would arrest a family and starve them until his fine was paid. The courts had been closed for months and law and order no longer existed.

Lawson's Nigerian brigade commander had only five companies of troops – under 600 men – available to deal with an area the size of Metropolitan France. Massively over-stretched, he decided to secure the capital and the airport with two companies and use the remaining three to cover the rest of the Province by a system of flying visits of teams of officers in light aircraft whose task was 'to try and persuade the local leaders to cooperate among themselves and ... concentrate on keeping the areas under their authority calm.'

'Sometimes the teams were received with coldness and politely told to leave', recounted Lawson, 'sometimes they were threatened with arrest if they did not leave immediately; sometimes they had to sprint back to their aircraft as the village drums summoned the warriors in from the bush. It was an exception to the rule when they received a friendly reception on the first visit.'

Slowly news of the happenings in the Congo filtered though to the outside world and with it came an account of a massacre at Kongolo in North Eastern Katanga on 1 January 1962. There followed rumours that, although twenty-two white missionaries had been killed, there was still one being kept captive.

It was decided to try and rescue that missionary, and to that end on 23 January Major Lawson landed from a light aircraft at a nearby airstrip. As it was unwise to leave the plane on the ground in hostile territory, Lawson sent it back to base and started to walk towards Kongolo, routinely carrying his regimental ash plant. He recalled:

> It was a nature ramble with a difference. I could see movement out of the corner of my eye. A feeling down the back of my neck told me that people

were coming up behind. When I eventually looked round there were some 800 soldiers and half-naked tribesmen who were closing in. Each with a weapon ...

Then I felt a sharp stab in the middle of my back. I wheeled round and struck with my ash plant the man standing close behind me with an arrow in his hand. He appeared to lose his balance and fell down in an ungainly heap. He was dressed in a pair of ragged shorts and a feathered headdress. We both looked at each other and he suddenly started to giggle. Then everyone was smiling and laughing and some pressed forward to accept a handshake. A most extraordinary business! I had not meant to hit him; it is just that I break out into an uncontrollable fit of temper when someone touches me from behind.

I have made a fool of myself before because of this failing, but this time it broke the ice. The crowd lost their immediate desire to shoot their little stranger. A few hours later ... it was possible to persuade them to let me take the missionary out of Kongolo. Within 3 days he was back in Brussels.

Later, Lawson, accompanied this time by a Nigerian officer, Major Nwawo, made a further attempt to rescue some more missionaries and nuns from a village behind the Katangese lines. The official citation recommending Lawson for the DSO and Nwawo for the MC, each for bravery, described the situation:

Early in January 1962 Major Lawson, having heard reports that some Belgian missionaries had been murdered in Kongolo and that the town was occupied by irregular troops, raping, looting and pillaging, repeatedly volunteered to make a personal reconnaissance. When he received permission to do so he was flown to Kongolo where he was last seen walking away from the airfield, alone, unarmed and surrounded by an excited crowd of armed and hostile men. No organized help was at hand and it was clear that the whole town had been wrecked, burned and pillaged.

Having again volunteered to rescue missionaries in danger, Major Lawson on 27 January re-entered the area although it was infested by armed bands ready to ill-treat or shoot on sight anyone unknown to them. On this occasion he was accompanied by Major Nwawo and a Congolese interpreter. Later at Mbulala they found some surviving priests and nuns. Here they were suddenly attacked by an armed mob shouting "Kill these spies."

Showing great courage and determination Major Lawson worked his way through the town seeking out the facts of the massacre in which twenty-two Belgians had been shot and their dismembered bodies thrown into the river. Hearing that one Belgian priest had survived he sought him out and by clever maneuvers led him to safety. On his return Major Lawson's report to the United Nations Force Commander was of the greatest value.

Eventually, by the intervention of some Congolese officers, Major Lawson was able to ensure the evacuation of the priests and nuns by air. On the way back to Kongolo the car broke down but the gallant party completed their perilous journey on foot.

These exploits were picked up by the media and widely reported. The *Daily Express* ran the story under the banner headline 'Lionheart Lawson' and Dickie became a hero. *The Times*, then a newspaper with international authority and renown, referred to Lawson's exploits in two editions. In the wake of the Suez debacle of 1956 and the ending of National Service the Army was feeling undervalued. National prestige had been badly knocked by Suez and by the opposition to our action of the USA, our principal ally. Dickie's brave, humanitarian exploits in a far-off land captured the public's imagination and was evidence that our soldiers abroad could still distinguish themselves.

Deservedly, Lawson was awarded the Distinguished Service Order (DSO), and his Nigerian colleague the Military Cross (MC). Foreign awards and further recognition followed: the Vatican appointed Lawson a Knight Commander of the Order of St Sylvester and he was made an Officer of the Order of the Crown of Belgium (the Leopold Cross). More importantly from a career perspective, Lawson was now being talked about widely in the Army, and considered for special advancement and future high command.

First, he had to prove himself at what is termed Regimental Duty: initially at squadron and then at regimental level in the Royal Tank Regiment. Initially, he took command of an Independent Squadron in Berlin, and later as a Lieutenant Colonel commanded with distinction an Armoured Reconnaissance Regiment along the British Sector of the so called 'Inner German Border', the fortified Iron Curtain between the two halves of divided Germany.

Between these two appointments, Lawson was embroiled in another fierce conflict, this time in Aden, where the former colony's transition to independence was prolonged and bloody. As Chief of Staff to the locally recruited Federal Regular Army – the FRA – Lawson experienced the tensions of a Force whose loyalty was split down the middle, as one tribal faction began to sympathize with the aims of one terrorist group, whilst their rivals aligned themselves with the other. The situation deteriorated to such an extent that the British officers and NCOs began to wonder how much longer they would be able to hold the FRA together.

One June evening, during the Arab–Israeli war of 1967, Lawson went into the Arab Officers' Mess in Aden to find the place in turmoil. As he crossed the hallway he was hurled against a wall and surrounded by shouting junior officers. For more than an hour and a half he was 'thrown about the room, shoved, slapped and spat upon by about twenty young madmen' who were reacting to false reports they had just heard on an Egyptian radio bulletin that British planes were bombing their Arab brothers in Cairo. He was eventually rescued by some older officers, who at the same time as they were attempting to calm down the younger men, were indicating the seriousness of the split in the FRA and urging Lawson to alert the British General Officer Commanding in Aden to the crisis. In the end, these senior officers got Dickie out of the Mess and into a Land Rover to convey their message to the General.

For his leadership and calmness during a period of crisis, and for the quality of his work in Aden, Dickie Lawson was in 1968 appointed an Officer of the British Empire.

A spell in the Ministry of Defence's Procurement Executive followed his two and half years in command of 5 RTR. Then, unsurprisingly in view of his success at regimental command, he was selected for one of the Army's foremost appointments: command of 20 Armoured Brigade. Here he was at the front of the British Army's shop window in NATO: 1st (British) Corps stationed in Detmold in West Germany.

He was now being groomed for the top. Command of 1st Armoured Division, one of three Divisions in BAOR, came in 1977, and then he was promoted to be the General Officer Commanding and Director of Operations in Northern Ireland in the rank of lieutenant general (a three-star general).

The selection and advancement of senior officers is much discussed within the Army, and it is followed too by those interested in Service matters. Lawson's appointment was a surprise because he had a Royal Armoured Corps background rather than the traditional infantry pedigree for the job; furthermore, although the 'Troubles' had being running for over ten years, Lawson had never served in Northern Ireland before. Informed commentators wondered how the appointment had come about, and how he would make out.

The Army's senior appointments are made by Number 1 Board, consisting of the military members of the Army Board under the chairmanship of the Chief of the General Staff. Unlike in other allied countries, the selection process for senior British officers requires no formal political or civilian input, although for procedural and constitutional purposes the names and appointments of those selected by No 1 Board are endorsed before promulgation by the Defence Secretary, and then approved by HM The Queen.

Field Marshal Sir Edwin Bramall (now Field Marshal Lord Bramall) chaired the Board that selected Dickie Lawson as GOC Northern Ireland, and he remembers the justification for that choice:

When Tim Creasey (the previous incumbent) came to leave, 'Police Primacy' was not working properly, as Tim had not been slow to point out; but equally relations between him and the Chief Constable and also with the PUS of the Northern Ireland Office were at very low ebb. This did not augur well for the future for getting the joint Police/Military effort on to a better and more effective basis.

On becoming CGS in 1979, I therefore chose Dickie Lawson (with the full support of No 1 Board) ... for two main reasons: first, because of his intelligence/politico background in Iraq and the Congo (where he had made his name and displayed courage and nerve) which I believed would help him take in his stride the complex and dangerous insurgency problems in Northern Ireland, with its vital intelligence content.

Secondly, because I believed he had the right sort of personality to work closely and constructively with the police and civil servants for the benefit of our joined-up effort.

I knew Dickie to be an intelligent, perceptive and subtle [sic] officer – all qualities likely to prove invaluable in the Northern Ireland scene. I remember that he once, much later, said to me of the people of Ulster, "the softer you whisper, the louder they hear", and I knew what he meant!

I also felt that his small stature and quite modest and relaxed demeanour, in such contrast to the bulk and domineering manner of the, albeit able, Creasey was just what was needed to work closely with the Police, without throwing them onto the defensive, and would thus enable the military points to be got across firmly without rancour or jealousy.

Much later on, as CGS, I was walking along the beach at Bangor with the, by then new, Chief Constable, Jack Hermon, and Dickie; and Jack (who I thought was an excellent Chief Constable) was sounding off in a rather Irish and expansive way on how he saw the problem and its solution. And with good relations in mind, I was listening and acknowledging in a very polite way – how interesting etc etc!

I heard Dickie Lawson interject: "CGS you don't want to believe all that rubbish Jack is putting over." Then I knew relations were just as they should be!

It was a very good appointment.

On 1 December 1979 Dickie flew to Belfast to take up his appointment. He was accompanied by his wife Ingrid and Berninia, their Saint Bernard.

Their first task was to settle into the large, imposing, Georgian style residence allocated to the GOC, called Cloona House, which was set in three acres of mature garden adjacent to the Nationalist Poleglass Estate on the edge of Belfast.

In many ways it was a delightful residence, which had traditionally been occupied by the GOC and his family since the Army acquired the property in 1940. However, as the potentially hostile Poleglass and Twinbrook estates expanded, Army Security pronounced it untenable, especially during periods of heightened tension and emotion, such as during the hunger strike. Indeed, during this period, the Lawson's twenty-year-old son Ulrik had to be withdrawn from Bangor University because a threat to him had been identified. Furthermore, at a time when the shortage of soldiers was acute, a whole platoon of the local Ulster Defence Regiment had to be deployed to guard the place, manpower that could be used more effectively elsewhere

The Lawsons were to be the last Army occupants. But the process of vacating Cloona was to be long drawn out and controversial. Ulster sensitivities demanded that giving up the GOC's traditional residence must not be portrayed as surrender; equally the Nationalist community could not be allowed to claim that they forced the GOC to withdraw. Eventually Cloona was disposed of by giving it to a Catholic charitable foundation.

Away from domestic issues, Dickie worked from an airy office in Headquarters, Northern Ireland – the Army's imposing brick-built Headquarters on the edge of the grey, Presbyterian town of Lisburn, County Down, some ten miles from the centre of Belfast.

For many years before the start of these Troubles, Northern Ireland's GOCs had been men in their last appointment before retirement, content to complete their service in an agreeable post which, whilst hardly taxing, was considered prestigious and carried a knighthood, even though the GOC had fewer than 1,000 troops under command.

Lieutenant General Sir Ian Freeland was the last of these 'old style' GOCs. Appointed in peaceful times prior to the Troubles, he was still in post in 1969 when the first soldiers were committed to the streets of Belfast in support of the by then exhausted Royal Ulster Constabulary, who had endured days of public disorder. A tall, urbane and shrewd officer, Sir Ian had perceptively warned Jim Callaghan (Home Secretary in Harold Wilson's Labour government) that it would be easy to send soldiers in "but it would be the devil's own job to get them out again." And so it proved; the Army was still operational nearly thirty-eight years later when Operation BANNER formally ended on 31 July 2007.

When the Troubles intensified in 1971, it was judged that because of increased activity and responsibility an additional general officer should be appointed to the HQ. A major general, subordinate to the GOC, and entitled the Commander Land Forces (CLF) was given responsibility for current operations. But his title was a misnomer as he had more than just land forces at his disposal. Day-to-day operational responsibility for the small Royal Navy and the larger Royal Air Force detachments was also his. Yet the GOC still shaped policy and was held responsible overall for anything that occurred under his command.

In practice, these two senior officers had overlapping functions and the division of responsibility between them was not always clear. What was today's current operation could be the subject of tomorrow's policy change. As visitors observed, it was a very Irish situation!

Most GOCs and CLFs managed to work well in partnership. But the partnership that really mattered was that of the Chief Constable and GOC. If this fell into disrepair it was reflected down both chains of command with adverse results.

This is where the personal qualities that had earned Lawson's selection counted. There had been significant discord in his predecessor's relationship with the former Chief Constable, Sir Kenneth Newman. Their discord was not due so much to a clash of personalities – although these were dissimilar – as to a fundamental difference of approach in how the campaign should be run.

But Lawson was a new broom. Before he had even set foot in Ireland, he had thought carefully about his overall strategy:

> I wanted to change direction and lower the Army's profile and, at the same time, reduce the number of soldiers routinely in evidence, thereby offering easy targets to the terrorists.

Next, my somewhat unusual background led me to believe that the acquisition, confirmation and protection of information were the essential tasks of any commander seeking to achieve success in the murky waters of a democratic government's response to terrorism. I needed to know more than the 'Spooks' if I was to command the way I wanted.

Lastly, I felt that the perception of whatever occurred on the Island of Ireland was far more important than the actual facts. Hence, I deduced that 'Public Relations' must be controlled by me on the spot and not by the Ministry of Defence in London. No one knew my leprechauns better than I did, especially as I soon started to think like them.

Lawson's immediate priority was to establish a direct and warm relationship with the new Chief Constable, 'Jack' Hermon, who had taken over the RUC in February 1980, a couple of months after Dickie's arrival.

Every inch a tribal Ulsterman with concomitant black and white views, Hermon was an experienced policeman who already had the confidence of the RUC. But he could be touchy and mercurial. According to Hermon's autobiography, a senior Englishman in the NIO once described him as a "truculent Irishman".

Jack and Dickie were different, both physically and temperamentally. The former was thickset and ebullient, whilst Dickie was bright, small and alert: a Jack Russell to Hermon's Doberman.

The Chief's job was lonely and exposed and so he needed friendship and reassurance from a confidant – someone who was independent with a light touch. What better friend could he find than the pint-sized GOC with a twinkle, who had just arrived and seemed to have no axe to grind?

In fact, Jack did not much care for small men and could be dismissive of them. Dickie must have sensed this and decided to grab his attention. Without telling a soul, he concocted a plan. He asked Jack to show him something of the lovely glens of Antrim and its attractive coastline, of which he had heard so much. The Chief Constable, although busy, could hardly refuse; besides he was proud of Ulster and liked showing it off. So the party set off with their wives, attended by their respective close protection teams – some four cars and twelve people in all. In the pretty seaside town of Portrush Dickie suggested they stop for an ice cream. He emerged from a wayside parlour with ice creams which every member of the party enjoyed on the beach.

On returning to their cars, a traffic warden was writing out penalty notices. Jack remonstrated with the man exclaiming, "It's all right; I'm the Chief Constable … "

Whereupon Dickie Lawson, still licking his ice cream cone, chipped in: "He always tells people that, you know!"

At this point the Chief realised – maybe for the first time – that here was a little fellow with a great and mischievous sense of humour. This was a man he would enjoy, and their friendship began.

Fortunately Lawson, unlike his predecessor, believed in the concept of 'Police Primacy', which conveniently tied in with Lawson's wish to reduce the Army's profile.

But it takes time and patience to effect change in large constituencies. Lawson began the process soon after his arrival by setting out his approach in a carefully worded speech to the Belfast Chamber of Commerce, reported in the *Guardian*:

The primary role and purpose of the Army is to defend the frontiers of the State against external aggression. However, when paramilitaries or armed groups get within the gates and threaten the internal fabric of the State, the police may need the support of the armed forces. And let me stress the word support. The Army do not stand in front of the police; nor do we stand behind them and certainly we do not stand in their place … The question is not just what we should do but much more importantly how we should do it. There are a few who out of sheer frustration and impatience say to me: "Go in hard, general! Flush out those terrorists whatever the cost. What we want are bodies and what we want are skulls and we do not care how you get them" Well! Let my reply to those people ring out loud and clear: I'm not in that business. I have not come here to destroy Ulster. For such a wild and totally impracticable course of action is not only a guaranteed recipe for disaster, it is a sure-fire way to give the terrorist his victory on a plate.

Having cleared his yard-arm in public, Lawson now needed to reassure Jack Hermon of the RUC's capability to take the lead. Moreover, they arrived jointly at a compromise which satisfied most sceptics in the RUC and the Army of the practicalities of the new policy.

Within the three geographical police Regions and the eight police Divisions, the RUC would formally be in charge, chairing each Regional and each Divisional Action Committee. These joint committees would authorise operations and allocate tasks. But, depending on the level of threat, each area would be free to operate as local commanders judged appropriate. In some 'normal' areas the Army would not be needed to support the RUC at all, whereas in other 'hard green' areas, like South Armagh, soldiers would run the operation with minimal RUC input. The level of military involvement would alter as the threat changed.

This arrangement lasted well for several years but eventually came under strain after Lawson had left. A new CGS, the renowned and much admired warrior Field Marshal Sir Nigel Bagnall, drew on his operational experience of the Borneo 'Confrontation'. There the importance of controlling the border was a key component of success. But the border in Ulster was far from tightly controlled and this, coupled with other factors, caused Bagnall to assess that the Army had become marginalized and that the counter-terrorist campaign was drifting. But Lawson, who had been appointed to be NATO's C.-in-C. Allied Forces Northern Europe, was in Oslo by then.

Lawson would have relished a bit of drift anyway. He distrusted certainty and had distaste for anything too formalised. Once he advised a newly arrived brigadier, "You must never have a short conversation with an Irishman and you must not have a plan."

"No plan, Sir? I must surely have a plan for I am a brigadier?"

"No plan," Dickie repeated firmly, "it's the one thing against which all Irishmen will unite."

Some wondered whether such unconventional attitudes and so informal a manner might indicate a lack of gravitas and steel in a GOC. But the death and continuing violence implicit in all terrorist campaigns continued remorselessly, and any doubts about the new GOC's strength and determination were quickly dispelled. He remained calm and resolute under pressure.

One of Dickie's brigade commanders remembers a mortar attack wrecking an important Army base and its surroundings in the heart of a small market town in South Armagh in the summer of 1980. This event heralded a new, unpredicted terrorist capability, yet Lawson remained unflappable and firm as the wires from London hotted up, as they always did following any major incident. Tensions caused by the hunger strike were already causing concern in London, and a lesser GOC could easily have buckled.

The same brigade commander also noticed how finely tuned were Lawson's antennae. He seemed to know exactly what was going on and developed unconventional sources for gathering information. He accurately predicted one incident and when subsequently asked how, replied, "Oh, the Mother Superior warned me!"

Lawson could be direct and forceful on certain issues. He abhorred the description 'Bandit Country', which was widely used to refer to Nationalist

South Armagh and the border with the Republic. He argued that if those living there were always associated with a place described as 'Bandit Country' they would feel and behave as outlaws. Psychologically the State was excluding them by undermining their sense of citizenship.

So, arbitrarily, he dissuaded soldiers and Army PR from talking about 'Bandit Country'. However, he was too late. By the mid-1980s the phrase had become so ingrained in the public lexicon of the Troubles that the media and others continued its use, and Lawson's intuitive initiative was never widely adopted.

Many of his ideas and policies were ahead of their time. He felt that soldiers routinely conducting patrols along the border just because it was there was a pointless and dangerous exercise, akin to redcoats trailing their Colours in front of the enemy. It invited challenge and so attracted trouble which often developed into full-scale cross-border incidents.

Furthermore, as the Army was forbidden to cross into the Republic, the incidents inevitably took place on ground advantageous to the terrorists, with the inevitable result that soldiers and policemen were unnecessarily harmed. Moreover, almost any border incident heightened the political temperature between Dublin and London.

In the aftermath of each cross-border incident, the British diplomatically attempted to avoid implying that the Irish authorities were unable – even unwilling – to exercise proper control on their side of the border. Nevertheless, mostly British tact failed, and political umbrage was taken to the detriment of future progress.

Lawson concluded that the whole process was self-defeating and, if he had had his way, would have banned outright patrols along the border. But that would have incurred the ire of the Loyalists (and in truth many a policeman) who would have interpreted such a policy as surrendering under pressure a legitimate part of the United Kingdom. Lawson was realistic enough to realise such constraints upon him, and so was content to encourage his soldiers not to behave like redcoats and to dissuade them from going down to the border just to see if it was still there.

Evidence of Lawson's goal of a reduced profile was the reduction of Army force levels from around 27,000 to 7,000. The need for more troops in the 1982 Falklands Campaign also contributed to the lowering of force level. But such a massive reduction would never have been possible had not the Chief Constable been reassured by Lawson that it was safe to allow military manpower to be reduced to the benefit of operations in the South Atlantic.

However, not everyone was comfortable with Lawson's approach. Some less gifted and more pedestrian souls were unsettled by his elliptical remarks and were unsure about what he really wanted. By the end of his tour, even some of the Army's top brass and certain civil servants in London were alarmed about the direction – or, as they saw it, lack of firm direction – of the campaign in Ulster. They could not always understand what Lawson intended, and wanted evidence of more vigorous and obvious action.

But the evidence of progress was overwhelming. The Chief Constable and the RUC grew immeasurably in self-confidence and stature under Lawson's support and nurturing. This enabled 'Police Primacy' to become established, never to be challenged again. Indeed, it was largely Lawson's ability to stiffen the resolve of the Chief Constable, and of his Secretary of State, in the early eighties which gave these two the confidence to face down Sinn Fein/IRA during the tricky period of the hunger strike, and to reinforce the Prime Minister's own resolve.

Over time, although it was not yet apparent externally, the Peace Process was starting to gestate in Provisional IRA minds. It would never have developed as it did without some evidence of a return to 'normality'. Promoting 'normality' was the most significant single achievement of the whole campaign, and it was Dickie Lawson's legacy. It is doubtful whether any other commander available at the time could have accomplished it.

7

The Civil Servant's Tale

Author's Introduction

After command I was promoted and, in Service parlance, was required to 'fly a desk.' That meant doing a staff job. I was fortunate to be sent to somewhere I already had some feel for the issues. I found myself back in Northern Ireland in 1982 for two years where, in the Command Headquarters as Chief of Staff, I was responsible for its work and output.

This was my fifth tour of duty in the Province and because I would be there for at least two years – the appointment was designated 'accompanied' – my wife and two young children could come too. We lived in a house within the Army compound in Lisburn, County Down, about ten miles from the centre of Belfast. Despite the continuing and unpredictable death and destruction perpetrated by paramilitaries, life in Lisburn was surprisingly normal. Our young children attended the local primary school, and off-duty we were free to enjoy, with the minimum of restriction, the abundant and generous local hospitality that was offered in the North.

My work as Chief of Staff put me at the interface where policy decisions were made on both sides of the water for us to implement locally. Civil Servants – both in the MOD and NIO – working on behalf of Ministers, shaped policy and drew up the priorities for the latter to endorse or change. The military, the civil servants and the intelligence services in the Province then set about implementing whatever policies Ministers had approved. The RUC, always mindful of their constitutional and operational independence, spurned political interference and insisted that their duties be carried out, as usual, under the law.

By the time I joined HQ Northern Ireland in 1982 the hunger strike had ended. But a residual bitterness over its terms and the cost in young lives had embittered both communities. I found myself working on projects with the dedicated civil servants at Stormont, whose job was to handle the complexities surrounding that emotive episode, as well as coping with the many and diverse pressures of their routine work.

As officers in the Armed Service become more senior, most harbour uncharitable views of civil servants, formed, at least in part, by the fact that they are conveniently blamed for unrealistic controls and shrinking budgets, which are perceived as constraints on the Services' morale and effectiveness. However, the officials at Stormont with whom I worked were professional and able, and I was struck by how patriotic they were and loyal to their ministers. One had to accept that they were the gate-keepers, and so one could not engage with ministers, or achieve anything, without the potential frustration of going through them. They were often criticised – unfairly I thought – for the decisions that ministers had made either on their advice or in face of it. Yet their professional loyalty was such that one could seldom determine which was the case. This meant that they deflected much criticism which would otherwise have been aimed at ministers.

John Blelloch, on his first tour in Ulster, was one of those senior civil servants. As a Deputy Undersecretary (DUS), one of his responsibilities was advising ministers on prisons; hence everything connected with handling the hunger strike involved him. Seven years later, in 1988, Blelloch returned for a second tour on promotion to that rare class of mandarin: a Permanent Secretary, appointed to the Northern Ireland Office with a presence both in Whitehall and at Stormont.

I was fortunate that John, and other senior civil servants, agreed to share with me some of their experiences at what were professionally challenging times. Blelloch, both as DUS(B) and as PUS, was twice at the hub of power and influence in Northern Ireland. Nothing new or important affecting security during the Troubles could be achieved without his input.

Civil servants sometimes felt their contribution in Northern Ireland compared to the military's, was undervalued. I remember, as GOC, reflecting with a senior member of Blelloch's staff, on the image of our respective Services.

"It's all right for you," he remarked wistfully, "You're seen as a shining knight on a white charger, whereas I'm just viewed as a dreary old official."

Hopefully, the Civil Servant's Tale can rectify such a false perception. Without the parallel contribution stemming from the Civil Service's wider perspective and wisdom, the fight against terrorism would have been greatly impeded, and would have taken much longer.

* * *

For fifty years, until the imposition of Direct Rule in March 1972, Northern Ireland had been governed by predominantly Unionist and Protestant elected politicians from Stormont, the vast grey Palladian building on the outskirts of Belfast.

Ulster had its own Prime Minister who, along with his junior ministers, was served by a local Northern Ireland Civil Service (NICS) which ran the day-to-day business of the Province. Crucially this included law and order and justice, without reference to Whitehall.

It was indicative of the remote relationship between Whitehall and Northern Ireland that the Division of the Home Office (E2) then responsible for Northern Ireland also handled the Channel Islands and the Isle of Man. One official remembers that his main task pertaining to Northern Ireland was "explaining to anyone who complained about conditions there that under the Government of Northern Ireland Act 1921 it was not the responsibility of Her Majesty's Government, but of Stormont."

When Stormont was suspended in 1972, the immediate consequence was that Westminster politicians and Whitehall civil servants took over many of the responsibilities previously exercised by local civil servants. Thus an additional layer of government was visited upon the existing NICS. This required a profound psychological readjustment by the Ulstermen and women, who would, among other irritants, lose their offices, along with their own way of doing things. Watching their work being handed over to incoming strangers fuelled their irritation, and to add insult to injury the accommodation for these incomers – dismissed locally as 'blow-ins' – was arranged initially in hotels at considerable public expense.

A senior incoming Whitehall civil servant remembers:

Almost nothing relating to the Northern Ireland Civil Service was handled with much sensitivity during that period. In the prevailing atmosphere of crisis too little thought was given to the long term implications of getting off on the wrong foot with our locally based colleagues.

One Permanent Secretary from the early days of Direct Rule recalls:

The NIO Brits who lived in the four-star Culloden Hotel in 1972/3 were driven to Stormont Castle in an old but nevertheless rather grand Daimler. What sort of impression did that give?

Another remembers that to most local civil servants:

Direct Rule was an affront. Westminster ministers and their Whitehall staff took charge; we came in as overlords and told them what to do. Senior NIO people living and eating in Stormont House (which was formerly the residence of the Northern Ireland Speaker) developed a sense of isolation. This accentuated the NICS feeling of our distancing ourselves from them, and our aloofness.

A third explained the practical differences between the two civil services:

> The essential professional difference between NICS and the incoming ex-
> Whitehall civil servants was that the former had in effect served a one-
> party state for fifty years and had had much less to do with politics than
> was usual in Whitehall.
>
> Furthermore, as these civil servants were born and brought up in the
> Province, they tended to have strong, ingrained views about how to go
> about politics. Conversely, the civil servants from Whitehall, although
> they had little or no local knowledge, were keen and accustomed to
> engaging confidently with political issues.

Michael Legge, an experienced public servant, reflected that many parallels
existed with the situation which had been described fifty years earlier by Sir
Henry Robinson Bt, who had spent a lifetime in the Irish Civil Service in
Dublin. He wrote in *Memories: Wise and Otherwise*:

> A number of officials came over from London with a lot of power, privilege
> and prestige. They quickly pushed aside those who had had their hands on
> the levers of power and grappled with a mixture of flair and naivety with
> formidable problems like decommissioning weapons and engaging
> Republicans in the political process … What was galling about it was that
> imported English civil servants were given substantial salaries and special
> 'danger allowances' and were surrounded day and night by barbed wire,
> sandbags and guards whilst the Irish officials, especially those who had to
> work in open country, unprotected and alone, such as resident magistrates
> and local government officials, received no similar considerations.

John Blelloch was one of the former Whitehall–based civil servants who was
posted to Northern Ireland at a crucial period of the Troubles. He had been
working at the Ministry of Defence as an Assistant Undersecretary, when he
was offered promotion to one of the two Stormont appointments at Deputy
Secretary level. The job would require Blelloch and his wife Pam to move
to Northern Ireland.

John, then fifty, viewed this as a potentially interesting professional
challenge. After discussing the position with Pam, who was teaching at a
London junior school and whose own career would therefore be interrupted.
Despite the resultant disruption of family life, John accepted the offer and
the Blellochs moved to Belfast in 1980.

Humphrey Atkins (later Lord Colnbrook) was Secretary of State for Northern Ireland at the time, and Blelloch became his principal adviser, through the Permanent Secretary, on security issues – in terms of both policy and implementation.

Blelloch himself is a neat, slightly stooped man, with a twinkle and a wry sense of humour. He looked, spoke and behaved like a quintessential civil servant. One felt he would have been at home on the Viceroy's staff in pre-war India; equally, he could have graced some post in academia, exuding experience, calm and good cheer.

At Stormont he moved into an office in the Castle a floor below his Secretary of State. He headed a small team of dedicated and experienced civil servants who found him to be a fair and kindly boss, albeit with a somewhat cautious temperament. Blelloch himself attributed the success of his Division to the quality of his subordinates.

John Blelloch is a Scot, born in Edinburgh in 1930, and was educated at Fettes. He did his National Service in the Royal Artillery in the UK, before going up to read Classics at Gonville and Caius College, Cambridge. On graduation, he entered the Civil Service.

The Civil Service in those days routinely exposed capable young graduates to the work of ministers. Blelloch was in due course appointed Private Secretary successively to Fitzroy Maclean and Julian Amery, who were Parliamentary Undersecretaries of State (junior ministers) in the then War Office in Anthony Eden's embattled Government at the time of Suez.

Later Blelloch attended the London Business School, anticipating his increasing responsibility for procurement and hence the management of public money. Promotion followed, and by 1968 Blelloch had attained the Civil Service grade of Assistant Secretary. By the time the Troubles in Northern Ireland began he was the equivalent in rank of a one-star military officer and had earned a reputation for approachability, competence and even-handedness among the Service community in Whitehall. He was considered to be able, patriotic and sympathetic, as the best civil servants are, and instinctively to have the interests of the Services at heart – not accolades attached to all his Whitehall colleagues.

Blelloch's father was the strongest influence in his early life. He had been a senior civil servant in Malaya during the Communist-inspired guerrilla campaign which afflicted that country from 1948 to 1960. During it Blelloch (senior) had for a time advised Field Marshal Templer, the Governor and Director of Operations, on local matters.

The absolute authority vested in the Field Marshal as 'Supremo' during that Emergency was often cited – by Army officers, and by the Prime Minister herself, among others – as a successful and appropriate model to be emulated in Northern Ireland.

The notion of the 'Single Campaign Authority' was discussed regularly in Whitehall and Westminster but would invariably be rejected on each occasion, on constitutional and practical grounds, by some of John's civilian colleagues, among others. Many Army officers feel that the failure to appoint a Supremo – not necessarily a Serviceman – was the greatest single mistake of the campaign. Blelloch himself often imagined what his father's stance would have been. He judged his father would have considered that the political input should prevail, whatever set-up applied.

Of all the issues confronting DUS (B) during Blelloch's first tour in Northern Ireland, the 1981 hunger strike was the most intractable. When the Permanent Secretary was in London, the Secretary of State looked to John for the formulation and implementation of security policy, and the prisons were always in focus.

Within the Republican movement there is a history of using the hunger strike as a weapon to coerce the authorities – be they in Dublin or Belfast – into conceding demands. There had been protests in 1972 at Belfast Jail and in 1977 at Portlaoise Prison in Dublin. The so-called 'Blanket' protest of 1976-8 at the Maze (previously named Long Kesh) on the outskirts of Belfast had been followed by the 'Dirty' protest started in 1978, which developed into the hunger strike of 1980. That strike ended on 18 December of that year when one of the seven hunger strikers, Kevin McKenna, who was near to death, was transferred at his sister's request to an outside hospital. At this point the strike leader, Darkie Hughes, called off the protest to save the life of his comrade.

Robert (Bobby) Sands, who was what PIRA termed their Officer Commanding (or OC) in the Maze, but not one of the seven hunger strikers, was bitterly critical of Hughes's decision. Sands recognised the intensity of the psychological pressure on the leader of a group when one of them became critically ill, so he determined to circumvent the problem next time by going first and alone on hunger strike, followed at substantial intervals by other volunteers. In this way, he reasoned, he could be sure that he would be near death first and would not be deflected by having responsibility for the life of a comrade.

Hence on Sunday 1 March 1981 Bobby Sands, aged twenty-six, refused breakfast and announced he was now launching a second hunger strike until the prisoners' demands were met. These amounted to what the Republican movement termed 'political status', which translated into five specific demands affecting their prison conditions, namely:

- The right not to wear prison uniform
- The right not to do prison work
- The right to associate freely with whom they liked
- The right to one weekly visit; one weekly letter in and out and one weekly food parcel
- The restoration of all remission lost as the result of the protest action.

The prisoners themselves strongly believed in their right to be recognised as prisoners of war. They did not see themselves as criminals, nor did their families.

The issue between the prisoners and the authorities was essentially one of principle: either, as the former insisted, they were recognised as prisoners of war and entitled to control their own lives within the prison, or, as the Government held, they would be treated as convicted criminals, with internal control of the prison exercised by the prison authorities.

To Blelloch inheriting this policy the matter was straightforward. It was not about decent prison conditions, on which this humane man would have insisted, but about the implementation of a coherent Government policy based on the principle of who should run the prisons. As one of Blelloch's staff wrote at the time, "The battle lines for a final confrontation had been drawn. Both sides clearly understood the other's position and in the end one would have to back down. Sands was determined that it would not be the prisoners and the Government had made clear it would not be them."

Indeed, the Prime Minister, whilst on a routine visit to the Province on 5/6 March, had stated categorically that the Government would not compromise on the issue of political status. Yet that did not prevent Francis Joseph Hughes refusing breakfast ten days later; and a week after that, two more volunteers, Raymond McCreesh and Patrick Joseph O'Hara, joined him.

The nature of the protest demanded resolve and intense commitment, and it generated among the prisoners strong feelings of group cohesion and common suffering. As far as they were concerned, the blame for the crisis lay with HMG and the prison authorities, who they believed were trying to break their Republican spirit. Unfortunately, poor communication and personal animosity between some prison staff and their prisoners only served to strengthen these feelings.

Initially, the prisoners were reportedly unhappy at the low level of public support for and media interest in their action. But this altered significantly when Frank Maguire, MP for Fermanagh and South Tyrone, died, and a by-election was called for 9 April 1981. Various Republican candidates with their eye on the seat withdrew or were persuaded not to submit their nominations, and Bobby Sands became the Sinn Fein candidate. He appointed Owen Carron as his agent, whilst Sands's sister, Marcella, publicly supported Sinn Fein's PR line, declaring, "Bobby's election will save not only his life and the lives of his comrades but will also give them their just demands."

However, Sands himself appeared to show little interest in the by-election and is reported to have said it would make no difference to the protest or hunger strike, although he was quoted as declaring, "The strikers will not stop until the Brits give in."

By the date of the by-election Sands had lost over two stone, having only taken salt water since 1 March, and he had been transferred to the prison hospital for observation. From the outset he had cooperated fully with both the medical and prison staff, being medically examined and weighed every day.

The medical care of the prisoners, both on hunger strike and elsewhere in the prison was in the hands of the prison doctors. As Blelloch observed, "It would have been a very serious matter if it had been suggested, let alone established, at any time that the prisoners were being kept alive by tampering with their liquid diet. In fact, there was never any suggestion that this could have been so, or that their care was anything other than scrupulously professional."

The by-election result produced a clear victory for Sinn Fein. Sands defeated the Ulster Unionist Party's (UUP) candidate, Harry West, by 30,492 votes to 29,046 – a majority of 1,446.

The result had some immediate consequences. Firstly, it inflamed the Unionists and led to an increase in public disorder; secondly, it generated national and international media interest, portraying it as a substantial victory for PIRA and a significant setback for the British Government, on whom the onus for resolving the hunger strike was now placed. Thirdly, the result opened the floodgates to a large number of official and unofficial individuals and delegations – churchmen, fact-finders, intermediaries and pressure groups – wanting to see Sands in hospital, all intent on exerting their influence.

The most significant long-term consequence, as Blelloch noted, was that the election result made it possible for Sinn Fein to embrace electoral politics fully much sooner than anticipated. This was the unexpected by-product of the hunger strike, seldom alluded to but presaging, nonetheless, an important breakthrough.

In the wake of the by-election a stream of visitors sought admission to the Maze, and the NIO was required to process each application. Three TDs (Members of the Dail) arrived from Dublin, followed by Members of the European Parliament; then the Papal Nuncio, Archbishop Gaetano Alibrandi asked to see Sands. Presumably his visit reflected the Pope's alleged view that Ireland's religious hierarchy should not address themselves merely to the British authorities (as they had up to then) but also to the prisoners themselves, which they had hitherto failed to do. Pope John Paul II was on public record as saying: "The Bishops are urged not only to insist with the British authorities, but also to do everything possible in order to persuade prisoners to adopt a more human attitude and, I repeat, one more in keeping with Christian principles."

Visits by 'foreigners', particularly those from the Republic, infuriated most Unionists who viewed their concern as disingenuous and a pretext – an improper one at that – to involve themselves in the domestic affairs of Ulster. Explaining difficult decisions on behalf of ministers is meat and drink to experienced civil servants. Their skill as wordsmiths is renowned and their ability to justify any course of action sought by ministers is legendary. This being Blelloch's domain, he would have cleared the following submission to the Secretary of State, which was released prior to the visit of the three Irish TDs to the Maze:

> There may be a possibility that the visitors Sands has asked to see will be able to persuade him to give up his hunger strike and for this reason it has been decided to authorize a special visit.

In fact, the TDs reported that Sands was determined to continue his hunger strike until death, unless the prisoners' five demands were granted. The TDs called on the International Red Cross to intervene, and on the European Convention on Human Rights (ECHR) to send a representative to the Maze immediately. But Sands declined to see any such visitor, on the grounds that it would achieve nothing.

Don Concannon MP, the Shadow Northern Ireland Minister, visited the Maze and spoke to all four hunger strikers, making it clear that there was no possibility of the Labour Party coming out in favour of granting special category status. David Steel MP, the then Liberal leader, spoke in similar terms on a later visit. These were significant interventions because they demonstrated that the bi-partisan approach at Westminster continued to hold.

By 30 April, having lost almost three stone (nearly a third of his original weight), Sands was gravely ill, and the condition of the other three strikers had deteriorated to such an extent that they had also been admitted to the prison hospital.

Sands's eyesight and hearing worsened and there was some evidence of heart irregularity. He was placed on a ripple bed and given two sheepskin rugs for warmth. He was afforded 'full family visiting rights', which meant that relatives could remain with him round the clock.

As Sands came closer to death, PIRA pulled out all their political stops. They used contacts with John Hume's Social Democratic Labour Party (SDLP) – the traditional Nationalist opposition party in Northern Ireland; with sympathisers in the South; the Catholic Church; and overseas supporters in North America, Australia and New Zealand. Owen Carron, Sands's election agent, was prominent in such manoeuvres. They were combined with increasingly dire threats of disorder if Sands died.

Two final interventions took place in Sands's last few days. First, his solicitor, Pat Finucane, and his sister, Marcella, who allegedly had formally contacted the ECHR on 23 April, citing breaches of three Articles of the Convention – right to life; prohibition of inhumane treatment; and freedom of expression – were present when the Convention's representatives arrived at the prison. However, at no time did Sands agree to see the ECHR members and he maintained his line that he would only do so if Danny Morrison and Gerry Adams, both of Sinn Fein, were present – a condition unacceptable to the NIO. As the Convention did not ask formally or informally that Sands's pre-condition should be fulfilled no meeting took place.

After the failure of the ECHR a further intervention was undertaken by Monsignor John Magee, one of the Pope's private secretaries, who visited on 28 April with a plea from the Pontiff. But Sands remained unmoved. Nevertheless, Father Magee made a second visit and spoke to each of the four hunger strikers in the prison hospital. But with nothing new to offer, he had no success in persuading them to give up, and left the prison a very disappointed man.

Sands's condition became critical when he lapsed into a coma on Sunday morning, 3 May, which was the 64th day of his fast. He did not regain consciousness and died early on Tuesday, 5 May, with five members of his family present in the hospital.

The final entry in his diary reads:

> I'm standing on the threshold of another trembling ... I'm a political prisoner ... I believe in the God-given right of the Irish people to sovereign independence and the right of any Irish man or woman to assert this right in armed rebellion ... there can never be peace in Ireland until the foreign oppressive British presence is removed.

His body was immediately taken to an outside hospital and a post-mortem performed, after which his remains were taken to his home in Twinbrook. His funeral at Belfast's Milltown Cemetery, where there is a special Republican plot, was set for 7 May. Some 30,000 people followed the cortège, PIRA provided a uniformed escort for the coffin and masked gunmen fired volleys over the grave. That night there were widespread riots, particularly in Belfast.

Inevitably, there was hostile political reaction within Northern Ireland and abroad to Sands's death, although a much more muted response was noticeable in Britain. John Hume criticised HMG for failing to show greater flexibility and sensitivity, and this line was taken up in North America by leading Irish-American and Irish-Canadian politicians. There were demonstrations at many British Embassies and Missions in Europe, and in more distant places, such as Cuba.

In the media Sands's death was accorded front-page headlines and detailed coverage throughout the world. All the Irish national newspapers viewed his death as avoidable but, anticipating her determination, the *Irish Times* warned that Mrs Thatcher's principle of no surrender would not be abandoned at one death but might if the number became intolerable:

> One death would shock millions and Britain might ride out whatever international criticism was hurled at her, but two or three or four? No government could survive world opinion in such a situation.

But it did. The second hunger striker, Francis Hughes, died a week later, followed on 21 May by both Raymond McCreesh and Patrick O'Hara. All four deceased were replaced on hunger strike almost at once by fresh volunteers. And so the clash of wills continued, whilst undercover efforts to find a solution, official and otherwise, were intensified.

The hunger strike dragged on through the summer of 1981, with accusations against the British Government of intransigence, bad faith and lack of imagination being levelled from various quarters. However, occasional support for HMG was expressed. In Eire a new Taoiseach, Garret FitzGerald, had been elected. Six weeks after taking office he launched a fierce attack on the role of the IRA leadership in continuing the hunger strike. "It is clear," he said on 31 July, "that the IRA could end the protest at any time, yet they have not done so. They cannot evade responsibility for the deaths of the hunger strikers."

That day, the family of Patrick Quinn, who had been refusing food since 15 June and had become confused, requested that he be moved to the Royal Victoria Hospital (RVH) in Belfast where he was medically treated and subsequently accepted nourishment.

Quinn's removal from the hunger strike at his mother's request represented the first incidence of strike-breaking. The NIO noted the evidence of the rift, already widely known to exist, between some of the strikers' relatives and the PIRA leadership. Meanwhile, Father Faul, the influential, independently-minded parish priest from South Tyrone, became a significant figure in attempts to persuade the relatives that the protest was hopeless and that the Government would not give in. Nevertheless, hopes for a breakthrough did not materialize, and over the next two days (1 and 2 August respectively) Kevin Lynch and Kieran Doherty, both replacement hunger strikers, died with all the private anguish and public disorder that engendered.

The level of street violence and terrorism escalated. Statistically, 1981 was one of the Troubles' worst years since the mid-1970s; 101 terrorist-related deaths occurred and around 30,000 plastic bullets were fired.

On the evening of 20 August, without warning, the condition of Patrick McGeown (a replacement hunger striker on day 42 of his fast) seriously deteriorated. Within a short time he lost mental and physical control, and the prognosis was grave. His relatives were summoned at once and, having spoken to the doctor, McGeown's wife and mother jointly gave the necessary written approval for medical intervention to save his life. Within an hour McGeown was recovering well and was sufficiently lucid to thank all concerned for saving his life.

Sinn Fein issued a statement critical of the Government on behalf of Mrs McGeown, presumably to deflect suggestions of any crack in the hunger strike. However, she herself subsequently admitted that she could no longer bear to see her son suffer and went on to demand that "HMG meet the hunger strikers and their representatives in Long Kesh, so that no more lives would be lost."

Meanwhile, pressure mounted on Sinn Fein as Father Faul again appealed for an end to the strike. He said that the prisoners should be advised by those outside that theirs was a 'hopeless situation.' This was certainly the prevailing view of the relatives, although rarely expressed in public.

On 4 and 6 September the families respectively of Matthew Devlin and Laurence McKeown (not to be confused with Patrick McGeown who had already ended his strike) gave the necessary written approval for medical intervention, and after the men's admittance to the Intensive Care Unit of the RVH both recovered rapidly. However, on 7 September John Henry Pickering refused breakfast, so the total number still on hunger strike went back to six.

A routine autumn Cabinet reshuffle saw James Prior appointed as Northern Ireland Secretary in September 1981. The arrival of a new ministerial team in any Department is a busy time for civil servants because numerous briefing papers have to be prepared. Civil servants' first impressions of the minister, and vice versa, are quickly formulated. Blelloch and his subordinates were impressed by the considerate yet shrewd Jim Prior. Equally, ministers are invariably grateful – and often surprised – at the unbiased and professional way in which their civil servants acquaint them with their new responsibilities and support their new political masters, and a mutual respect and loyalty is usually established.

On 17 September 1981 the new Secretary of State, accompanied by Lord Gowrie, newly appointed as Prisons Minister, and Mr Nicholas Scott, a Catholic – all three perceived as sensitive politicians – visited the Maze as one of their first official duties.

Ten days later Gowrie arranged to meet ten relatives of the hunger strikers. According to the official record:

The Minister, while being personally sympathetic to the families, made it clear that he opposed the granting of political status and would not negotiate with prisoners on hunger strike, though he hoped to improve prison conditions when the hunger strike ended.

It did, five days later. With defiant rhetoric and recrimination, a statement was issued on 3 October on behalf of the prisoners:

We the protesting prisoners … being faced with the reality of sustained family intervention are forced by this circumstance, over which we have little control at the moment, to end the hunger strike. This [strike-breaking] campaign was orchestrated by clerics who received approval from the Catholic Church, and, according to earlier accusations by Danny Morrison, 'by people within the Irish Establishment ... the SDLP and particularly by the Irish Hierarchy ... working on the emotions and putting moral pressure on the understandably distressed relatives.'

On 6 October James Prior emphasised that there would be no return to a special category or political status. However, he did announce important changes for all prisoners in Northern Ireland: in future, prisoners would be able to wear their own clothes at all times; concessions would be made on lost remissions; and some provision would be made for wider association of prisoners on adjacent wings.

Although the IRA had been faced down, these concessions were greeted with outrage by the DUP and OUP (Official Unionist Party), and many of the prison staff themselves expressed deep bitterness at the outcome. Ian Paisley and Peter Robinson went to see the Secretary of State and expressed their views that the changes were "a complete sell-out to the IRA", and an acrimonious meeting ended with their walk-out. Even the mild-mannered future Privy Counsellor, Jim Molyneaux, leader of the Ulster Unionist Party (UUP) and MP for Antrim South, accused Mr Prior of "snatching defeat from the jaws of victory."

These reactions must have struck Blelloch and his staff, who had worked hard on this grisly business for over six months, as an apt reflection on Northern Irish politicians' inherent intransigence. Encapsulating their frustration, one civil servant remarked in despair, "Whatever one does, it's absolutely impossible to satisfy everybody!"

Reflecting years later on the course of the hunger strike, Blelloch pondered whether the whole thing could have been avoided if the British Government had conceded the wearing of 'prisoners' own clothes' from the outset.

He concluded that, whilst the issue had enormous symbolic importance, it was but one – and arguably by no means the most important – of the prisoners' five demands. He felt that 'free association' would have been their higher priority.

Blelloch neatly summarized the Government's dilemma: "for the British Government to have conceded 'own clothes' in those circumstances would, in my view, not only have failed to end the protest but the prisoners might well have been encouraged to believe that by threatening further hunger strikes they would have got the remaining demands."

Furthermore, it was Blelloch's judgement that Jim Prior's appointment in September 1981 as the new Secretary of State, and Lord Gowrie's sympathetic but firm stance with the prisoners' relatives, helped greatly to reinforce the families' belief that their best option was to assist the ending of the hunger strike.

Blelloch's experience in Northern Ireland of working on these high-level and sensitive matters that required constant ministerial input, including briefing the Prime Minister, stood him in good stead. He was recalled to London in 1982 and appointed to the key post (at three-star equivalent level) of Deputy Undersecretary (Policy and Programmes) in the Ministry of Defence. Unsurprisingly, he was then selected to attend the prestigious Royal College of Defence Studies Course in 1984 at Seaford House in Belgrave Square. This was an internationally recognised year-long course for senior officers of all three services, as well as some police, diplomatic and Civil Service high flyers, plus a few 'rising stars' from the worlds of commerce and industry.

Blelloch was subsequently advanced to be the MOD's Second Permanent Undersecretary and the overseer of its substantial budget. He was now the department's number two civil servant.

His upward progress, reflecting in large part his successful first tour in Northern Ireland, meant he had been in the Province for only three years before being recalled to Whitehall. This reinforced the perennial and sceptical view of some local critics who often complained about what they termed the 'short tour-ism' of British officials. Such critics viewed too many high-flying 'Brits' as leaving just when they were beginning to understand the place. Such criticism, widely expressed in influential circles in Northern Ireland and Dublin, was levelled not just at civil servants but at able ministers, army officers and all those 'blow-ins' from the Mainland who were accused of using the Province's troubles as a stepping stone to advance their own careers.

Senior NIO officials in particular caught the brunt of it and were the target of occasional and disobliging public comment. Many Unionists felt the upper reaches of the NIO and FCO were largely responsible for what they saw as the 'feebleness' of HMG's policy on Northern Ireland. According to his biographer Dean Godson, David Trimble, for example, attributed to the present Marquis of Salisbury the remark that "decades of Imperial decline had brought about a cast of mind of British officialdom of assuming that the most expedient way of tackling any difficulty is finding the most elegant path of retreat."

Blelloch was sometimes infuriated after being berated for the umpteenth time with the accusation over dinner that the present state of Northern Ireland was all the fault of the Brits. Mainland Brits also noted that their most vocal critics were often those who themselves stood aloof from the fray, making no personal contribution or commitment to alleviating or resolving the Troubles, by enrolling, perhaps, in the UDR or RUC Reserve, or by entering democratic politics.

Notwithstanding the occasional disagreeable exchange or experience, some of Northern Ireland's most hospitable and engaging hosts wanted to make ministers, soldiers and civil servants feel at home. Invitations to take part in country pursuits, to play golf or to sail were widely extended – often to virtual strangers on the basis of some distant connection – and the warmth and generosity shown on these occasions compensated for some of the downsides of family separation and service in Northern Ireland. For example, the Blellochs were both invited to become members of the prestigious Royal Belfast Golf Club, without joining the waiting list, and accepted this generous offer. By the same token, others temporarily stationed in the Province, were able to enjoy some of the finest sport available in the British Isles in spectacularly beautiful surroundings.

On their first tour, John and Pam lived in attractive Helen's Bay overlooking Belfast Lough. It was here that tragedy struck the family. Their son Niall, who was reading Medicine at Aberdeen University, was killed in a tragic accident, and the Blellochs bravely bore their anguish whilst John was grappling with the heavy workload imposed by the hunger strike and his other responsibilities. Although some detected an unsympathetic attitude by locals towards NIO civil servants in general, the Blellochs recall that their neighbours were friendly and in several cases extremely helpful and welcoming.

Back in London, Margaret Thatcher, in the face of mounting Army casualties, Warrenpoint and the hunger strike, resolved that "something must be done about Northern Ireland." Robert Andrew, who was then the Permanent Secretary in the NIO (the job Blelloch would later inherit), noted that "all attempts to solve the problem had been manifestly unsuccessful so far." Consequently, the Prime Minister was prepared to collaborate with Dr Garret FitzGerald, the newly appointed Taoiseach in Dublin, in a way that would not have been possible with Charles Haughey, his predecessor. In a radical departure from previous policy it was decided to involve the Dublin government to represent the interests of the Nationalist minority in the North.

The lead in negotiating what came to be known as the 'Anglo-Irish Agreement' was taken in London by Robert Armstrong, then Secretary to the Cabinet, and in Dublin by Dermot Nally, his opposite number. On the British side, the FCO, and the NIO at Permanent Secretary level, were closely involved. The negotiations took two years and inevitably there were differences in approach. In principle, all parties wanted an agreement from the outset, but for the NIO, with its painful memories of the Ulster Workers' Strike, it had to be an agreement that would be accepted, however reluctantly, by the majority in the North, and one that would not again reduce the Province to a state of ungovernability. This was eventually achieved by discarding concepts like joint sovereignty and limiting Dublin's involvement to a consultative role.

Nevertheless, when the 1985 Anglo–Irish agreement was signed it was bitterly opposed by the Unionists, who felt betrayed by Mrs Thatcher. However, their opposition was not taken to extremes, and the government of Northern Ireland could be carried on with some improvement in cross-border cooperation and a reduction in terrorist incidents. In Robert Andrew's opinion, "It may not have been a great achievement for so much effort; but arguably it laid the foundations for future progress; and without the contribution of UK civil servants it would not have happened."

Andrew further recalls, as did Blelloch, that plenty of other immediate and practical issues impacted upon the lives of civil servants, especially the continuing terrorist incidents and resulting casualties which darkened the atmosphere. Others recall always being on the move and commuting between London and Belfast. One PUS remembers without affection "the awful plane and helicopter journeys – the Andover landing at windswept RAF Finningley to pick up Roy Mason" [Secretary of State 1976–79].

Then there was domestic separation and the demands of personal security, always high on the agenda. Andrew received an IRA letter bomb which was defused before any harm could be done. But, Sir Brian Cubbon, his predecessor, was blown up and badly injured in 1976, and his private secretary killed, in the course of a visit to the British Ambassador in Dublin. More outrageously in diplomatic terms, the ambassador himself, Christopher Ewart-Biggs, was also killed. Later, following a PIRA threat to senior civil servants, a bomb attack took place at the home of Ken Bloomfield, the Head of Northern Ireland's Civil Service (NICS). His home was destroyed in the blast, although neither he nor his family were injured.

Mindful of the morale of local civil servants, Robert Andrew in particular remembers seeking to improve relations and to involve NICS more in the current initiatives to bring peace to the Province, to which traditionally they were not privy. Moreover, he sought to break down the perceived 'them and us' barriers by mixing on social occasions the more junior members of NICS with mainland-based civil servants, and he was the first Permanent Secretary formally to recognise the contribution and sacrifices of NICS by attending the funerals of staff killed on duty.

Summarising his time in Northern Ireland prior to his handover to Blelloch, Andrew recalls that for two years his main role had been negotiating the Anglo–Irish Agreement, followed by a further, even more tricky two years implementing it in the face of the Unionist campaign summed up in the slogan 'Ulster says No'.

When in 1988 Blelloch returned to Northern Ireland as PUS, he had reached the very pinnacle of the Civil Service and had become one of that select breed: a top mandarin. The Troubles were in their twentieth year and he was the first Permanent Secretary to have served at Stormont in a previous capacity. Hence he enjoyed the professional bonus of knowing the background to almost all issues that arose.

Blelloch now reported directly to the Secretary of State, initially Tom King and then, when King left to become Defence Secretary, Peter Brooke. His experience, working for both, was that they had their own views on how things should be run, and the stereotypical notion that it was the Civil Service that really ran things, not ministers, was a myth.

Certain factors distinguished Northern Ireland's Permanent Secretaryship from other top civil servants' appointments. Sir John Chilcot, who succeeded Blelloch as PUS NIO in 1990, and went on to serve as such for another six years, making him then the longest-serving Permanent Secretary in post, remembers the human factor which coloured so much of his job:

> My very first, and lasting, memory of being PUS at the NIO was to be woken in the flat in Stormont House in the small hours of my first morning to be faced with the terrible news of the deaths of five soldiers in a series of proxy bomb attacks.
>
> As Permanent Secretary I was now faced with hard choices: fly, as planned, to London that morning. Go? Or stay? Be visible or be useful? Risk being thought to flee the scene, or support the Secretary of State in his necessary appearance in Parliament that afternoon?

In the event, the PUS flew to London but did not decide to do so until he had the latest incident reports delivered while awaiting the plane, in case late developments made his the wrong choice. Chilcot continued:

> That awful morning foreshadowed one, to me special, feature of the job. It mattered where you were, London or Belfast, in terms not only of what you could do but also how you saw and assessed the same situation from those two perspectives. It coloured one's emotional temperature, as well as one's rational judgment, and was a constant reminder that neither a

London nor a Belfast (let alone a Dublin) picture was complete in itself. Ministers, officials, others of our governing community were all at risk of losing the essential binocular vision of the Northern Ireland situation, without constant and conscious self-awareness of it.

Constant travel across the Irish Sea – with on occasions double or even triple return journeys – and the sheer pace of the typical day were aspects of the job I had not anticipated. A crisis to manage, video-conference meetings between the London and Belfast offices, and a string of meetings as the day wore on became routine. I remember how different things could look, depending whether the locus of the crisis was political, and if so where – Stormont or Whitehall – or whether it was operational, and therefore almost certainly in Northern Ireland. Such considerations were never-to-be-forgotten as a critical element in any judgment.

One side-effect for me was that because of the physical exertion involved in all that travel I cannot remember losing much sleep throughout my time as PUS, despite the strains and difficulties. I can though still remember vividly the experience, which had not happened to me before or since Northern Ireland, of being woken by the telephone at an ungodly hour and being completely uncertain for some moments where on earth one was.

A final reflection of that hectic and significant time is that the task, common in some measure to all high level responsibility, but for me especially so in Northern Ireland, required a very careful management of one's own mood and feelings, so as to keep a steady and level state of mind amid the violence, high emotion and human tragedy of the situation, while remaining open and seeking honest and empathetic communication with apparently irreconcilable people.

Such reflections strike responsive chords with all those who served in the Province and bore weighty responsibilities during the final three decades of the last century. They, too, felt their work was fulfilling and satisfying, although the content and circumstances were sometimes disagreeable.

Occasionally their motives were questioned, and they were often misunderstood. But they took their responsibilities seriously and were even-handed, conscientious and patient in fulfilling them. They acted both personally and officially with all the wisdom, compassion and generosity for which their years of experience and training and their responsibilities fitted them. A tribute to them is overdue.

8

The Secretary of State's Tale

Author's Introduction

After a six-year gap my involvement with Northern Ireland was reawakened when I returned there in 1990 as the GOC and Director of Military Operations.

In addition to exercising command in an operational theatre, my work involved balancing and finessing the sometimes conflicting interests and priorities of two ministries – Defence and the NIO.

In London, the MOD was preoccupied with the uncertainties implicit in the collapse of the Soviet Union. The Berlin Wall had been demolished in August 1989, and some of the States previously behind the Iron Curtain had already declared their independence, hence the opportunity for a potential 'Peace Dividend' through 'Options for Change', whereby with extensive restructuring, and cuts, millions could be saved on Defence.

'Options for Change' had an unexpected impact in Northern Ireland because it offered a practical resolution to the dilemma of the long-term future of the Ulster Defence Regiment (UDR).

The Hunt Report of 1970 had recommended the disbandment of the USC, or B-Specials, (see Tales 1 and 10) and the forming of the UDR as an integral unit of the British Army, but for service in Northern Ireland only.

Soldiers in the UDR quickly distinguished themselves by their bravery and commitment, which no one ever doubted. Indeed, this was recognized by the award to the whole Regiment by the Queen herself of the rare unit citation the Conspicuous Gallantry Cross (CGC). The part-time soldiers were especially vulnerable to assassination – many living at home in exposed and isolated places.[6] But sadly, no matter how professional UDR soldiers were, or how well they behaved, the regiment could never entirely shake off its antecedents in Nationalist eyes: as the B Specials under another guise. Some still perceived the UDR as a

---

6. The UDR suffered a disproportionately high number of casualties, with 197 killed, of whom 162 were murdered off-duty (pp. 2–12 *Operation Banner – Analysis of Military Operations in NI*).

hostile, sectarian force, drawn predominantly from the Unionist community which they could not trust to act impartially.

Members of the Regiment fiercely rejected these accusations, emphasising their strong and genuine desire to attract recruits from the minority community. They pointed out that many potential Catholic recruits were intimidated from joining. But this argument was circular: many Catholics doubted the Regiment would welcome them and, whatever the reason, they never came forward in the numbers that would alter perceptions. Accordingly, 'what to do with the UDR?' remained one of the complex unresolved issues on the political agenda.

The opportunity to resolve it, however, came with 'Options for Change' under which cuts to, or the disbandment of, the Royal Irish Rangers – an existing infantry regiment with impeccable Irish credentials – were being contemplated. Hence the suggestion that the UDR should merge with them and change its title to 'The Royal Irish Regiment' had many attractions. The new regiment, with an Irish ethos and tradition anchored in both the North and South of Ireland, would have a long-term future; soldiers could enjoy wider career opportunities, yet would still retain the option to serve locally.

Had the proposal not been adopted, and had not the new regiment formed on 1 July 1992 quickly become well established, the 'Future of the UDR' would undeniably have become a major issue during the subsequent Peace Process. Inevitably it would have become a 'show-stopper' during negotiations on decommissioning. Even the RUC's title and identity had to be sacrificed as part of that process (see Tale 10) and so there would have been scant chance of the controversial UDR surviving unchanged.

Headquarters Northern Ireland (HQNI) were consulted locally about the arrangements, but once the logic and feasibility of the UDR proposals had been accepted politically, the HQ's job was merely to ensure, with the assistance of NIO, that the proposal was not torpedoed by Unionist resistance.

Apart from this issue, our preoccupation remained to support the RUC in safeguarding the lives for which we were still responsible. The risk had not diminished and it kept soldiers on their toes. As ever, they gave of their best.

Strategically, by the 1990s the Army was holding the ring, with the RUC ever more confidently taking up the lead. Street disorder and the nightly confrontation with rioters were distant memories, except during the marching season when every year thousands paraded to commemorate distant triumphs over the 'other side'.

Occasionally, horrendous incidents still took place, mostly along the border, like the car bomb driven across it and detonated in the North at a permanent Vehicle Check Point at Buncrana outside Londonderry which killed five soldiers.

As GOC, I worked successively to two Northern Ireland Secretaries: Peter Brooke (later Lord Brooke of Stoke Mandeville) and Sir Patrick Mayhew (later Lord Mayhew of Twysden), both of whom put their wisdom and energies into kick-starting the peace process. That their successors eventually managed to deliver something recognisable as peace is, I believe, a tribute to their imaginative and skilled endeavours.

For the 'Secretary of State's Tale' I invited one of their predecessors, Tom King (later Lord King of Bridgwater), whom I had known in Northern Ireland and at Defence, to be my subject. I did so for three reasons. Firstly, he was in harness when the Anglo-Irish Agreement of November 1985 was unveiled. Ulstermen were so taken aback when that initiative was announced that King, who had only recently taken up his appointment, soon felt their fury. Here was evidence of how passionate politics in Ireland was and how any peace initiatives needed to be handled with great delicacy – fundamentals to an understanding the Troubles.

Secondly, King was Secretary of State when persistent accusations were made that elements of the Security Forces had been operating illegally on his watch and during his predecessor's time. It was alleged that they had adopted a ruthless 'shoot-to-kill' policy whereby unarmed citizens, confronted in suspicious circumstances, were shot dead rather than arrested. These were followed by accusations of 'collusion', meaning that elements within the RUC and the Army were allegedly furnishing Protestant paramilitaries with the necessary intelligence to enable them to target and then murder opponents.

Both accusations were hugely damaging and, quite properly, required thorough investigation. But for Tom King, a man who had been a Somerset Light Infantryman himself and had seen active service with King's African Rifles against the Mau Mau in Kenya, and who had always shown solidarity with those in the front line, the allegations were unsettling. It was unpleasant for any Secretary of State, ultimately responsible for everything that occurred on his 'patch', to have to contemplate that his own security forces might have been acting outside the law. But he did not flinch from instituting a thorough investigation.

Other unhelpful consequences arose from the accusations. They accentuated inter-communal suspicions and tension, already running at a high level. In addition, the ensuing investigations diverted the attention of RUC and Army commanders away from current business, thereby impairing the progress of operations and demoralising relationships.

Tom King, whilst Northern Ireland Secretary, was, uniquely, the target of a failed terrorist assassination attempt, which is the third reason for choosing him, to portray the risks – mostly unstated – that went with the job.

By chance, King was also present when 10 Downing Street was mortared by the Provisional IRA on 7 February 1991. By that time he had moved from Northern Ireland to Defence and was attending a Gulf War Cabinet Committee Meeting. For a minister to experience two such episodes in as many years gives some taste of the physical risks which the holders of high office during this period accepted.

Most of the top appointment holders in Northern Ireland had full-time protection. It went with the job and was accepted as such. But having close protection did heighten profiles and tended to draw attention to the individual concerned, and sometimes by its intrusive nature alarmed and inconvenienced family, friends and neighbours.

Not that any such holders of high office could reasonably have complained, for those who held senior appointments during the Troubles were generally delighted to be in post. They derived satisfaction from knowing that, although their own contribution, viewed through the prism of history, might be transitory and puny, for a time they had the opportunity to try and influence the situation for the better.

Tom King's story well illustrates the point.

* * *

The role of the Secretary of State for Northern Ireland, following the demise of Stormont in early 1972, was described by Dr John Oliver, a former NICS Permanent Secretary, as "the king-pin: governor, prime minister, commander-in-chief, negotiator, arbiter, host, all rolled into one." That may gild the job too brightly, but what is undeniable is that the Northern Irish – of all persuasions – take a keen interest in their Secretary of State.

Traditionally, before the Troubles, a resident Governor had represented the Queen. Following the imposition of Direct Rule, he was replaced by a Secretary of State, so it is understandable that the nature of the man or woman perceived (inaccurately in constitutional terms) as replacing the Governor would be closely observed. Moreover, the community quickly forms strong views about anyone holding a responsible appointment, and his or her character and suitability for office are widely discussed. Once minds are made up – for better or worse – they are rarely altered.

For the incumbent at Hillsborough Castle, once the Governor's imposing official residence and now that of the Secretary of State, this could be daunting, but most former Northern Ireland Secretaries seemed to agree that, despite the domestic upheaval and the intrusions of full-time protection, professionally theirs was the best and most fulfilling job in politics. Nevertheless, some political perceptions from the past remained: either that Northern Ireland was a kind of punishment posting to which ministers would be banished who were out of favour with the Prime Minister, as Jim Prior (SSNI 1981-84) was said to have been with Margaret Thatcher; or that it was where worthy yet otherwise hard-to-place Party elders, like the late Merlyn Rees (Labour's SSNI 1974-78) or Humphrey Atkins (SSNI 1979-81), would end up.

Tom King became the second longest serving Northern Ireland Secretary during the Troubles, after Sir Patrick Mayhew who served from 1992 to 1997. Conservative Member of Parliament for Bridgwater in Somerset since 1970, King had been appointed to ministerial office in Prime Minister Margaret Thatcher's first administration.

Late in the summer of 1985, Margaret Thatcher had conducted one of her Cabinet reshuffles. King, who was then Employment Secretary, remembers receiving a telephone call from Robin Butler, the Cabinet Secretary, inviting him over to 10 Downing Street to hear of his future, following an August of media speculation about who would be promoted or fired.

The reshuffle advanced Douglas Hurd from Northern Ireland to the Home Office, and King was appointed to replace him. In *The Downing Street Years* the Prime Minister confessed that she had previously misjudged King, based on her time in Opposition. Perhaps she remembered, as King does, that when he was Minister for Local Government from 1979 to 1983, he had been the only Government minister to understand the intricacies of the 'block grant', the mechanism by which the Community Charge would be calculated. Whatever her reasoning, she wrote that he "was a man with a taste for detail ... I then made the uncomfortable discovery that detail was not at all Tom's forte ... " Nevertheless, she had resolved that he should take over in Northern Ireland where, she continued, "the other side of his character, which was a robust, manly good sense [would win over] hardened opponents to his point of view, at least as far as is possible in Northern Ireland."

She acknowledged that, from the standpoint of Ulster, in reality it was a "slightly difficult time to put in a new Secretary of State, with negotiation of the Anglo-Irish Agreement in its final stages." Douglas Hurd had been intimately involved in its genesis, and King, who took up his appointment on 3 September 1985, five weeks before it was unveiled, was, as a result, to have a tough baptism.

The Anglo–Irish Agreement had come about (in circumstances described in Tale 7) partially as a result of Mrs Thatcher's despair of getting any movement, let alone agreement, from the Ulster Unionists in response to any of her initiatives. It seems that her identification with Unionism – a Tory instinct – and her resolve in facing down the hunger strikers, had gained her little credit or latitude. Moreover, she had come under pressure from an ally, President Reagan, to take an initiative in Northern Ireland, an issue about which the large Irish–American constituency was always concerned. Additionally, she herself believed that it was right to explore every avenue to improve security with the Republic, and under the terms of the Agreement she was optimistic that this looked feasible. There was one further not insignificant factor. Thatcher was charmed by Garret FitzGerald, the Taoiseach, who persuaded her that surely together they would be able to ameliorate the present unhappy situation.

On 15 November 1985 the Anglo–Irish Agreement was signed at Hillsborough Castle, to the fury of large numbers of Ulstermen. King caught the immediate flak, which he did not deserve. As Margaret Thatcher acknowledged in her memoirs, 'Tom was initially highly sceptical about the value of the Agreement – indeed within weeks of taking office he had sent me a minute arguing that [its] balance as drafted was heavily in favour of the Irish.' From then on Tom King was perceived to be ambivalent about the value of the Agreement, although in public he loyally supported it. 'Loyalty is for him the highest virtue – disloyalty the unpardonable sin', wrote Bruce Anderson of King in *The Times*.

The Agreement acknowledged that there was an Irish 'dimension' to the interests of both Ulster and the Republic on subjects such as legal issues, security and cross-border incidents. For the first time, the South assumed a role in the governance of Northern Ireland, thereby widening the scope for Dublin's involvement in areas from which it had previously been excluded.

In exchange, the Republic agreed that there could not be – and would not be – any change in the status of Northern Ireland without first gaining the consent of the majority in the North. This confirmed Northern Ireland's position as part of the United Kingdom, thereby undermining the very essence of one of the IRA's justifications for conflict, namely that the island of Ireland should be a single entity. Gerry Adams denounced this betrayal as "a disaster for the Nationalist cause."

Meanwhile, at the other end of the political spectrum, the prospect of the Republic's 'interference' in the affairs of the North provoked outrage among hard-line Unionists. Between 100,000 and 200,000 Loyalists gathered in protest outside Belfast's City Hall; as Bardon's *History of Ulster* claims, "Nothing like it had been seen since 1912."

By coincidence, King had been invited to the City Hall that day for lunch as a guest of the Independent Broadcasting Authority (IBA), who had flown in to review UTV's operation in Northern Ireland. Being an inquisitive minister who liked to see things for himself, he was glad of the opportunity to assess the mood of the crowd. But some hotheads discovered where the Secretary of State was lunching and started banging on the door and issuing dire threats, much to the consternation of the IBA's mainland-based members. Without too much difficulty, King was extracted unharmed via the back stairs by his RUC Protection Team before the crowd en masse could react to his presence. But the event was noteworthy for the fright it gave the IBA members from the 'Mainland', and the insight it gave King into the raw strength of Unionist protest.

Unionist sense of betrayal by the Anglo-Irish Agreement was palpable and, as in previous crises, it was Ian Paisley who articulated it most vehemently. As Professor Lord Paul Bew describes graphically in *Ireland – the Politics of Enmity*, he made a vitriolic attack at the City Hall on the Prime Minister, and another from his pulpit at the Martyrs' Memorial Church in Belfast, where he accused her of being the architect of "this betrayal". Leading his congregation, he prayed:

> We pray this night that thou wouldst deal with the Prime Minister of our country. Oh God, in wrath take vengeance upon this wicked, treacherous and lying woman: take vengeance upon her, oh Lord, and grant that we shall see a demonstration of thy power.

Bew comments that much anger was also focussed locally on the NIO, though in fact "the Foreign Office, and more particularly the Cabinet Office, had taken the decisive role in committing Britain to the Agreement, whilst the NIO had been profoundly sceptical."

In perhaps just the sort of demonstration Dr Paisley had in mind, a series of formal protests took place. Fifteen Unionist politicians resigned their seats, thereby precipitating by-elections; UK Ministers and officials were boycotted; and 'consent' was withdrawn from Government with the refusal by protesters to pay rates and other dues.

The Loyalists organised a 'Day of Action' which sought to bring the Province to a standstill. It inconvenienced many, but achieved no lasting result. In contrast to their somewhat feeble efforts during the 1974 Ulster

Workers' Strike, the RUC ensured the Province kept running, for which there was relief in Government circles, and the RUC gained credit.

There were no more Days of Action. But neither were the anticipated improvements in security cooperation with the Republic forthcoming. Moreover, the expected strengthening of the SDLP – John Hume's constitutional Nationalist party and rival to Sinn Fein – in the 1987 Election was only temporary.

It soon became clear that the advantages which the Prime Minister had anticipated as flowing from the Anglo-Irish Agreement were not forthcoming, and she became disillusioned. Indeed, her Memoirs noted (*The Downing Street Years* p. 403) her surprise at the ferocity of the Unionist response, claiming that, 'their reaction was worse than anyone had predicted.' An additional personal blow was the resignation of Ian Gow in protest at the signing of the Agreement. He had been her able, former Parliamentary Private Secretary, and was her confidant and political soul-mate. (He was later murdered by a PIRA car-bomb at his home in East Sussex on 30 July 1990).

Meanwhile, detached observers at home and overseas, noting the reactions on both sides of the divide in Ireland, concluded that, with Unionists and Republicans equally unhappy, a good balance had been struck. Surely both London and Dublin had made important concessions which would isolate those seeking to achieve their aims by violence?

This was the perception in the United States where President Reagan noted that, given Thatcher's determined leadership (and, by implication, given his influence), the British were at last attempting to do the right thing over Ireland.

In fact, with hindsight, the groundwork involved in establishing the Anglo-Irish Agreement of 1985 paved the way for achieving the Good Friday Agreement, signed on 10 April 1998, which formally ended the Troubles. Unfortunately, between these milestones, the paramilitaries on both sides, far from reducing their violence, embarked on increased activity.

The bombing by PIRA of the Remembrance Day Ceremony in Enniskillen, County Tyrone, in November 1987 was particularly horrific. Eleven were killed by a car-bomb placed near the War Memorial, and sixty-three were injured, nine seriously. One of the victims was fifty-nine-year-old Gordon Wilson. He was trapped in the wreckage with his daughter and they held hands to comfort each other. But his daughter died, whereas he was extracted from the devastation and survived. Having recovered, Gordon's remarkable dignity and words of forgiveness in the wake of what must have been unbearable grief were broadcast world-wide. He told the BBC: "I have lost my daughter, and we shall miss her. But I bear no ill will. I bear no grudge. Dirty sort of talk is not going to bring her back to life."

He forgave her killers, he said, and prayed for them every night. His moving and conciliatory words attracted much admiration, and they were believed to have persuaded the Loyalist paramilitaries, intent on retaliation, to desist.

King suggested that the Prime Minister should show her solidarity with the community by attending the delayed Remembrance Service in the town two weeks later. As Mrs Thatcher was due to fly to a European Union meeting in Paris that day anyway, it was easy to re-route the aircraft via Belfast. She arrived in Fermanagh in a downpour, and King recalls that, despite everybody's soaking, her visit uplifted the local community.

Behind the scenes, even before the Enniskillen bombing, developments were undermining confidence in aspects of the Security Forces' work. Accusations that the Army and RUC had adopted a 'shoot-to-kill' policy were voiced in the wake of a number of covert operations. The accusations were that the RUC and Army had sanctioned the use of lethal force against suspects, who were subsequently discovered to be unarmed, rather than first seeking to arrest them.

In response King had to make defensive statements in the House of Commons on events which were unclear and still shrouded in secrecy. He found this uncomfortable, and, of even greater concern, the shoot-to-kill controversy involved him in increasingly unsatisfactory exchanges with Sir Jack Hermon, the RUC's Chief Constable, to the detriment of their mutual confidence. The Chief Constable considered the matter to be an operational issue and thus, on principle, his business to sort out with his Police Authority, rather than something involving a politician. This tends to be the automatic response of policemen when controversial aspects of their role arise, but it was unhelpful for the Secretary of State to be at odds with his police chief, especially as constitutionally he was required to answer to Parliament for the smooth running of the Province.

The complexities of public accountability are often frustrating. In the immediate aftermath of a major incident the situation is invariably confused and the facts hazy. Initial accounts take time to verify, and frequently the first report is found to be inaccurate. Often, within hours of a statement being made, it has to be corrected. But the very act of correction can appear inept – even suspicious – and the authorities are consequently wrong-footed.

Moreover, all covert operations are sensitive by definition. Either there is an intelligence interest which cannot be revealed, or there is some sensitive technical aspect which cannot be declared. Also, by convention of long standing, mention of SAS operations and the function of the UK's various security services is taboo. Yet the unfortunate minister or spokesperson, who should have been briefed on all the known facts, has either been deliberately kept in the dark about facets of an operation too sensitive to reveal or, worse, having been given the facts, urged never to declare them.

Yet those to whom ministers must account in a parliamentary democracy wish to know what has happened; why it has happened; who was involved; and, importantly, if fatalities occurred, how the incident could have been avoided or handled better. Often an assumption is made that a mistake must have occurred, and that therefore someone should be to blame.

Fortunately, Tom King was a robust minister and could give a good account of himself and those for whom he was answerable, even if, some felt, he tended to bluster when challenged. Had he not been robust, he would not have lasted to become the longest-serving Secretary of State for Northern Ireland up to that time. However, he was frequently faced with just the sort of challenges which ministers find awkward and their civil servants dread. As a minister renowned for being supportive of commanders in the field – particularly those in the front line – he wanted openly to support the Chief Constable and GOC, but in practice he found himself rather too often on the back foot responding to criticism of the Police and the Army.

Following a series of controversial incidents from 1982 onwards, and particularly in the aftermath of the shooting dead by the Security Forces of Michael Tighe, an unarmed youth, in what became known as the 'hayshed' incident, the Chief Constable had been persuaded to invite Mr John Stalker, Deputy Chief Constable of Manchester, to investigate the ensuing 'shoot-to-kill' allegations.

In May 1986, however, before his Report could be published, John Stalker was removed from the Inquiry when his Police Authority controversially suspended him in connection with alleged breaches of discipline. Prior to his suspension, Stalker claimed that he was about to uncover the truth about what happened in the hayshed. He claimed that a contemporary tape, which he had unearthed, would finally reveal whether or not a warning had been given to Michael Tighe before he was shot.

Stalker was replaced by Sir Colin Sampson, the Chief Constable of West Yorkshire, who continued to investigate the shoot-to-kill allegations where Stalker had left off. But mysteriously the key 'hayshed' tape had disappeared, and was never found. Sampson duly completed his report, which was delivered to Northern Ireland's Director of Public Prosecutions; but it was never made public, because it contained sensitive material bearing on national security.

As Secretary of State King was privy to the Report, although what legal action to pursue was not his responsibility but that of the then Attorney General, Sir Patrick Mayhew. He told the House of Commons in January 1988 that he had consulted with ministerial colleagues, as he was constitutionally required to do after the so-called 'Shawcross precedent', and had agreed with the Director of Public Prosecutions (DPP) that prosecution would not be in the public interest by virtue of the security factors involved.

King concurred, judging on balance – as was entirely proper for the Secretary of State to judge – that a prosecution which might destabilize the fragile relationships in Northern Ireland would itself be undesirable.

But high-profile and controversial incidents did not stop, and King was to be involved in the aftermath of several. The next occurred on 8 May 1987 when an undercover operation at Loughgall in County Tyrone engaged and killed eight PIRA terrorists (one uninvolved civilian was also killed, and another was injured). The terrorists were about to launch a mortar attack against the local police station and kill those inside.

PIRA never sought to deny their planned attack; they merely vowed to retaliate later for their severe losses. Worryingly for them, they had to admit that their plans must have been known 'to the Brits' in advance. Their suspicion of having been penetrated, despite their tight discipline, was to have an increasingly detrimental effect and arguably advanced the peace process (see Tale 9).

The retaliation for Loughgall came nine months later when a PIRA team of three – one woman and two men – travelled to Gibraltar. Their intention was to detonate a car-bomb to catch the daily changing of the guard ceremony outside the Governor's Residence which attracted many tourists.

Their plot was foiled on good intelligence – although, as so often occurs, not every piece of the jigsaw was known. On 6 March 1988 three terrorists – Mairead Farrell, Sean Savage and Danny McCann – were identified by an SAS sub-unit, and shot dead. Yet again, the dead were found to be unarmed, and witnesses denied they had even been challenged. Furthermore, the car suspected of carrying the explosive and discovered adjacent to where the ceremony was due to have taken place, did not contain a bomb. On the face of it, here was another shoot-to-kill incident. But the initial accusations of foul play by the 'Brits' were undermined by PIRA's defiant admission that their team in Gibraltar was on active service intent on killing British soldiers.

Nevertheless, international controversy raged about the legality and morality of the British action. Thames Television commissioned a programme entitled *Death on the Rock*, which pre-empted the Inquest and enraged Mrs Thatcher. The Foreign Secretary, Geoffrey Howe, led on the international aspects of the incident, but King was kept in the loop as it affected the Province.

The Government tried, but failed, to prevent the screening of *Death on the Rock*. Notwithstanding, the Inquest seemed to be unaffected because on 30 September 1988 the jury concluded by a majority of nine to two that the three IRA members had been 'lawfully killed'. This was partially contradicted seven years later, however, by the European Court of Human Rights which ruled that the killings were 'unnecessary' and that the three IRA personnel 'could have been arrested.' Nevertheless, it ruled that the soldiers had not been operating under a policy of shoot-to-kill.

The funerals, ten days after the three terrorists had been killed in Gibraltar, took place at the IRA's hallowed plot in Milltown Cemetery in West Belfast. This became the scene of the next major incident, one with a horrific sequel.

During the well-attended and emotionally charged Requiem Mass and military-style funeral, an unknown assailant, identified later as a thirty-three-year-old, unstable, Loyalist paramilitary from East Belfast named Michael Stone, ran amok, firing into the crowd. He claimed to be acting in retaliation for the earlier Enniskillen bombing and intended to assassinate Gerry Adams and Martin McGuiness, both present as mourners.

Firing two hand-guns and throwing grenades indiscriminately, he killed three and injured more than sixty (but not Adams or McGuiness) before escaping, pursued by a small section of the crowd. Understandably, the incident caused alarm and confusion because no one could determine what was happening.

An RUC mobile patrol on the adjoining motorway passing the cemetery caught up with and rescued Stone, who had been run to ground by a small section of the crowd who were about to kill him. Stone was duly arrested, charged and sentenced to a long period of imprisonment. (He was released under the Good Friday Peace Agreement, having served thirteen years.)

An even more shocking event, considered to be the most brutally and publicly harrowing of the whole campaign, was to follow. On 19 March 1988, three days after the Milltown Cemetery killings, the body of one of Stone's

PIRA victims was being taken in a funeral procession to the same cemetery when two unidentified men drove into the path of the funeral cortege. They pulled over, having been waved down by the marshals, who tried to question them. In panic and distress, the driver attempted to break clear. But he stalled the car and failed to get free. His attempt alerted the suspicions of the crowd, who, understandably, were already alarmed and tense after the earlier incident.

It transpired later that the two men were Corporals Derek Wood and David Howes from the Royal Corps of Signals, in plain clothes and driving an unmarked VW Passat on an unauthorised, but otherwise innocent, journey.

The mourners and stewards, presumably seeing this as another Protestant paramilitary attack, especially when Corporal Wood pulled a pistol and fired it in the air, surrounded the vehicle and dragged the occupants out. The two men were bundled into a Black Taxi (as the Belfast cabs are known) and driven to some waste ground nearby. Here they were stripped, identified as soldiers, severely beaten up and eventually removed to face terrifying and lonely deaths at the hands of executioners who had been summoned to do the job.

Watching journalists reported that the soldiers were first tortured before being killed. Mary Holland, writing for the *Irish Times*, felt disgusted and helpless. "How did we let it happen?" she wrote. "Corporal Wood, wearing a green jumper, passed within a few feet of me and dozens of other journalists. He did not cry out, just looked at us with terrified eyes as if we were all enemies in a foreign country who wouldn't have understood what language he was speaking if he called out for help."

The whole harrowing and graphic sequence was recorded by Army HeliTele (CCTV). But it all happened so quickly that no intervention could be mounted in time to save the soldiers. In response to earlier complaints that the RUC's presence at the previous funeral had been intrusive and had antagonised the mourners, the RUC had agreed to stand off and observe this one from a distance using an Army helicopter fitted with HeliTele to monitor the funeral. Thus no physical security presence was on hand to intervene.

The horrific pictures and the accounts of journalists present were widely distributed. The barbarity of the incident caused revulsion and ensured world-wide condemnation, despite PIRA's attempted spin that these were members of the SAS (Corporal Wood was said to have documentation on him referring to Herford in Germany – the location of his parent unit –

which led mistakenly, according to an account in the book *Lost Lives*, to his alleged association with the SAS base in Hereford).

The Secretary of State had to account for all these incidents to the House of Commons, including having to explain why the two corporals were roaming in West Belfast. (After the incident, it was established that Corporal Wood, who was in the process of handing over to his colleague, was probably taking the opportunity to show the latter around Belfast, when they accidentally came upon the cortege.)

It would be wrong to imagine that King's time focussed solely on security. Most of it was spent running and supervising the business of the Province through the ministerial team which he headed. This was not merely a routine or passive function. For example, in January 1986 he enlarged his ministerial team by one and by October he had rearranged his ministers' responsibilities. He himself took on political and constitutional matters, security policy and operations, broad economic questions and other major policy issues. His deputy, the Minister of State, the late Nicholas Scott MP, continued to hold day-to-day responsibility for law and order, particularly relating to prisons, police administration and compensation, and for the Northern Ireland Department of Finance and Personnel. Of the four junior ministers (Parliamentary Undersecretaries) one, the late Lord Lyell, was responsible for Agriculture as well as for fielding all Northern Ireland matters in the House of Lords; another, the dynamic, impetuous, Richard Needham, was in charge of Health, Social Services and Environment; Dr Brian Mawhinney MP, an Ulsterman and Tom King's former PPS, handled Education and Information; and Peter Viggers MP was responsible for the Northern Ireland Department of Economic Development.

One of the headaches for ministers was the high and ever rising costs of the Troubles. A reference to the largesse being channelled across the Irish Sea at the expense, particularly of England's South East Region was highlighted by Graham Gudgin, the distinguished Belfast-based economist, who quipped that a statue should be erected in Belfast to commemorate the "Unknown British Taxpayer as the Unsung Hero of the Troubles."

There were four main streams of revenue: the first was the standard 'Block Grant', which emanated from HM Treasury to cover the provision of all routine areas of expenditure, such as health, the police and transport. Part of this was covered by tax revenues raised in Northern Ireland, but there was always a need for a large top-up, or subvention, from the Treasury covering about half of the cost of public spending. In 1984/5 the total subvention, excluding Army costs, was £1,491m (*Hansard*, July 1985).

The second contribution came from the MOD and related to the extra costs of operations in Northern Ireland, of keeping troops there and maintaining facilities (like border checkpoints and equipment) specifically for the purposes of countering the terrorist threat. During the full financial years covering King's tenure of office (1985/6 – 1987/8), the Defence Vote allocated a cumulative £447 million of public expenditure to the Northern Ireland budget.[7]

A third source of revenue came from the EU. In 1977 Northern Ireland had been designated as a priority objective EU Region on the basis of its peripheral position and disadvantaged status. The Vice President of the European Commission commented later that "Northern Ireland received more per capita from the EU than any other area except Greenland." Even so, EU funds contributed an amount equivalent to only around 2% of Northern Ireland's public spending.

Records show that from 1990 to 2005, under the programme for funding Europe's poorer regions, Northern Ireland received some £2.3 billion, plus £500 million allocated for 'peace' purposes. However, the Treasury reduced the block grant in line with incoming EU funds. This can be said to count as part of the British contribution towards the cost of Northern Ireland but one for which the UK received a 'rebate' from Brussels to offset its net contribution to the EU.

One element of the EU funding which was clearly 'additional' was the Peace Funds, which were awarded in three tranches from 1995 to 2013. These added around 0.5% per annum to public spending.

The fourth stream derived from Criminal Injuries and Compensation legalisation and was provided for that specific need. Technically, these sums should not be considered to be part of Northern Ireland's budget. Yet, manifestly they can be included in the real cost of the Troubles, and were significant. Even in the financial year 1999/2000 when the Troubles were declining, the total cost of compensation for Criminal Injuries and for Criminal Damage amounted to £76.1 million.[8]

There was a history to this. On Partition in 1921 it was intended that Northern Ireland should be self-funding, but the unfavourable economic conditions of the 1920s and 1930s meant that the Province struggled to

---

7. Costs of Military Operations in NI – 1985/86: £135m; 1986/87: £144m; 1987/88: £168m = £447m (Hansard, 16 June 1988).
8. NIO 1999–2000 Estimates Provision Ch 3 sub para G.

maintain public expenditure from locally raised taxes. Hence there was inadequate funding for things like housing, a deficiency which came back to bite Stormont in the 1960s when decades of under-investment became entangled in Nationalist accusations of discrimination in the allocation of publicly owned houses.

During the inter-war and post-war periods, Northern Ireland suffered the slow economic collapse of traditional industries such as textiles and shipbuilding. This was countered by new investment stimulated by generous public grants injected into industry by the government from the 1950s. But with the onset on the Troubles new investment dried up until the 1980s, inflicting even more economic damage.

Northern Ireland's economy was, however, saved by a continuing high level of public expenditure, much of it financed by taxpayers in Great Britain. Public spending had built up to a high level during the Labour governments of the 1960s, and Northern Ireland gained under the general principle of parity of public services throughout the UK.

Public spending was initially allocated to Northern Ireland on the basis of need, and the Province was always able to argue that it had a higher level of need than existed elsewhere in the Kingdom. For example, large families meant the need for a large number of school teachers; generally poor health meant an increased need for medical and hospital provision; and marginal farms posed a need for higher subsidies. Hence in almost every government programme Northern Ireland's needs could be demonstrated as justifiably high.

This high share of UK public spending was subsequently entrenched by the introduction of the so-called Barnett formula in 1979 (named after the former Labour Chief Secretary to the Treasury) whereby a new and simplified allocation of public spending across the UK was adopted. Barnett's formula ensured that regions like Scotland and Northern Ireland received a share of any national increase in spending in proportion to their population. However, these annual increases were built upon already high levels of spending in these regions, especially in Northern Ireland where it was around 35% higher per head than in GB.

In this way, Northern Ireland required large infusions of UK tax-payers' money, irrespective of the Troubles. Twelve years after the Good Friday Agreement the position has changed little. Northern Ireland continues to enjoy public spending per head 25% above the UK average, and the inflow of funds, the so-called 'subvention', has now reached £9 billion, or almost £5,000 for every person in the Province.[9]

Notwithstanding this largesse, economists like Graham Gudgin believe that the Troubles were financially affordable within the UK's large economy. He concludes: "In truth the burden was easily manageable and this was surely a major reason why the Troubles lasted so long."

Meanwhile, security concerns did not decrease. Those whose jobs put them at personal risk of assassination tended not to dwell on them. Occasionally, however, they were confronted by the reality. This happened to King following an incident at his home in Wiltshire in August 1987. He and his wife Jane were in Scotland at the time but his twenty-five-year-old daughter Elisa was riding with a friend in the woods on the Kings' estate near Chippenham in Wiltshire. She noticed a man and a woman seated on the parapet of a bridge; a tent was nearby. Something about them made her suspicious and she averted her gaze as she rode by, to avoid confrontation.

Returning to the house, she alerted one of her father's Protection Officers, always on duty from the Wiltshire Constabulary. He happened to be a former Royal Marine who had served in Ulster. Going to the spot, he asked questions of the couple, who gave what later transpired to be false names; they claimed to be merely camping at this agreeable spot, but the policeman became suspicious when their answers did not tally with his own experience of Northern Ireland and his observations. He arrested the couple on suspicion of poaching, and in the ensuing search of their possessions £4,500 was found sewn into the tent lining.

Some scribbled notes helped pinpoint a third person, twenty-four-year-old John McCann from Dublin, who was arrested in a campsite at nearby Wookey Hole in Somerset. Here a yellow Datsun with false English plates was found, which on investigation was discovered to have been bought at a Whitechapel car auction under the false name of Pat Kelly. Additionally, documents were found which allocated the trio a budget of £11,400 to fund their activities until December 1987.

These activities were to mount reconnaissance on a target list of nineteen names of various high-profile politicians, soldiers and judges for potential attack. Five of the names – Tom King, Rhodes Boyson MP, Nicholas Scott MP, retired Major General Richard Clutterbuck, a well known authority and broadcaster on terrorism, and Lord Justice Scarman – had asterisks against their name signifying, it seemed, primary targets. In addition, maps and

9. Department of Finance and Personnel, Belfast. *Northern Ireland Net Fiscal Balance Report*, Sept 2009.

descriptions were discovered pinpointing several Army establishments in the West Country, like the Regular Commissions Board at Westbury, Wiltshire, and the Royal Armoured Corps Centre at Bovington, in Dorset.

The trio were charged with 'conspiring to murder Mr Tom King and other people between 1 May and 31 August 1987'. The trial opened at Winchester Crown Court on 8 October 1988 and lasted fifteen days. The jury had difficulty in reaching a verdict but eventually found the three defendants guilty by a majority of 10:2. They were each sentenced to twenty-five years imprisonment. But on appeal the verdict was found to be unsafe because during the trial King, speaking in the House of Commons during a security debate, had been critical of the abuse of rules of evidence relating to rights to silence, which the Government wished to change. His remarks were deemed to have prejudiced the jury, who coincidentally had then retired to consider their verdict, and therefore the Appeal Court determined that King's views invalidated a fair trial, and the defendants were released.

King recalls that a senior civil servant whose responsibility was to ensure that nothing blew his minister's statement to the House off track, apologised for the embarrassment caused. Although the incident was clearly an irritant, equally it demonstrated the length to which British justice went to be fair.

King left Northern Ireland, as he had arrived, at the bidding of the Prime Minister. In July 1989 he was appointed Defence Secretary and was to be absorbed almost immediately in the preparation and planning, then the direction of, the First Gulf War.

After Defence, King was made a Life Peer in 2001. As Lord King of Bridgwater, one of the appointments he was offered and accepted was as Chairman of the newly created Parliamentary Intelligence and Security Committee to oversee matters of national intelligence. Here again he would have exposure to ongoing work in Northern Ireland.

From the start of the Troubles to the end of the century eleven Secretaries of State completed their period in office. Inevitably the issues confronting them waxed and waned as priorities changed, but all would have recognised Tom King's preoccupations and imperatives. Memories of the intransigence of Irish politicians of North and South, the disharmony within the Provinces' two main communities and the horrific death, destruction and lives lost will remain with them. Equally, the fact that peace of a kind has emerged after all these years is a tribute to successive Secretaries of State, and those in support of them, who can generally be proud of their various contributions.

9

The Spook's Tale

Author's Introduction

When Willie Whitelaw was appointed to be the first Secretary of State on the dissolution of the old Stormont Parliament in March 1972, he insisted on having as his right-hand man a specially selected intelligence officer from MI6. Years later, that officer told me that he had been appalled at the time by the poor state of the RUC's local intelligence records and by their lack of organisation.

From the outset, the Army had been puzzled and frustrated at the lack of timely and reliable intelligence. Previously, Army officers who had been engaged in operational planning around the world had routinely been accustomed to having intelligence on tap. During the 'emergencies' of the sixties, Malaya, Kenya, Aden, Cyprus, there might have been deficiencies in intelligence – there always are – but at least basic and accurate information existed to enable soldiers to do their job properly.

As Northern Ireland was initially perceived as yet another of those 'emergencies', it was a shock to find so little useable intelligence available. 'Useable intelligence' means intelligence which can be acted upon straight away without the risk of revealing its source or how it was obtained. Useable intelligence is precious because it enables law enforcers to be selective and to identify wrongdoers accurately, whilst leaving the innocent or uncommitted alone.

Initially Army officers were told that these shortcomings were the consequence of the RUC's Special Branch being tired and demoralised. Later we discovered that they knew almost everything there was to know about the history of past IRA campaigns and the identity of the previous generation of Republican families, but their records had not been kept up to date, and a lack of 'penetration' of the contemporary Republican community was revealed.

Dissatisfaction within the Army over the lack of useable intelligence was a running sore throughout the Troubles, and caused more bad blood between the various arms of the Security Forces than any other single shortcoming. The reasons, from an Army perspective, emerge at the start of the Tale that follows.

As GOC, I was not privy to any of the tentative peace overtures or negotiations that were starting as I took up my new post. Nor should I have been, since, quite properly, the important 'need-to-know' principle governing the dissemination of intelligence was observed. Nevertheless, I sensed from the tone of successive political pronouncements and from wider observation that peace feelers were being put out in both directions. The inside story of how and by whom the process was effected is remarkable and reflects much credit on some individual members of the intelligence community.

My appointment gave me a ringside view of both that community and the political one. To capture the flavour of them, and to account for the importance of the work he and others on his team did, I chose the late John Deverell CBE, Northern Ireland's former Director and Coordinator of Intelligence (or DCI) to be the subject of this Tale. It ends tragically with his death and that of twenty-eight other young and talented servants of the Crown. It is a sombre tale of the sacrifice suffered by those engaged on routine duty far from the front line.

* * *

Since the advent of Police Primacy in 1976, soldiers working in the specialized and close-knit world of intelligence had been viewed rather as 'country cousins'. Kept at arm's length and given only the essentials needed to complete whatever task was required, Army officers believed they could contribute far more to the overall benefit of the campaign if only 'intelligence' were better integrated. After all, the Army had enviable resources to contribute: unlimited manpower – which then did not have to be accounted for in budgetary terms – and useful state-of-the-art equipment. Furthermore, they had a high work ethic, enormous enthusiasm and skills honed by months of intense training prior to posting to Northern Ireland.

It was held by some diehards, on the other hand, that using soldiers, rather than those traditionally involved in intelligence, was unconstitutional, an unnecessary departure from the norm and an unacceptable risk. Soldiers were answerable to a different chain of command – a military one – ultimately headed by the Secretary of State for Defence rather than by the Home Secretary, who constitutionally was answerable to Parliament on all internal intelligence matters. Altering this longstanding arrangement risked not only duplication of effort and widening the knowledge of secrets but, worse in Whitehall terms, providing an opportunity for a separate agenda to develop, and even a competing power base to become established.

John Deverell, who as Director and Coordinator of Intelligence at Stormont was responsible for the overall intelligence capability in Northern Ireland, was no diehard. But there were plenty around him who felt it wise to maintain the status quo and keep the Army at arm's length, except where the occasional use of lethal force was required.

From Deverell's title one might assume his role was to direct and coordinate the intelligence effort; in other words, to take charge of various intelligence agencies and pull their operations together. But this was not John's style, which was instinctively consensual; nor was it the way MI5, to whom Deverell was now professionally accountable, liked to conduct its business. They favoured a more indirect approach.

At the time, MI5 had not yet been authorised to take the lead nationally, or even provincially, in intelligence matters relating to Irish terrorism. In the early 1990s that role in Northern Ireland was still the job of the RUC's Special Branch. But the RUC's intelligence people faced a Herculean task. Firstly, there were four separate and largely autonomous external agencies contributing to the picture: MI5, MI6, GCHQ and the Metropolitan Police's Special Branch (MPSB). But that was not all. Within the Province, the RUC's Special Branch and Army Intelligence were also major contributors to the local picture. Additionally, within the Army itself there were also several providers, such as the regimental intelligence cells at one level and, at a higher level, the source-handling unit of which Peter Jones (Tale 4) was part.

Faced with such a plethora of agencies, each working hard and diligently within its own remit, the DCI became in effect *primus inter pares,* sharing the lead with the RUC's Head of Special Branch. This burden-sharing was undeniably pragmatic: the Police were still in the lead and the Army, which had already acquiesced in the arrangement, adopted a subordinate role.

In practice, Deverell functioned rather more as an adviser and enabler than as an executive director and coordinator of intelligence. He jollied people along and eventually got them going in the right direction, in the manner of a sheepdog, not that he habitually performed as his master expected. Indeed, colleagues and those close to him recalled Deverell's independent nature and observed that he regarded his work as a vocation not just a career.

Lower down the intelligence structure were three Tasking and Coordination Groups (TCGs) – one to each of the three geographical Police Regions under an RUC Superintendent. It was here that the coordination of operations was supposed to take place. But unfortunately the TCGs, initially at least, did not have real-time access to all the intelligence material available. Yet on this issue the RUC were in denial, even when operationally experienced Army officers, who knew something of real-time battle management, tactfully tried to point it out and suggested possible improvements.

Discussions at the highest level about these shortcomings were the catalyst for the annual 'Machrihanish' seminars and earlier a series of informal gatherings, hosted by the GOC and attended just by him, the Chief Constable, the Permanent Secretary NIO and the DCI.

Later this developed into a brain-storming session, conducted by the senior intelligence staff alone to promote better outcomes. Gradually a consensus was reached on how improvements might be made, and these were implemented when the opportunity arose. John Deverell, hosting these sessions, presided with a light touch and was good at encouraging discussion and getting the best out of those attending.

John had been born in Kenya in 1936. He was the son of a Colonial Civil Servant, whose postings were in idyllic spots – Jamaica as Chief Secretary; the Windward Islands as Governor; and finally as Governor of Mauritius. John was the eldest of three boys and he spent his early life, including a spell at boarding school, in Kenya. He developed the self-reliance and maturity which often marks out those who grew up in East Africa, and this was evident when he came home and entered St Edward's, Oxford in 1949. John shone there as a popular and responsible boy, a proficient swimmer and sailor, and an enthusiastic actor. His entry to read law at Trinity College, Oxford was no surprise – it was what intelligent and rounded boys from St Edward's did.

In late 1955 National Service came first. Deverell did his basic training in his local regiment, the Oxford and Buckinghamshire Light Infantry, before being commissioned into the Duke of Cornwall's Light Infantry. Eager to return to Kenya and experience active service, Deverell seconded to the King's African Rifles (KAR), joining 5 KAR at the tail end of the Mau Mau emergency – he led patrols into the forest, and while off-duty enjoyed the social life. It was during this time that he met his future wife Margie.

On demobilization he was accepted into the Colonial Service and at some stage was recruited into national intelligence. By dint of the traditional selection methods then in vogue, John was admitted to a secret world closed to outsiders. Closed it might be, but no organisation providing a valuable service can be entirely isolated from its customers, and as John progressed up the Service professional interest in him and his past achievements was inevitable. The Irish, in particular, enjoy mystery and like to explore the background of those with whom they are going to work. So John's past record and accomplishments were scrutinised.

His important role relating to various overseas operations was already widely known in the upper reaches of the Province's intelligence community. He had been the favoured internal candidate to take over as Director General from the uncharismatic (according to MI5's authorised History) Sir John Jones in 1985. In addition, he was credited with playing a leading part in the origins of a notable intelligence success.

As Director K – the Head of the Security Service's Counter Espionage Branch – Deverell debriefed the Soviet double agent, Oleg Gordievsky, who had escaped from Russia to the West in July 1985, having fallen under KGB suspicion. Gordievsky in his best seller *Next Stop Execution* paid tribute to Deverell, describing him as "a man of exceptional intelligence and charm, who became a staunch friend and ally."

Earlier, before his escape to the West, Gordievsky had been posted to the Soviet Embassy in London. There he had dramatically assisted our national security by exposing an MI5 traitor, Michael Bettany, who had taken hundreds of classified documents to his flat, including material relating to operations in Northern Ireland, where Bettany had once worked. Again it was Director K who was responsible for the unmasking of Bettany, who was sentenced on conviction to twenty-three years imprisonment.

Most details of the 'Bettany affair' were already known to the Province's intelligence community, among whom Deverell's fine reputation was familiar before he arrived. There was some mystification caused by an article in *An Phoblacht*, a Republican propaganda sheet produced in Dublin, which claimed correctly that John Deverell 'had once been the natural candidate to head the Security Service'. The article reported that John had allegedly been involved in a recruitment operation in Germany to persuade two Irishmen to work for the Security Service. The article claimed that the operation had gone awry and had transgressed German law in some way, creating a diplomatic incident. Its conclusion was that John had been held responsible for the 'incident', which was why his nomination to head the Service had not succeeded.

Whether or not this was accurate, he was now to become closely involved in one of the most important and historic developments of the Troubles: the functioning of a secret conduit to the Provisional IRA, notwithstanding the government's avowed ban on talking to terrorists whilst they continued to perpetrate violence.

The very existence of any communication with those wishing to destabilise by violence existing democratic institutions seems disagreeable – even traitorous – but in practice unofficial means of communication are routinely established during most conflicts so that the issues at the root of the conflict can be addressed and, hopefully, resolved.

Hence, Governments and groups in armed conflict regularly establish a process or mechanism by which they can communicate covertly through intermediaries. But getting this secret process to work in Northern Ireland was particularly difficult, because suspicions by one community that a deal might be being struck behind their backs with the other ensured that few secrets remained so for long.

Nevertheless, for years a remarkable secret conduit or 'Link' – as it was referred to by the few who knew – did exist, based in Londonderry. At the Republican end of the Link was an unlikely peacemaker: a middle-aged Irish Republican pacifist named Brendan Duddy, who, as a modest businessman, ran a popular fish and chip shop serving the Catholic community. Amongst those who called there had been a young teenager named Martin McGuiness, who had made regular deliveries of hamburgers from the neighbouring butcher's shop in which he worked.

Although Deverell did not establish the Link himself, twenty years later he was responsible for overseeing its function and effectiveness when it purported to convey an unusual message from PIRA to HMG. Although there is now some doubt about the authenticity of the message, it was accepted at the time as genuine. The effect was dramatic and arguably for the good, in that it triggered a Government response that led eventually to the Downing Street Declaration of 1993, the Good Friday Peace Agreement of 1998, and the creation of the Northern Ireland Assembly in the same year.

The first public evidence of the existence of links to the IRA had come when Willie Whitelaw, the then Northern Ireland Secretary, met in London (ostensibly in secret) some Provisional IRA leaders in the large, centrally placed Cheyne Walk flat of the Conservative millionaire Paul Channon.

The meeting was not a success; it turned out to be a one-off encounter from which both sides withdrew in suspicion and disarray. It had been set up by an MI6 officer called Frank Steele, who had a strong belief in the opportunities for resolving intractable issues that such secret meetings gave their participants. However, news leaked out of the meeting with the IRA and caused public dismay. Whitelaw's own assessment was, "an unpleasant experience", and no further official talks took place under that Conservative Government.

In view of the important roles they would later play, it is of interest that Steele was struck by the prominent characteristics of the two most junior IRA delegates. He noticed that Martin McGuiness had the coldest, most penetrating eyes he had ever seen, and of Gerry Adams he remarked to a colleague, "That young man is extremely bright!"

In 1974, in conditions of even greater secrecy, such that even Merlyn Rees, the Labour Government's then Northern Ireland Secretary, was unaware of them, Prime Minister Harold Wilson authorised the same back-channel using Frank Steele's successor, the independently minded and determined Michael Oatley, who had taken over as MI6's man in the Province on the Secretary of State's political staff. Oatley described the initial function and purpose of the back-channel as analogous to a pipe. The action of blowing down the pipe at one end can be felt at the other; and, if minded to communicate, the far end can blow back and an exchange can begin. The beauty of the arrangement was that, as nothing but air passed down the pipe until it was brought into use, it was possible truthfully to uphold HMG's policy of non-communication.

At the Republican end of the pipe in Londonderry then was Rory O'Bradey, President of Provisional Sinn Fein, soon in discussion with the more influential strategist David O'Connell, believed to be the IRA's chief of staff. Holding the pipe and making the connection was the pacifist Brendan Duddy, who was deeply committed to ending the violence and destruction.

Jonathan Powell, Prime Minister Blair's Chief of Staff, describes Duddy: "as a brave and ingenious intermediary … among the most persistent and effective of the unsung heroes of the peace process." Arguably, Oatley deserves to have been included in such a tribute, but as a public servant perhaps he was considered merely to have been doing his job.

After Steele departed, Oatley was left to ponder his role. Gradually the need to establish some contact with the PIRA leadership developed, but like everyone else he was under clear instructions not to consider any such thing. Notwithstanding, he formed the view that something might be achieved by contact, in view of his assessment of the high quality of the recruits who were now joining the IRA, thereby increasing its potency.

He was not alone. Many independent observers noted that in areas like the Creggan all the best kids were getting involved (this did not accord with contemporary Government propaganda, which portrayed these volunteers as mindless thugs). Furthermore, it was evident that many members of the local Nationalist community accepted that the IRA had some justification for its activities and even had some respect for those who were running it.

With such thoughts churning in Oatley's head, he made his way alone into Republican areas like the Bogside to meetings with people who would not leave their homes. He sensed strongly that the situation had become crazy and that greater realism was needed. Moreover, he felt that the peculiar freedoms which he enjoyed gave him opportunities – and therefore responsibilities.

Yet he was fully aware that what he was doing was unauthorised and that he was acting alone in circumstances of high risk. The physical danger he was in was brought home on one occasion by a senior republican who remarked: "Don't tell us when you are coming, then we can't be blamed when they kill you!"

At times of uncertainty when Governments are feeling their way, anonymous officials like Oatley enjoy an advantage over their more identifiable colleagues: instant, direct access to those able to take decisions of national importance without further reference to others.

Oatley took his beliefs direct to the then Permanent Undersecretary at Stormont, the late Frank Cooper, who was a wise, robust and, later, a famed public servant. Cooper, who was a tough Mancunian and had been a wartime fighter pilot, could instantly see the value of trying to influence the situation through guarded communication which might or might not lead somewhere. He soon obtained the agreement of Prime Minister Harold Wilson, himself an equally gritty northerner, who trusted Cooper to pursue the initiative.

In this manner the so-called 'Christmas ceasefire' of 1974 was negotiated, using the Link through Duddy and Oatley.

But some nine months later this was torpedoed by an autumn resurgence of Loyalist violence. As a result, the IRA felt duped and in their mythology 'talks' and 'negotiations' got a bad name. Some commentators believe this background explained Sinn Fein/IRA's hesitations and suspicions in finessing the recent peace process. Whether or not this was the case, back in the mid-1970s there was a general loss of confidence in the IRA's existing leadership which occasioned the ascent of a new generation of leaders, including Adams and McGuiness, as the old guard of O'Bradey and O'Connell lost influence and were replaced.

The Link was again used as a conduit for negotiations during the first hunger strike in 1980. But the negotiation of a peaceful outcome, which was said by those involved to have been possible, failed due to inflexibility on the part of the prison management and staff.

Oatley had left the Province in mid-1975 but kept privately and unofficially in touch with Duddy. After PIRA broke off the ceasefire in 1975, Roy Mason, the then Secretary of State, ordered all contact with Duddy and any other 'go-between' to be ended.

At this point, Duddy and Oatley jointly agreed that the former should tell his PIRA contacts that with the resumption of their campaign there would be nothing to talk about, perhaps for a very long time. But whenever they might in the future wish to communicate, the Link represented by Duddy's access to Oatley and the latter's assumed ability to contact Downing Street night or day, remained in being wherever in the world Oatley happened to be. Oatley confidently believed that the personal trust which had been established between him and his interlocutors, and all parties' proven ability to keep secrets, was too valuable an asset to waste.

In this way the Link lay unused until November 1980, when it was activated briefly in the attempt to end the first hunger strike, and thereafter remained dormant until 1991. Sensing a possible change of mood, Duddy and Oatley at that stage agreed to use the latter's imminent retirement as a reason to arrange a meeting. Duddy argued that the Link, a reassuring facility in existence for so long, would lapse unless it was renewed. Surely this could not be in the Republican interest? On this basis, Martin McGuiness, now a leading member of the Provisional Army Council, sanctioned an exploratory meeting at which he provisionally agreed to a resumed secret dialogue.

Strategically, from a Republican perspective, any honest assessment of their situation had to acknowledge that the Provisional leadership was not getting any younger; neither did the prospect of having to pass on the conflict unresolved to the next generation appeal. Their intention had always been to get the 'Brits' out of Ireland on their watch. But although the Provisional IRA was a potent force still able to cause pain, the Army was clearly unbowed, and realistically Britain would be able to sustain its present commitment indefinitely.

Additionally, several recent IRA operations had come unstuck, and there was an undeclared realisation that the movement had been penetrated by informers, not on the mainland perhaps, but locally. Although discipline remained tight, and the certainty of execution was known to be the fate of anyone suspected of informing, setbacks were occurring with increased frequency. Confidence within the movement had been shaken and trust, that important glue which binds all combatants in a common purpose, was eroding.

In February 1993 Prime Minister John Major was interrupted in the Cabinet Room in 10 Downing Street with a startling secret message purporting to come from the Provisional IRA leadership via the Link. John Major recalls that the message, the provenance of which has been endlessly contested, read:

The conflict is over but we need your advice on how to bring it to a close. We wish to have an unannounced cease-fire in order to hold a dialogue leading to peace. We cannot announce such a move as it will lead to confusion to the Volunteers, because the press will misinterpret it as surrender. We cannot meet the Secretary of State's public renunciation of violence, but it would be given privately as long as we were sure that we were not being tricked.

Major claimed to have thought long and hard about the message, about which he harboured suspicions. From his intelligence assessments he already knew that there were splits in the PIRA leadership, that they had been deeply penetrated by British intelligence and that some senior IRA members were rethinking their approach.

Indications and rumours of peace feelers had reached him through the Link since he took over as Prime Minister. But he had also experienced direct evidence of PIRA's murderous intent – the mortar attack on Downing Street in December 1991 being its most obvious manifestation. He was advised that, although the IRA might offer various proposals for peace, inevitably at some stage extreme violence would be used in parallel. Apologists for the IRA always tried to explain this inevitability as the IRA's way of demonstrating to their volunteers that they were negotiating from a position of strength and were not just surrendering.

Major also had to take into account wider political factors. Peter Brooke, his first Northern Ireland Secretary, was engaged in the important 'Three Strands' talks involving Dublin and the constitutional political parties.[10] Brooke had made an important speech in November of that year in which he declared that the British Government had "no selfish strategic or economic interest in Northern Ireland ... Britain's purpose was not to occupy, oppress or exploit."

His speech had infuriated hard-line Unionists who chose to interpret it as another prelude to a sell-out. Major, aware of how carefully he must tread, recalled the Unionist opposition that Margaret Thatcher had faced over the Anglo-Irish Agreement of 1985. At the time, her initiative had seemed straightforward and practical enough through English eyes, but in Northern Ireland it had been ill received. Now her successor could imagine the

---

10. The Ulster Unionists led by Jim Molyneaux, Paisley's DUP, the SDLP led by John Hume and the small Alliance Party of John Alderdice.

certainty of extreme Unionist alienation if any secret negotiations or betrayal of their interests were uncovered.

Government policy in Northern Ireland did not change after the 1992 general election returned Major to power. Sir Patrick Mayhew replaced Peter Brooke as Northern Ireland Secretary, and in feeling his way forward in pursuit of peace he insisted in a speech at Coleraine recorded in Paul Bew's *Ireland*:

> The reality is that if Northern Ireland's position as part of the UK is ever going to change, it will only be by the will of a majority of its people ...
> We are not indifferent, we are not neutral in our resolve to protect and deliver the people of Northern Ireland from terrorist violence. We are not neutral in defending [their] right ... to democratic self determination.

Statements of that kind and various other messages via Dublin and through John Hume, who was known to be talking to Sinn Fein, created an atmosphere in which everyone seemed either to be engaged in talks, or anxious not to be left out of them.

In consultation with Mayhew and others, Major agreed that the safest political response to the peace overture received would be to take no risks, and to insist that PIRA first demonstrate their goodwill by calling a ceasefire. But Major, and those advising him, felt that in the interest of peace and humanity he should respond to any feelers put out by PIRA, even though the chances of success were not encouraging.

To respond as he did in the circumstances was brave and far-sighted. In due course it would lead to the establishment of various confidence-building measures and eventually to the 1998 Good Friday Peace Agreement under a different Prime Minister, who was able to build on the patience and vision of his predecessor. It is often overlooked that the imagination to respond positively to PIRA's initial peace feeler was John Major's, not Tony Blair's.

The path connecting overtures, negotiations and talks was neither straightforward nor predictable. Oatley's retirement was a blow to Duddy because together they had been the key initiators and facilitators in whom the IRA had confidence. Oatley was replaced by a man known to Duddy only as 'Mr Henderson' or 'Robert', and by others as 'Fred'.

In appointing 'Fred' one of those irritating but predictable turf wars developed high within the intelligence community: to whom should Fred be answerable? In his office at Stormont, John Deverell was frustrated by the argument. He did not mind who 'owned' Fred as long as the momentum of the peace overtures for which he was responsible was maintained.

A graver anxiety afflicted the Provisional leadership when it became public that they had allegedly been sending out messages that might be interpreted by the Volunteers as surrender. When Patrick Mayhew revealed to the House of Commons on 29 November 1993 all the exchanges that HMG had had with Sinn Fein/IRA, Martin McGuiness flatly denied that the 'conflict is over' message had come from him.

The message could certainly have been interpreted as injurious to IRA prestige and to their negotiating stance, hence the denial. In its aftermath, the IRA's wrath and suspicion fell initially on Duddy as the most likely perpetrator of the 'wishful' text of the message. Duddy was interrogated by Martin McGuiness and three senior Army Council men for four hours at his home about the provenance of the message. He convinced them that he had not initiated or altered it. But he found the whole experience terrifying, to the extent that he concluded that if he had engaged in any freelance peace initiatives on PIRA's behalf without their authority he would have been executed.

'Fred' also came under suspicion and, in intelligence circles, so too did Deverell, but equilibrium was eventually restored and 'talks about talks' leading to a temporary ceasefire continued direct between the IRA and the Government. 'I regretted the loss of the back channel,' John Major wrote in his autobiography. 'It gave us some difficult moments, but it played its part. Making peace is a tricky business.'

On several occasions the peace talks were nearly aborted by the British. On 20 March 1993 the IRA detonated a bomb in the centre of Warrington in Cheshire, killing two young boys, Tim Parry and Jonathan Ball, and injuring 56 people. The following month a huge bomb exploded in Bishopsgate in the City of London, causing one death and damage of over £800 million. It is hard to comprehend how those purporting to seek a peaceful solution to the conflict could have behaved so callously and cynically. As an exasperated Duddy remarked, when asked to explain in Peter Taylor's BBC TV documentary *Peacemaker*, "You must understand that's how the IRA works: this department bombs; that department talks. That's just how it works!"

John Deverell's role during this time came under critical scrutiny. Along with the rest of officialdom, he had been unaware that Duddy and Oatley had been conferring, until the result of Oatley's unauthorised meeting with McGuiness in February 1991 landed a hot potato in his lap.

This was a very uncomfortable situation for Northern Ireland's Director and Coordinator of Intelligence, professionally answerable to the Security Service. That Service's Director General, Stella Rimington, was not at all pleased to learn of Oatley's unauthorised activities in her area of responsibility. The fact that Oatley was an officer from a rival intelligence Service (the SIS) made matters worse. But what had been done could not now be undone. The requirement was for the DCI to manage its consequences deftly.

His task was delicate. Given the PUS NIO's decision to use the new opportunity for dialogue that the Link presented, Deverell had to control and manage it. In this he would have been guided by his instincts as a past colonial service officer, brought up in an atmosphere of 'can-do' and accustomed to taking responsibility. His strength of character and persuasive powers would have enabled him to overcome the lack of enthusiasm for his task from his own Director General and to ignore the innate suspicions among his contemporaries and rivals for promotion.

The political context against which these overtures were developing was not propitious, and presented a high hurdle for Deverell to clear. There was no sympathy in Parliament or the Government as a whole for the idea of dialogue. John Major's slender majority and Unionists' acute suspicions did not make this a time for taking political risks. Yet Deverell held his nerve and supported a course he felt as a patriot was in the national best interest. Without his conviction of the Link's value and his ability to represent that it was now being securely and safely managed, it would not have survived.

John Major maintained his resolve to talk if and when a cessation of hostilities occurred. In the end it did. Around the same time, successful negotiations with the Irish Government, helped by Major's high regard for Albert Reynolds, the Taoiseach, led to the signing of the Downing Street Declaration on 15 December 1993. Hansard recorded his remarks that day, to the effect that this was another milestone on the path to peace as it affirmed "the right of the people of Northern Ireland to self-determination, and recognised an 'Irish Dimension' whereby all the people of the island of Ireland had the right to solve by mutual consent, the issues between North and South."

Less than six months after the Downing Street Declaration had been signed, a tragic accident befell many of those who had striven so hard to make peace possible. The effects of the accident were felt throughout the entire intelligence community. The Army, the RUC and the RAF were all badly affected by it too, and its ramifications are still being felt fifteen years later.

The accident, on the Mull of Kintyre at the western extremity of the Scottish coast, where millennia ago Scotland and Ireland were joined, occurred on the evening of 2 June 1994. A Chinook helicopter piloted by Flight Lieutenants Jonathan Tapper and Richard Cook, RAF, with an aircrew of two and twenty-five passengers, including John Deverell, was flying from RAF Aldergrove, near Belfast, to Fort George in the Scottish Highlands, where an intelligence conference, known as a 'Machrihanish' after the first such gathering, was to be held. When the helicopter crashed, all those on board were killed. All the passengers were senior specialists in various aspects of intelligence and came from the Army, the RUC or various departments of the Security Services.

In the immediate aftermath there was surprise that so many experts were travelling together, and there was conjecture that the IRA had brought down the helicopter by planting a bomb on board or by missile attack.

No specific decision had been made to authorise the flight and allow so many important eggs to travel in one basket. Nor would it have been. Throughout the Troubles busy people travelled by helicopter, particularly when first they had to be drawn in centrally from widely dispersed bases to be briefed before continuing on a long journey. Furthermore, hopping across the water from Ulster to Scotland by air was far quicker, much more convenient and cost-effective, as well as being considered statistically safer than travelling by any other available means.

Accident investigators at the scene quickly ruled out the cause of the crash as being sabotage or terrorist attack. Determining what actually happened in the final moments of the flight, however, proved to be much more difficult and controversial. Various inquiries have considered the evidence, numerous opinions have been expressed and judgements been made. Nevertheless, contradictions have arisen and some findings have been disputed.

Under Scottish law, a Fatal Accident Inquiry conducted by the Sheriff of North Strathclyde, Sir Stephen Young, on 21 March 1996 at Paisley examined the best witness. He was the lighthouse keeper who described the conditions and the poor visibility over the Mull. He stated: "visibility was 400 to 500 metres and in places below 20 metres."

From this, and from post-mortem evidence, the Sheriff determined the nature and place of death. He found that those on board "were rendered unconscious at once and died more or less instantaneously" from the impact of the Mark 2 Chinook (ZD 576) on a rocky outcrop on the side of Beinn na Lice, 810 feet above sea level and under a mile east of the Mull of Kintyre lighthouse. But this did not explain the cause of the crash.

That judgement was attempted by an RAF Board of Inquiry that sought to discover what had occurred to the aircraft and in the cockpit as they approached land. They examined every aspect of the flight and every bit of wreckage but were hampered in that neither a black box nor a cockpit voice-recorder were fitted (Service aircraft were not then required to fit them), and by the fact that much of the wreckage had been destroyed by fire. Thus, the Board was only able to reach an open verdict.

In due course, this was reviewed, as their Service's regulations require, by the RAF chain of command. Two senior Air Marshals (Air Chief Marshal Sir Bill Wratten, as Air Officer Commanding-in-Chief Strike Command, and Air Marshal Sir John Day, as Air Officer in Command of No 1 Group), as well as the professional head of the Service, the Chief of the Air Staff himself (Air Chief Marshal Sir Michael Graydon), read all the evidence and attributed the cause of the crash to the pilots being 'grossly negligent.'

This was unusual. Traditionally in the RAF such a verdict, for reasons (among others) of compassion and morale, is delivered only when there is 'absolutely no doubt whatsoever' that any other cause could have been possible. Partly because of this departure from custom, the Reviewing Officers' verdict became highly controversial.

Their finding was queried by various influential bodies, such as the House of Lords Defence Committee and the Public Accounts Committee, and by individual politicians, former Prime Minister John Major and former Defence Secretaries Malcolm Rifkind and Michael Portillo among them. Experienced aviators, as well as serving and former RAF officers, weighed in, while the families of the deceased pilots were (and still are) understandably assiduous in defending the reputation of their sons. Controversy continues to this day.

All these critics of the Air Marshals' findings pointed out variously that the Chinook's introduction into service and its safety record had been controversial; the computer software was unreliable; 'uncommanded engine run up' had caused the test pilots at Boscombe Down to pronounce the aircraft to be 'positively dangerous', and further test flights there had been halted. There were accusations that 'fresh evidence' of malfunctions had been overlooked or dismissed. Finally, critics of the Reviewers set great store by the training and experience of the Special Forces pilots, which, they believed, made an absurdity of the verdict of gross negligence.

The *Pilot* magazine of 15 March 2000 carried a powerful justification by Air Chief Marshal Wratten, one of the Reviewing Officers, of the findings. He pointed out that the Reviewers had independently agreed:

> that the sortie was planned to be a low-level, daytime ... transit flight clear of cloud under Visual Flight Rules. Yet when it crashed, the Chinook was flying at high speed, well below safety altitude, in cloud (in Instrument Meteorological Conditions) in direct contravention of the rules for flight under either Visual Flight Rules or Instrument Flight Rules.

Specifically, Air Marshal Sir John Day, himself an experienced helicopter pilot, had pointed out that with less than a mile to go before impact a navigational waypoint change was made. This proved, Wratten wrote, that:

> the pilots were in control of their aircraft at that moment, a fact undisputed by even our most vociferous critics.
> The essence of our critics' theory is that in something less than twenty seconds after the waypoint change but before impact the Chinook could have suffered a major emergency. Before impact, however, they claim it must have cleared itself because it left no trace of having happened.

Wratten commented that there was no 'new' evidence; everything germane to the incident had been weighed and taken into account. In particular, the serviceability and maintenance of that aircraft, and of Chinooks generally, had been considered, and all past technical and trial reports from Boscombe Down and elsewhere had been assessed.

The article declared that the Chief of the Air Staff in referring to the Special Forces background of the pilots had written: 'Any assertion that experienced pilots would never commit ... a fundamental error is without foundation and unsustainable, as flight safety records sadly reveal.'

In conclusion, the Reviewing Officers, declared Wratten, 'stand by every word we wrote in reaching our judgement.'

The Ministry of Defence has consistently upheld their verdict.

One other puzzle remains: not so much about the crash but about its wider consequences. Given the fact that the crash destroyed a large part of Northern Ireland's intelligence capability, and many a secret went to the graves of those in possession of them, why did not IRA/Sinn Fein and the Loyalist paramilitaries capitalize on this debilitating setback to their adversaries?

Both groups already knew, or strongly suspected, that they had been compromised and that informers were in their midst. It was surprising therefore, in terms of military advantage, that within weeks of the crash PIRA had declared a cessation of hostilities, and that the Protestant paramilitaries mounted no further significant operations.

The answer presumably must lie in their genuine yearning for the peace, one that had been so elusive and had taken so long to establish. Hence, John Major's decision to press ahead with the peace process, supported by the advice of his two Secretaries of State, was vindicated. His and their patience was even more remarkable against a background of violence that never seemed to stop.

The Spook's Tale illustrates the crucial part played by a tiny number of individuals in intelligence, or functioning in that field – Duddy, Oatley, Deverell and not least the unidentified 'Fred' – who were involved in these historic and far-reaching events. In their separate ways these men provided the conduit to enable the peace process to be established, and the mechanism by which it could develop.

The skill and persistence involved in creating this opportunity, and the process by which, once established, it could be nurtured and developed, despite all manner of setbacks, were fine examples of statecraft, patience and persistence.

10

The Policeman's Tale

Author's Introduction
At the outset of the Troubles in 1969, relations between the Police and Army had got off to an indifferent start. Although the exhausted RUC officers on duty in Londonderry in August 1969 must have been delighted to see the Army arrive in force to relieve them, once the dust had settled many viewed the next seven years as a humiliating time for a once proud and independent police force.

In effect, the RUC had been 'taken off the streets', and their failure to maintain the peace in Londonderry had been shockingly exposed to criticism in the media, particularly on television, where footage of baton-wielding officers wearing quasi-military uniform whilst exhibiting signs of panic made uncomfortable viewing. The inevitable inquiry into what had gone wrong was undertaken by Lord Hunt, who as Brigadier Hunt had led the successful ascent on Mount Everest at the time of the Queen's Coronation in 1953.

The Hunt Report was critical of the RUC as a supposedly impartial police force and recommended the immediate disbandment of the paramilitary, tough 'B Specials' (or Ulster Special Constabulary) who were widely feared and loathed in the Nationalist community. Many Ulstermen, however, believed the 'B-men' were an essential component of the RUC, robustly underpinning law and order. One of their strengths was believed to be their intimate knowledge of who the local terrorists actually were. Hence, it was said, the IRA's strenuous efforts to get them disbanded.

Critics of Hunt's recommendations viewed the B Specials' disbandment (and their replacement by the Ulster Defence Regiment, as an integral unit of the British Army under national control) with dismay, believing it to be politically motivated, or at best naïve. But Lord Hunt's recommendations were accepted.

The RUC were then further dispirited under the less than inspiring leadership – as many saw it – of Sir Arthur Young, a chief constable imported to effect change and restore morale. He manifestly failed to do so and resigned after less than a year in post.

Nor was the Army always helpful in soothing the bruised feelings of the RUC in those early days. A few of the older officers – mostly with past experience of colonial service – could be arrogantly dismissive and patronising about the RUC.

Equally, some RUC officers let their resentment of and impatience with what they referred to as 'blow-ins' from the Mainland, who were generally ignorant of Irish affairs, cloud their relationships with those engaged in the same demanding endeavour.

By 1976 the RUC had been revitalised. Individual police officers had earned widespread admiration and respect for their courage and loyalty under dangerous circumstances. Furthermore, the government's policy of dealing with terrorism as an extreme outbreak of lawlessness to be dealt with through the civilian courts, as with any other crime, propelled the RUC to the forefront of the conflict. 'Police Primacy' logically followed (as described in the introduction to Tale 6), whereby the RUC took over from the Army the operational lead in the fight against terrorism. In practice, this meant that the two Forces worked in partnership, each contributing what it did best.

On all my operational tours I worked with the courageous and resilient officers of the RUC, now the corporate holder of the George Cross. The more senior I became, the closer our partnership grew, so that as GOC I was hand in glove – available at an instant – with my opposite number, Hugh Annesley, the Chief Constable.

For my Policeman's Tale, I sought someone who could complete the story of the Security Forces' involvement towards the end of the conflict, after Hugh and I had left. I realised that from the point of view of many former, loyal RUC officers the extended peace process, with its many false dawns and its wishful political thinking, was anathema, and consequently this was a dispiriting period.

I was fortunate that Chris Albiston, an experienced former Assistant Chief Constable in Northern Ireland, a United Nations Commissioner of Police in Kosovo, and a candidate for the leadership of the newly formed Police Service of Northern Ireland (PSNI), was prepared to be the subject of my last Tale.

* * *

During the Troubles, the Royal Ulster Constabulary was the second largest police force (or police service, as all Constabularies are now termed) in Great Britain and Northern Ireland. At its height there were some 8,500 full-time police officers and 5,000 reservists, almost all recruited locally. Only a handful of policemen, and the occasional woman, were seconded or transferred from the Mainland, and those were appointed to senior positions, or achieved them subsequently.

Distinguished Chief Constables, like Sir Kenneth Newman or Sir Hugh Anneseley, originally came from the Metropolitan Police. Some, like the late

Colin Cramphorn and the late Ken Masterton, had enhanced their careers by attending the prestigious one-year course at the Royal College of Defence Studies in Belgrave Square. These two officers were being groomed for the top as future Chief Constables or Metropolitan Commissioners, but died prematurely before they achieved the high office for which they were well fitted. Sir Paul Stephenson, now the Commissioner of the Metropolitan Police, was seconded to the RUC as a Superintendent in Northern Ireland in the 1990s, where he was a Sub Divisional Commander in Banbridge, County Down. Service in Northern Ireland was undoubtedly a feather in the cap of any police officer from the Mainland aspiring to high office.

One such was a young man from a strong, liberal background, with no Irish connections, whose ambition in 1975 was to join the Metropolitan Police. Subsequently, he too transferred to the RUC, and that stood him in good stead professionally also. The son of a middle-ranking civil servant, Chris Albiston came originally from London and had lived a peripatetic life, in the Cotswolds, Birmingham, Ayrshire and Yorkshire, as well as London itself. By the time he went up to Exeter College, Oxford to read modern history in 1972, he was widely travelled and had experienced more of his own country than most of his contemporaries.

With a father steeped in the values of Keir Hardie and a believer in the desirability of Irish reunification, and a mother whose family traditions were of Gladstonian liberalism, Albiston arrived at Oxford predictably sporting long hair and left-wing views. Studying contemporary history, he was interested in observing student demonstrations as a manifestation of dissent. Unexpectedly, Albiston discovered that the police were what they claimed to be: impartial upholders of the law. Then the father of a close friend was murdered by the notorious Donald Neilson, known as 'the Black Panther', and Chris decided that what he really wanted in life was to be a policeman, rather than a civil servant or a diplomat as had been in prospect.

At the time, the police were actively recruiting university graduates and Albiston was accepted by the Metropolitan Police. After swearing in as constable, he entered in 1975 the training school at Hendon in North London for a four-month basic training course. All Metropolitan police officers began their careers at Hendon (those from other Forces attended regional training establishments) on beat and patrol duties, with identical status and training. It is widely felt within the Service that one of the strengths of British policing is to start all ranks on an equal footing, thereby ensuring a level playing field and inculcating a common bond from the outset. Conversely, some laymen judge that the arrangement instils a 'canteen culture' in which the practice and ethos of serving the community competes with an overriding sense of loyalty to one's fellow officers.

PC Albiston's early years in uniform were spent as a constable in the Camden Town and King's Cross areas of the capital, dealing with petty crime, hooliganism and prostitution. Promoted within three years to Sergeant, he transferred to the West End, which was an intensely busy Division by day, with a unit (including attendant interpreters) dealing exclusively with shop-lifters, public order, traffic, traders and tourists. But the area lacked the presence of any significant resident population, so was less frenetic by night.

Albiston then attended the Police College at Bramshill in Hampshire. The academic and residential nature of this course encouraged him to share his experiences with officers from all over the country, and he developed a keen interest in the struggle of the RUC against terrorism.

He realised that Irish terrorism had existed for over a century without making much impact on the Mainland, but that police colleagues – the men and women of the RUC – were living daily with the threat of violence, not only at work but also at home with their families and at leisure with their friends. A long weekend spent in Northern Ireland as the guest of an RUC officer during August 1979 made a deep and lasting impression on Albiston.

It was the weekend of the main parade of the Royal Black Preceptory, the most senior and prestigious organisation within the Protestant Orange Order, when thousands of marchers and supporters, wearing bowler hats and sashes, parade to the accompaniment of flute and pipe bands. Strutting and swaggering – and thumping out the beat of their big bass drums – they asserted their ascendancy over the neighbouring Nationalist and Catholic community, rather like male animals marking out their territory.

That bank holiday weekend chanced to coincide with the Mountbatten murder and Warrenpoint atrocities (see Tale 5). The ferocity and violence of both these attacks, so foreign to his previous police experience, shocked and moved Albiston. He returned to the peace and detachment of Bramshill with a profound admiration for the RUC, and nurturing the desire one day to be part of it.

Without his realising its significance at the time, further preparation for his subsequent move to Northern Ireland occurred when Chris was appointed to the CID as a detective inspector in 1983 and transferred to Southall in West London.

Here he played a leading role in investigating a spate of significant sectarian killings in the aftermath of Mrs Gandhi's assault on the Golden Temple of Amritsar. He established the clear links that connected those who orchestrated political violence with those involved in general crime. As a keen CID officer, like generations before him, he felt that those responsible for intelligence – i.e. Special Branch (SB) – should share more of their product. Those working in the front line – whether police or soldiers – invariably hold such opinions; however, with increasing seniority and maturity their views tend to moderate.

Albiston's proficiency at handling Southall's violent, racially motivated crimes was noted, and he was promoted to detective chief inspector in charge of the CID in neighbouring Ealing, one of the Met's busiest divisions. From there he moved to Scotland Yard's 'Specialist Operations Department' which, although it sounded exciting and glamorous, in reality involved Chris in making policy, handling administration and processing staff issues. No real police work was involved, and Albiston's thoughts turned again to Northern Ireland.

At the time, Ulster and its policing were particularly topical. The RUC was under severe scrutiny and the then Chief Constable, the late Sir John Hermon, recorded in his autobiography *Holding the Line* that 1986 was his 'Hardest Year'. There had been three separate incidents during which the RUC, acting on sensitive intelligence and with Army support in one case, had shot dead suspected terrorists who subsequently were found to be unarmed. The routine follow-up investigations had been ineptly handled, and allegations that the RUC had embarked upon a 'shoot-to-kill' policy began to circulate.

The Deputy Chief Constable of Greater Manchester, John Stalker,[11] was called in to investigate, but he and Jack Hermon crossed swords before Stalker's report had been delivered. It was the beginning of a fractious period in the fortunes of the RUC which Albiston would deplore.

For the moment, he observed these travails from behind his desk in New Scotland Yard. He worried about the implications of failure to hold the line against terrorism in one part of the UK, and felt that many of his colleagues were insufficiently alert to this danger. More to the point, he wanted to involve himself in events that he foresaw as a threat to the stability of the United Kingdom.

---

11. Stalker was subsequently suspended and investigated over allegations, amongst others, pertaining to his friendship with a Manchester criminal outfit known as 'The Quality Street Gang'. He was never reinstated.

His opportunity came as he studied one of the reports recommending that the RUC open its selection for superintendents to candidates from other British police forces. Albiston duly applied but his application was rejected out of hand. He never understood why, and it took another application and eighteeen months, during which lobbying by sympathetic, if somewhat puzzled, senior officers occurred, before Albiston was able proudly to don in July 1989 the olive-green uniform of an RUC chief inspector.

The move to Northern Ireland involved his whole family. His wife and three daughters joined him in Lisburn on the edge of the City of Belfast, mostly in Co Antrim with a small part in Co Down. On the outskirts of Lisburn was a large military camp from where the Army was commanded. RUC Lisburn was a high-profile police station.

The largely business-oriented Protestant community in Lisburn was close-knit and very different from what the Albistons had known in London. A bleak picture of day-to-day life was depicted on British television screens and described in national newspapers. Northern Ireland was perceived as a place of unremitting violence – daily bombings, shootings and terrorist attacks. But the reality was that large parts of the Province seemed normal – normal, at least, once one got used to being stopped at checkpoints by armed police and soldiers and routinely searched when entering shopping areas. Scrutiny by CCTV was routine in Ulster long before it became so on the Mainland. But for an English policeman to have to carry a concealed gun when taking the children to school or walking the dog was as unusual as it was unwelcome.

Experienced RUC officers kept their occupations secret from their neighbours, and in some cases even from their own children. The Albistons merely told their children that 'it was best not to mention that Daddy was a policeman.' But even this straightforward approach could invite complications. One child, when asked by a friend what her daddy did, replied that she couldn't say because it was a secret!

Furthermore, the family's English name was unique in the Province, and this caused practical problems with legal documents such as land registry, electoral rolls and utility contracts. It also meant that Mrs Albiston, a doctor, had to practise her profession under a different name. That she did so successfully in neglected areas of local healthcare provision indicated how, with some improvisation and ingenuity, a degree of normality was possible.

And there were plenty of compensations among these irritants. The air outside Belfast was clean and invigorating. Living was considerably more affordable than in London. Houses were cheap to buy, and rents were low.

The grammar schools were excellent; the theatre, opera and restaurants were easily accessible and good value; the roads were uncrowded, and travel was quick and easy.

The RUC, Chris discovered, was an even more closed and introspective community than he had imagined. It was proud of its long history stretching back to the days of the Constabulary of Ireland, through the grant of a Royal Warrant to be renamed the Royal Irish Constabulary after the Fenian Uprising of 1867, and thence to the creation of the Royal Ulster Constabulary after Partition in 1922.

The men and women of the RUC had experienced terror without flinching throughout the violence of several IRA uprisings. Similarly, the RUC had suffered at the hands of the other dissident faction, the so-called Loyalists, who had tried to render the Province ungovernable during the 1973/4 Ulster Workers' Strike and in the wake of the 1985 Anglo–Irish Agreement. Then scores of police families, notably in Lisburn, had been intimidated and burnt out of their homes by Loyalist thugs. The RUC stood resolute throughout, tempering even these distressing events with some black humour. One advertising slogan for the Coal Board ran: 'Come home to a real fire.' Some wag amended it to: 'Come home to a real fire – join the RUC.'

Albiston found that he was quickly accepted by most of his colleagues. Evidence of this emerged when years later, in conversation with a constable who had been present, Chris learnt that a prank – a sure sign of acceptance – had been played on him. His flak jacket, with which he as an English officer was unfamiliar, had been 'loaded' with two extra solid metal protective plates, thereby making him not only the best protected chief inspector in the RUC but the one with by far the heaviest load to carry.

Initially, most of Chris's work in Lisburn involved him in getting to grips with routine Northern Ireland policing. Loyalist parades had to be marshalled away from sensitive areas, unpleasant sectarian attacks on perceived Nationalists, or even just on random Roman Catholics, had to be prevented or cleared up; and for many weeks there were nightly attacks on the homes of prison officers. Feuding among paramilitary gangsters was rife. On one occasion, the leader of such a gang contemptuously dismissed the warning Albiston gave him of a threat to his life and spurned all the precautionary advice and measures offered, only to be gunned down shortly afterwards by men who had previously been his associates.

On a personal level Chris had some near scrapes himself. He was called out to take charge of an incident where the Provisional IRA had abandoned a petrol tanker with an affixed incendiary device in the middle of Lisburn's busy shopping centre. When the device failed to explode the Army's bomb disposal team (ATO) were routinely tasked to defuse it. Whilst the RUC cordon of which Chris was part was waiting for ATO's technical procedures to begin, a process which takes time, the Duty Inspector decided to move away from below the street lamp, under which he was standing, to the other side of the street, lest the glass shatter following ATO's controlled explosion – whereupon a kilogram of Semtex high explosive concealed inside the concrete pillar supporting the street lamp itself exploded. Moments before, the policeman had been at that spot.

As an incomer, Albiston was particularly interested to gauge local attitudes. Some people supported the police, whatever their faults. Others hated the RUC, whatever it did. But most just judged each incident and individual on merit. He found there were some Unionists who cherished the English as symbols of that tradition; and there were others who expected perfidious Albion to betray them because the English could not be trusted to maintain the Union, and never even tried to understand their predicament. Conversely, there were Nationalists who saw the presence of any Englishman in Ireland as the root cause of all their problems, whilst others felt that at least an Englishman might deal more even-handedly with them than Unionists would.

Albiston observed too the differences between soldiers and policemen. He noted the police's slow, methodical approach with its attention to detail and need for evidence, compared with the enthusiastic and energetic attitude of soldiers, particularly the officers, who wanted to achieve demonstrable success during their relatively short tours of duty. This meant that with each changeover of soldiers new relations of trust and understanding had to be established with the RUC; but, Albiston judged, "relationships depended more on individual attitudes than on accents or backgrounds."

After two years Albiston's tour in Lisburn ended and, much as he regretted leaving this front-line post, he appreciated that, in the interests of career development and widening of experience, able commanders get called to higher things. He was appointed to RUC HQ as Superintendent Force Command working on policy matters and liaising with the Northern Ireland Office and HQ Northern Ireland.

Among his responsibilities was the Joint Secretariat of the Province Executive Committee (PEC), working alongside a keen, young Army colleague imbued with that Service's agenda. The Army had invested considerable time and energy in establishing the PEC (Tale 9) as the instrument by which better coordination of intelligence and operations could be arranged. This implied that they had not been – and still were not – well coordinated: an admission which was hard for the Chief Constable and the DCI to accept. So the establishment of the PEC had been difficult to sell.

The practical issue was how such a body would improve the effectiveness of operations in the face of continued terrorist attacks. Army commanders with recent operational experience knew that the decision-making process at the highest level would be quicker and more effective if the latest intelligence and specialist advice was available on tap in real time. They knew from experience that any operation must be run that way if the best results were to be obtained. Indeed, they were thoroughly frustrated that after two decades of the Troubles such fundamental arrangements were not already in place.

The reason that they had not been adopted earlier was that in non-military circles the spectre was raised of an attempted Army takeover, and with it the danger, first, of breaching constitutional propriety, and second, of compromising sources and intelligence. Albiston's clear direction from his bosses was that any attempt by the Army to try to run operations via the PEC should be politely thwarted.

But the violence and mayhem continued, although neither Albiston nor members of the PEC, other than John Deverell of course (Tale 9), were aware of the unusually well kept secret that the peace process had begun.

A new spate of killings started on 23 October 1993 with the bombing at Frizzell's fish shop on the Shankill Road perpetrated by the Provisional IRA, who believed, wrongly, that a meeting of Loyalists, including the notorious Johnny Adair, a leading Ulster Freedom Fighter, would take place upstairs that Saturday afternoon. The Provos believed this gave them the opportunity to remove several of their most senior enemies with one blow. But the bomb intended to annihilate them exploded prematurely as it was carried into the crowded shop by Thomas Begley and Sean Kelly, two junior members of the IRA. Nine civilians, uninvolved in any aspect of the Troubles, were killed, as was Begley.

This incident unleashed a wave of 'tit-for-tat' murders which culminated on 30 October 1993 in what came to be known as the Greysteel Massacre, when three Ulster Freedom Fighters (UFF) gunmen entered the Rising Sun Bar in a village outside Londonderry frequented by Catholics, and where a Halloween Party was taking place. The gunmen fired into the crowd, killing eight civilians, including two Protestants, and injuring thirteen. None of the victims was involved in any aspect of terrorism.

Albiston recalls that within as many days some thirty-one murders had taken place and tension on all sides was at boiling point. That October was the worst month for deaths since 1976. The fact that the peace process was underway added to the wickedness and futility of this communal blood-letting.

In the spring of 1994 Albiston attended the Senior Command Course at the Police College, Bramshill. This was a mandatory course for promotion to Chief Officer rank. After the day's work students chatted round the bar into the night, gossiping and assessing careers. One evening a visiting RUC officer hinted that Albiston's future lay in Special Branch. Such predictions can be unreliable, but not in this case. On returning to Belfast Albiston found himself posted to Special Branch and set to work on the Intelligence Desk.

He was now at the very centre of counter-terrorism in Northern Ireland, sitting on various important committees, such as the National Current Intelligence Group in London whose task it was to prepare the weekly Joint Intelligence Committee (JIC) assessments for the Prime Minister, which were distributed throughout Whitehall.

Albiston's arrival in Special Branch occurred just after the Mull of Kintyre tragedy, and as he walked the corridors and toured the offices on his introductory rounds he noted a scene reminiscent of the *Marie Celeste* – empty places and evidence of abandonment, yet everything left as it had been before the disaster struck.

By September 1999 Albiston had been promoted to be the Assistant Chief Constable in charge of the RUC's Northern Region (and designated ACC North) with responsibility for eighty miles of border with the Republic of Ireland. The previous year, under the Good Friday, or Belfast, Agreement, PIRA had declared a cessation of hostilities,[12] and so ACC North's police, and the soldiers from the co-located 8 Infantry Brigade who supported them, monitored the whereabouts and status of former activists. During the verification process, accurate knowledge of who and what crossed the border was one of the significant indicators that contributed to confidence building.

Albiston loved the job and forged a particularly harmonious relationship with the Army, but he observed a dark cloud on the horizon as his arrival in Londonderry coincided with the publication of the Patten Report, about which the RUC already had misgivings.

---

12. PIRA's 'cessation of military operations' was first declared on 31 August 1994, abandoned on 9 February 1996 for the Canary Wharf bombing, and reinstated 17 July 1997. It was breached locally several times thereafter.

Lord Patten of Barnes, a recently retired Governor of Hong Kong, a former Conservative junior minister in the NIO and, relevantly in relation to the task ahead, a Roman Catholic, was considered to have the ideal experience and credentials to determine how policing in Northern Ireland should take account of the Good Friday Agreement. An implicit understanding was that the status quo ante in respect of policing and security was no longer acceptable.

Hence the Independent Commission on Policing in Northern Ireland was charged with making recommendations to reflect this fact. Its report entitled *A New Beginning: Policing in Northern Ireland*, better known as the Patten Report, was published on 9 September 1999. It contained 175 recommendations, including some contentious and symbolic ones, such as changing the Royal Ulster Constabulary's name to the 'Police Service of Northern Ireland'; replacing the old cap badge with its crown and harp; altering the Oath of Allegiance; and removing all vestiges of association with the British Crown, such as flying the Union Flag and hanging the Queen's portrait in police stations. Similarly, any past connections or association with the Irish Republic – the RUC sprang from the original Royal Irish Constabulary – were also removed.

The changes profoundly shook the proud RUC. Patten's more contentious recommendations, and his implied criticism of the RUC's tradition and ethos, caused offence. Police officers felt betrayed, unappreciated and unfairly portrayed. Many Unionists were outraged too. Loyal policemen and women felt they did not deserve what they interpreted as a slap in the face at the end of an arduous campaign – almost five times longer than the duration of the Second World War – during which they had shown themselves steadfast and unbowed. With over 300 killed on duty and 9000 injured, many with life-changing injuries such as the loss of limbs or sight, they had suffered a far higher number of casualties than any other British police force. During the Troubles they had been assailed from all sides, attacked both by the various IRA groupings and by Protestant paramilitaries. At home they had had to endure the wrath and disrespect of their neighbours, the threat of 'under-car booby traps' and of other kinds of off-duty attack. Notwithstanding, they knew that professionally the RUC had become widely admired by police services throughout the world.

Like many a structured and disciplined organisation – the British Army was the example closest at hand – the RUC were attached to their symbols and lived by their ethos. They were proud of their badge, worn by all ranks. It served as a unifying identity and mattered to them; it was emblematic of their traditions and history. The Union flag flying outside RUC stations and the portrait of the Queen which officers passed as they came on and off duty were symbols of their loyalty and identity.

Policing is a lonely and at times dangerous business. Pride in being a police officer and acceptance that the calling is not just another job but entails a sense of service, commitment and occasionally sacrifice, are at the heart of the profession. Serving police officers do not view flags and emblems as demonstrations of triumphalism, or of the ascendancy of one part of the community over another. They see them as the manifestations of their unique profession, as a means of identity and common purpose, and as recognition of their history and sacrifice.

Ronnie Flanagan, the RUC's popular and respected Chief Constable, spoke for the majority of his officers when he said that he was not convinced that the new RUC title would attract more Catholics into the Force, which, apparently, was the *raison d'être* of the change. Nor did he believe that it would necessarily bring about the acceptance of Northern Ireland's police force by the Nationalist community predicted by Patten. He added, with an obviously heavy heart: "If we are to endure this great hurt as proposed then I hope the gains envisaged are demonstrable and achievable."

Albiston, along with most intelligent, pragmatic officers, realised that under the Good Friday Agreement changes to the RUC were inevitable, even essential. They were not about to fight them; indeed, most agreed that for the sake of future generations they should embrace change.

Albiston's own attitude was that the leaders should lead and if the Government was prepared to accept a policy of 'constructive ambiguity', so was he. 'Constructive ambiguity' he took to mean that all parties to the Agreement would have to accept for the greater good some equally uncomfortable adjustments. He envisaged a period of 'equal misery', during which all parties to change would be treated even-handedly.

But Albiston found that in practice things did not work out that way. When past events and incidents were officially investigated under processes such as 'Cold Case Reviews', the assumption of equal treatment was breached. Former RUC officers found themselves being investigated with greater zeal and more resources than were the original suspects. Indeed, it often appeared too politically awkward to investigate the latter at all. Soon irreconcilable bones of contention developed; however, they had not yet surfaced as Albiston turned his attention towards an unusual assignment with the United Nations.

In February 2000 he was tasked by his Chief Constable to conduct a routine disciplinary investigation that ACCs were occasionally required to perform. Unusually, this investigation took place in Kosovo, where a large number of RUC officers were attached to the United Nations. During his time there, Albiston was attracted to the Balkans and was able to identify with many of their security problems which were similar to Northern Ireland's – civil disorder, ethnic tension, racketeering and crime organised by paramilitaries.

Unbeknown to Albiston, Prime Minister Tony Blair had already agreed to provide the UN in Kosovo with a police contingent from the UK. Apparently, Blair had spoken to Ronnie Flanagan on the basis that by virtue of training and experience the RUC was the Force best able to provide suitable volunteers. This left the prestigious post of the Police Commissioner, United Nations Interim Administrative Mission in Kosovo (UNMIK) to be filled. Albiston, who was coming to the end of his command tour, volunteered for it and was selected by Kofi Annan, the UN Secretary General.

The UN Commissioner's task was to exercise operational command of 4,500 police officers from 52 nations in Kosovo. In addition, he was responsible for training a local force of a further 4,500 to replace those serving on attachment. It was a short but tough assignment, one for which Albiston was ideally suited. In post by January 2001, he found it to be a stimulating and satisfying appointment. He relished both the variety of the issues that confronted him and the people he worked with. Enthusiastically, he pronounced it to be "the best job I ever had".

But his contract only lasted a year, and when he returned to Northern Ireland he found a dispirited Police Service very different from the one he had left a year before. The implementation of the Patten Reforms and the investigations into various incidents, particularly the handling of the Omagh bombing, had soured the atmosphere and sapped confidence both within the Force itself and in how it was perceived from outside.

The Omagh bombing in County Tyrone had occurred on 15 August 1998, before Albiston went to Kosovo, so he was familiar with the incident. It was a particularly shocking one, perpetrated by dissident Republicans and coming a few months after the Agreement which was meant to have ended the Province's long running conflict, but of which the bombers were not part.

It took the lives of twenty-nine people, including the mother of unborn twins. Among those killed were eleven children, twelve women and six men drawn from all walks of life and from across Northern Ireland's sectarian divide. Additionally, some 220 were injured. But Albiston had not been involved in the original investigation of the crime, still less the subsequent investigation by the Police Ombudsman into the handling of various facets of it.

On 12 December 2001, a retrospective report by the Police Ombudsman Nuala O'Loan[13] concluded that people had been "let down by defective leadership, poor judgement and a lack of urgency" in the Royal Ulster Constabulary. Her damning report stated that RUC officers had ignored warnings, failed to act on crucial intelligence and had been uncooperative and defensive during her enquiry. Her report concluded by recommending the setting up of a new investigation team, under a senior officer from an outside Force, which would be independent of the new Police Service of Northern Ireland (PSNI).

The RUC's Chief Constable Ronnie Flanagan called the report "grossly unfair" and "an erroneous conclusion reached in advance and then a desperate attempt to find anything that might happen to fit in with that." So great was his outrage at O'Loan's claims that the Chief Constable commented that if the Ombudsman's judgement was proved to be correct, "I would not only resign, I would go and publicly commit suicide."

He later withdrew his remarks as seemingly insensitive to those who had been affected by suicide, but he pointed out his words were "indicative of how strongly I felt at that time."

Into this unhappy atmosphere of rancour and bitterness Albiston returned to Belfast to take on the cherished job of ACC Crime, PSNI. He was responsible for all Headquarters Crime Units (including the Serious and Organised Crime Squad, the Drugs Squad and the Fraud Squad), plus Specialist Operations Branch and Special Branch. In effect, there was no human condition or frailty of which Albiston was professionally unaware.

By now the RUC's name had disappeared and, in the eyes of many, the Service had lost its identity for no appreciable gain. The Force had been severely criticised and publicly humiliated by the Police Ombudsman, who was openly at odds with the outgoing Chief Constable. Those who had previously served in Special Branch had been picked out for particular disapproval and felt especially aggrieved. Criminal investigations, such as the Stevens Inquiry into alleged collusion by the RUC Special Branch and Army Intelligence with paramilitaries, were ongoing. These investigations were unsettling for those involved, and debilitating for the operational units

---

13. Dame Nuala O'Loan was appointed to the House of Lords in 2009 having completed a controversial tour as the first Police Ombudsman.

concerned. Finally, in terms of decisive leadership and a 'New Beginning', there was a vacuum. The PSNI awaited the appointment of a leader, and the process of selecting a Chief Constable was already generating speculation and uncertainty.

Throughout the United Kingdom the selection of Chief Constables is conducted under the public gaze and tends to be hotly contested. The process of becoming a candidate, of obtaining the right backing and references, and of competing at interview can be an exhausting and bruising experience. In the goldfish bowl of Northern Ireland, selection of the first Chief Constable of the PSNI was guaranteed to generate wide public interest, and be highly political too.

By February 2002, even before nominations had been formally requested, the names of five likely candidates were appearing in the press, of which one was Chris Albiston. As a senior police officer with international experience and a series of testing operational jobs in Northern Ireland, such as ACC North, under his belt, Albiston was seen as a very strong internal candidate. But, unbeknown to him initially, he carried a significant handicap from the outset: some of those involved in the selection process viewed him as tainted by having worked in Special Branch and by the very fact that he was an internal candidate.

A reasonable prerequisite for achieving a peaceful future in Northern Ireland following the Good Friday Agreement was that the arrangements for law and order and justice should command widespread confidence and be acceptable to the Nationalist community. It was a politically uncertain time and strenuous efforts were made to iron out, or eliminate, those issues which might impede political progress or become a bar to peace.

Despite these laudable aims, suspicion took root among many of Albiston's colleagues that the agenda of the political establishment was to paint the RUC, and Special Branch in particular, in the most unfavourable light so as to placate Nationalist feelings. More sinisterly, some felt an intention to legitimise (or at least overlook) the criminal activities of terrorists, thereby paving the way for their integration into the political mainstream.

Whatever the reasons, Albiston was not selected. The appointment as the first Chief Constable of the Police Service of Northern Ireland went to a police officer from outside Northern Ireland who had already been investigating the RUC, and for whom Albiston and his colleagues had no professional regard.

Despite his disappointment, Albiston remained as ACC Crime until his retirement in August 2003, although he did not find the arrangement congenial. On leaving PSNI, he took up a range of public service appointments in Central and Eastern Europe in EU 'candidate' and 'new accession' states – work which was much in demand.

Albiston continues strongly to defend the reputation of the former RUC officers for whom he was responsible. He is suspicious of what he and others perceive as one-sided investigations, with a vested interest to appease, by the Historic Inquiry Team and such bodies. In their investigations into allegations of criminality by the Security Forces they seem to accord them a parity of esteem with convicted terrorists. Despite an allegation made under parliamentary privilege to the contrary, he gave evidence and helped with various inquiries, yet he considers such investigations can be politically motivated and breach the understanding of 'constructive ambiguity' sold to him during the peace process.

On 28 September 2007, Albiston, now an *eminence grise* and long out of harness, made a speech at a large gala dinner in Belfast at which many former colleagues were present. He said:

> I salute the achievements of the RUC GC, Special Branch and the PSNI Intelligence Branch, in partnership with unstinting and courageous colleagues in mainland forces, the Security Service, Her Majesty's Armed Forces ... and the Garda Siochana. Without all your efforts the public and the security forces would have sustained far greater losses, and we might never have emerged to where we are today.
>
> I acknowledge the complexity of the political issues surrounding the future structures [for policing] which will be required to continue to deliver effectiveness, efficiency, accountability and acceptability. The threat has changed: so must we. We must seek to anticipate rather than to react.
>
> Finally, I wish every success to those who must carry the torch of light and decency into the future.

These are fine sentiments – devoid of bitterness – from an English police officer who in mid-career crossed the Irish Sea to volunteer for service in the Royal Ulster Constabulary and typically, in good times and bad, devoted himself to their cause.

During the Troubles, there were numerous Brits of like mind. Some felt so in harmony with Northern Ireland and the contemporary scene that, like Albiston, they now reside there and are fiercely protective of its history, identity and charm.

11

Postscript

When I left the Province for the last time, peace had not come, nor did it appear to be round the corner. But I never doubted that the Army and our colleagues in the RUC and Security Services would remain steadfast until it did. Now peace – or what passes for it – has arrived; and exported Irish terrorism no longer afflicts mainland Britain whenever its perpetrators want to heighten the political temperature.

Yet defining peace and judging its durability are difficult. Incidents of violence carried out locally by armed groups still occur, and the aims of many of those who took up arms originally to bring about a united Ireland have not been realised, any more than the aims of earlier generations in the late nineteenth and early twentieth centuries were fully achieved. Furthermore, the emotionally charged centenary of the Easter Rising will occur in 2016, and it is almost inconceivable that the occasion will pass off without some spectacular outbreak of violence.

The formal intelligence assessment is that 'dissident republican groups such as the Real IRA and the Continuity IRA ... continue to pose a threat to Great Britain, and to Northern Ireland in particular.'

Dr Martyn Frampton, a leading authority on dissident republicanism, records that the 32 County Sovereignty Movement (32 CSM), which is emerging as another disaffected Republican group, viewed the Provisional IRA involved in the Peace Process as engaging "in a collective act of gross betrayal" and stressed the impossibility of there being any end to the conflict in Northern Ireland short of a British commitment to withdraw.

So, if a 'peaceful' outcome cannot be said conclusively to have been established, what can the Security Forces claim to have achieved during the Troubles? And do the findings of the various investigations that have been concluded, or may yet emerge, invalidate such claims?

In January 1998, against the advice of the then Chief of Defence Staff, General Sir Charles Guthrie, Prime Minister Tony Blair initiated Lord Saville's Bloody Sunday Inquiry, the aim of which was to supersede the original, allegedly discredited, Lord Widgery Tribunal and, if possible, to assuage its 'hurt'. Guthrie was not alone in imaging that it would not succeed in changing entrenched opinions. However, its intention was 'to provide a definitive version of events surrounding a civil rights demonstration in Londonderry on 30 January 1972, in which thirteen civilians died after the Army opened fire.' (A fourteenth civilian died later).

Twelve years later, Lord Saville's Report was published and Prime Minster David Cameron in his statement in the House of Commons on 15 June 2010 brilliantly defused the whole issue by making with unusual force and frankness, yet in a manner widely acknowledged as statesmanlike, the following key points:

> Its conclusions were absolutely clear. There was no doubt, and there was nothing equivocal about them. What happened on Bloody Sunday was both unjustified and unjustifiable. It was wrong.
>
> For those looking for statements of innocence, Saville says: "The immediate responsibility for the deaths and injuries on Bloody Sunday lies with those members of Support Company [1st Battalion, The Parachute Regiment] whose unjustified firing was the cause of those deaths and injuries" and, crucially, that, "None of the casualties was posing a threat of causing death or serious injury, or indeed doing anything else that could on any view justify their shooting."
>
> Some of our Armed Forces acted wrongly. The Government is ultimately responsible for the conduct of the Armed Forces. And for that on behalf of the Government – and indeed our country – I am deeply sorry.
>
> Lord Saville finds no evidence that the events of Bloody Sunday were premeditated ... he concludes that the Government and the Army neither tolerated nor encouraged "the use of unjustified lethal force."
>
> Bloody Sunday is not the defining story of the service the British Army gave in Northern Ireland from 1969-2007. Theirs was the longest, continuous operation in British military history, spanning thirty-eight years and in which over 250,000 people served.
>
> Our Armed Forces displayed enormous courage and professionalism in upholding democracy and the rule of law in Northern Ireland. Acting in support of the police, they played a major part in setting the conditions that have made politics possible ... and over 1000 members of the security forces lost their lives to that cause. Without their work the peace process would not have happened.

The Prime Minister further commented on the serious failings that had occurred, in saying: "You do not defend the British Army by defending the indefensible" and, "Those wrongs cannot be allowed to cloud the reputation of our Armed Forces and the pride they inspire."

Bloody Sunday was an aberration. However, the shaming events of that day do not invalidate the claim that the overall British contribution in Northern Ireland was laudable. Moreover, the mark of a healthy organisation is one that can look back on its mistakes, learn from them and ensure that they are not repeated. They were never again repeated.

Assessing the course of the conflict in the round, the military, in conjunction with their colleagues in the police and security services, created the opportunity for peace to take hold. They confronted the violence; they underpinned law and order; and they sustained the community; giving politicians and civil servants the time to develop the processes and understanding necessary for progress.

As the Bishop of London pointed out at the service in St Paul's Cathedral to mark the end of Operation Banner: "Civilizations perish invisibly in the night when no one is prepared to risk their lives for them."

All of those who worked in Northern Ireland during the Troubles put their lives at risk and, indeed, civilization did not perish.

Glossary

Ulster – historically, Ulster was originally one of the four, and the most northerly, of the Kingdoms of Ireland. Centuries later, Ulster consisted of nine counties, the existing six plus Cavan, Monaghan and Donegal. When Ireland was partitioned in 1922, these three predominantly Catholic counties were hived off from Ulster and retained in Southern Ireland. Had this not happened, Ulster might not have had a predominantly Protestant population.

GOC NI (General Officer Commanding Northern Ireland) – a lieutenant general (a three-star rank) who was Head of the Army in Northern Ireland and Director of Operations.

The 'B Specials' (or Ulster Special Constabulary) – when called out, an armed element of the Royal Ulster Constabulary. Drawn almost exclusively from the Unionist community, they had a reputation for sectarianism and robust action, and were generally feared and hated by the minority community. Following criticism in the Hunt Report they were disbanded on 30 April 1970.

The UDR – superseded the B Specials as a local militia in 1970. They were incorporated into the British Army to provide a disciplined outlet into which could be channelled the Ulsterman's wish to serve.

CGS – a four-star general and the professional head of the British Army.

The Yellow Card – sets out succinctly the conditions under which a soldier legally may or may not open fire or use force. It was carried by every soldier and learned by heart.

Source – the term used to denote the provider of information to assist the security forces. The term is synonymous with agent or informer. The IRA used the term 'tout', and to be declared a tout invariably led to execution.

Craic – a Gaelic term denoting good stories in amusing company. Hence the vernacular 'he's good craic' indicates someone who is fun to be with.

Green Army – the term used to distinguish those soldiers in uniform, who operated openly, from those working undercover, often in civilian clothes to blend undetected with the locals.

Battalion – denotes a single infantry unit of some 650 men made up of four rifle companies.

Company – a rifle company of around 120 men consisting of three platoons around thirty strong. Each platoon consisted of a number of bricks.

Brick – the basic unit in an infantry role usually consisting of four men. A multiple consisted usually of three bricks.

Police Primacy – the government policy which restored the 'lead' over operations to the RUC from the Army. Merlyn Rees, the then Labour Government's Secretary of State for Northern Ireland, launched this 'Way Ahead' policy in the House of Commons in January 1976 following the disastrous (for HMG) Ulster Workers' Strike of 1974.

Operation Banner – the codeword given to the Army's operation in Northern Ireland.

Permanent Undersecretary (PUS) – a top post in the Civil Service and the head of a department, like the NIO. The 'four-star' job rates, in terms of protocol, as a full General (or equivalent).

Deputy Undersecretary – a senior civil servant equating to a three-star post in the Army. The NIO had two DUSs reporting routinely to the Permanent Secretary (PUS).

Special Branch – in the UK the lead in counter-terrorism nationally was vested in the Metropolitan Police's Special Branch until June 1992, when responsibility was formally transferred to MI5. Historically, the Metropolitan Police's Special Irish Branch was established in March 1883 expressly to counteract the threat of Irish terrorism.

MI5 – whose proper title is the Security Service. Answerable to the Home Secretary, its role is to safeguard the UK from threats posed from within the country.

MI6 – the Secret Intelligence Service, answerable to the Foreign Secretary, safeguards British interests from external threat, and actively promotes those interests by the covert collection of intelligence and the exercise of influence.

GCHQ – Government Communications Headquarters, which provides intelligence gleaned from electronic intercept and is answerable to the Foreign Secretary.

Widgery Tribunal – the Inquiry conducted by the then Lord Chief Justice in the aftermath of Bloody Sunday. He found that although the actions of some soldiers had bordered on the reckless, "there is no reason to suppose that the soldiers engaged in the arrest operation would have opened fire if they had not been fired upon first."

Bibliography

Andrew, Christopher, *Defence of the Realm: the Authorised History of MI5* (Penguin, 2010)

Arthur, Max, *Northern Ireland: Soldiers Talking* (Sidgwick & Jackson, 1987)

Bew, Paul, *Ireland: the Politics of Enmity* (Oxford University Press, 2007)

Birrell, W.D., *Direct Rule and the Governance of Northern Ireland* (Manchester University Press, 2009)

Dewar, Michael, *The British Army in Northern Ireland* (Arms & Armour, 1985)

Flackes, W.D., and Elliott, Sydney, *Northern Ireland: a Political Directory 1968-93* (Blackstaff Press, 1994)

Frampton, Martyn, *Legion of the Rearguard* (Irish Academic Press, 2011)

Godson, Dean, *Himself Alone: David Trimble and the Ordeal of Unionism* (Harper Collins, 2004)

Gordievsky, Oleg, *Next Step Execution* (Macmillan, 1995)

Harnden, Tony, *Bandit Country: the IRA and South Armagh* (Hodder & Stoughton, 1999)

Hermon, John, *Holding the Line* (Gill & Macmillan, 1997)

Hudson, Miles and Stanier, John, *War and the Media* (Sutton Publishing, 1997)

Ingram, Martin and Martin, Greg, *Stakeknife* (The O'Brien Press, 2004)

Judd, Alan, *Breed of Heroes* (Hodder & Stoughton, 1981)

Lawson, Richard, *Strange Soldiering* (Hodder & Stoughton, 1963)

McKittrick, David, Kelters, Seamus, Feeney, Brian, and Thornton, Chris, *Lost Lives* (Mainstream Publishing, 1999)

Major, John, *The Autobiography* (Harper Collins, 1999)

Mason, Roy, *Paying the Price* (Robert Hale, 1999)

Murphy, Dervla, *A Place Apart* (John Murray, 1978)

Needham, Richard, *Battling for Peace* (Blackstaff Press, 1998)

O'Callaghan, Sean, *The Informer* (Bantam Press, 2005)

Powell, Jonathan, *Great Hatred, Little Room: Making Peace in Northern Ireland* (Bodley Head, 2008)

Robinson, Rt Hon Sir Henry, *Memories: Wise and Otherwise* (Cassell, 1923)

Rutherford, Edward, *Princes of Ireland: the Dublin Saga* (Ballantine Books, 2004)

Thatcher, Margaret, *Downing Street Years* (Harper Collins, 1993)

Index